Windows Vista™
FOR
DUMMIES®
QUICK REFERENCE

by Greg Harvey, PhD

BICENTENNIAL
1807
WILEY
2007
BICENTENNIAL

Wiley Publishing, Inc.

Windows Vista™ For Dummies® Quick Reference

Published by
Wiley Publishing, Inc.
111 River Street
Hoboken, NJ 07030-5774

www.wiley.com

About the Author

Greg Harvey, the author of a slew of *For Dummies* books running the gamut from *Excel For Dummies* to *The Origins of Tolkien's Middle-earth For Dummies*, has had a long career of teaching business people the use of IBM PC, Windows, and Macintosh software application programs. From 1983 to 1988, he conducted hands-on computer software training for corporate business users with a variety of training companies (including his own, PC Teach). From 1988 to 1992, he taught university classes in Lotus 1-2-3 and Introduction to Database Management Technology (using dBASE) in the Department of Information Systems at Golden Gate University in San Francisco.

In mid-1993, Greg started a new multimedia publishing venture, Mind over Media, Inc. As a multimedia developer and computer book author, he hopes to enliven his future online computer books by making them into true interactive learning experiences that will vastly enrich and improve the training of users of all skill levels. In 2006, he received his PhD in Comparative Philosophy and Religion with a concentration on Asian Studies from the California Institute of Integral Studies in San Francisco, California. When he isn't busy writing, Dr. Greg works as a patient care and bereavement volunteer with the Hospice of Marin in Larkspur, California and Hospice by the Bay in San Francisco, California and a home and hospital volunteer with the Center for Attitudinal Healing in Sausalito, California.

Dedication

To my alma mater, the University of Illinois at Urbana-Champaign, Illinois, birthplace of NCSA (National Center for Supercomputing Applications) Mosaic, the great-grand-daddy of Microsoft Internet Explorer 7.

Thanks for helping me gain the analytical, language, and writing skills that all came into play in the creation of this work.

Author's Acknowledgments

Many thanks to Christopher Aiken at Mind over Media, Inc. for all his help and support with this revision of *Windows Quick Reference*.

I want to thank the following people at Wiley Publishing, Inc. who have worked so hard to make this book a reality: Katie Feltman for her consistent and inspiring help in getting this revision off the ground; Linda Morris for her dedicated editorial assistance; and the amazing layout folks in Production. Thanks, too, to Joyce Nielsen for the technical review.

Last, but never least, I want to acknowledge my indebtedness to Dan Gookin, whose vision, sardonic wit, and (sometimes) good humor produced *DOS For Dummies,* the "Mother" of all *For Dummies* books. Thanks for the inspiration and the book that made it all possible, Dan.

Greg Harvey

Point Reyes Station, California

Publisher's Acknowledgments

We're proud of this book; please send us your comments through our online registration form located at www.dummies.com/register/.

Some of the people who helped bring this book to market include the following:

Acquisitions, Editorial, and Media Development

Project Editor: Linda Morris

Acquisitions Editor: Katie Feltman

Copy Editor: Linda Morris

Technical Editor: Joyce Nielsen

Editorial Manager: Jodi Jensen

Media Development Manager: Laura VanWinkle

Editorial Assistant: Amanda Foxworth

Composition Services

Project Coordinator: Adrienne Martinez

Layout and Graphics: Denny Hager, Joyce Haughey, Stephanie D. Jumper, Barbara Moore, Barry Offringa, Lynsey Osborn, Erin Zeltner

Proofreaders: Laura Albert, Techbooks

Indexer: Techbooks

Publishing and Editorial for Technology Dummies

> **Richard Swadley,** Vice President and Executive Group Publisher

> **Andy Cummings,** Vice President and Publisher

> **Mary Bednarek,** Executive Acquisitions Director

> **Mary C. Corder,** Editorial Director

Publishing for Consumer Dummies

> **Diane Graves Steele,** Vice President and Publisher

> **Joyce Pepple,** Acquisitions Director

Composition Services

> **Gerry Fahey,** Vice President of Production Services

> **Debbie Stailey,** Director of Composition Services

Contents *at a Glance*

Table of Contents

Part 1

The Vista User Experience

If such a thing as a *beautiful* user interface for a personal computer operating system exists, Microsoft's Windows Vista, shown in the following figure, is surely at the top of this list. However, as you find out in this part, the Windows Vista desktop is much more than just a pretty face. Indeed, Vista is also Microsoft's most powerful and usable personal computer interface to date (and this is coming from someone who really liked Windows XP).

In this part . . .

- ✔ **Meet the Aero Glass Interface**
- ✔ **Guide for displaced Windows XP Users migrating to Windows Vista**
- ✔ **Personalizing your copy of Windows Vista**
- ✔ **Using the Start Search and Search features**
- ✔ **Using the Vista taskbar**

Aero Glass Interface

In Windows Vista, A is for Aero Glass, the name given to the operating system's graphical user interface (GUI). The name is a combination of the acronym AERO — Authentic, Energetic, Reflective, and Open — which describes the original design goals for the new operating system, and glass (the stuff of which actual windows are made), this stunning new user interface is all about clarity, in the sense of both brightness and simplicity.

The first thing to note about the Aero Glass desktop when first installed (and after you close the Welcome Center window that automatically appears) is the overall openness of the screen (due to a decided lack of program icons) and a rather minimalist Start button and taskbar, as shown in Figure 1-1. This open screen makes the most of your screen space, whatever the size of your monitor, by accommodating more open windows and more information within each open window.

Figure 1-1

The second thing to notice is the relative transparency and high degree of reflectiveness displayed by the various Vista screen elements, especially the taskbar, Start menu, and title bars of open windows (depending upon the graphics capability of your computer). You notice the transparency most in the title bars of windows and in the right column of the Start menu (especially when the menu is on top of another open window, as in Figure 1-2). You notice the reflectiveness most when you position the mouse pointer over buttons and desktop icons — they actually appear to glow. This effect is accomplished by backlighting the graphic with various contrasting colors — blue for most buttons and icons and bright red for a window's Close button.

The third thing to notice about the Aero Glass interface is the extremely smooth way in which screen elements change and the high degree to which this version of the operating system supports live visual previews.

You notice the screen smoothness whenever you open or close a new window and resize or move it on the Windows desktop. When Vista opens a window, it does so in a much more fluid manner than previous Windows versions. So too, when you drag an open window around the Vista desktop (even one playing a video or showing a music visualization), the graphics don't break up and become pixilated as they pass over other screen elements.

Figure 1-2

The live visual previews in Vista show up in several really cool desktop features: live taskbar thumbnails, Flip, and Flip 3D, which are used to switch between open windows. The live taskbar thumbnails feature enables you to see a thumbnail version and name of any window that is currently minimized on the Vista taskbar simply by positioning the mouse pointer over its icon. That way, you can get tell whether a particular window icon on the taskbar contains the particular application or Vista window you want to restore to its previous position and size on the Vista desktop.

Note that the Flip feature is a more graphic version of a switching feature first introduced in Windows XP (and still activated by pressing Alt+Tab). This feature enables you to activate a particular open window from among those currently minimized on the Windows taskbar by selecting its icon and window name in a band that appears in the middle of the desktop. In the Vista version of the Flip feature, however, rather than just a generic window icon, you see an actual live thumbnail of the contents of the window along with its window name (see Figure 1-3). This live preview helps you immediately identify the window you want to open on the desktop.

Figure 1-3

The Flip 3D offers an even faster visual method for activating an open window among those you have open. It accomplishes this by showing a stack of live 3-D representations for all the windows you have open in Vista (see Figure 1-4). You can then quickly flip through this stack until the thumbnail of the window you want to activate is displayed at the front of the stack. *See* "Flip and Flip 3D" later in this part for details on how to use Flip and Flip 3D to select a window.

Visual previews also show up in windows that contain file folders when using the Extra Large Icons viewing option. Figure 1-5 illustrates such a situation. Here, you see the contents of a few of the folders inside an Excel Wrkbk folder on my computer's hard drive after selecting Extra Large Icons on the window's Views pop-up slider. When any size between Large Icons and Extra Large Icons are selected, Vista actually shows a live preview of the first few documents within that folder so that you see a thumbnail of an actual graphic image, if the folder contains photos, and a worksheet, if it contains spreadsheets.

As you can begin to see from this brief overview, the Aero Glass interface in Windows Vista offers you an extremely visual and highly dynamic environment in which to work. All around, when coupled with the many less glitzy enhancements that the Microsoft software stuck under the hood, Windows Vista makes for a very satisfying user experience.

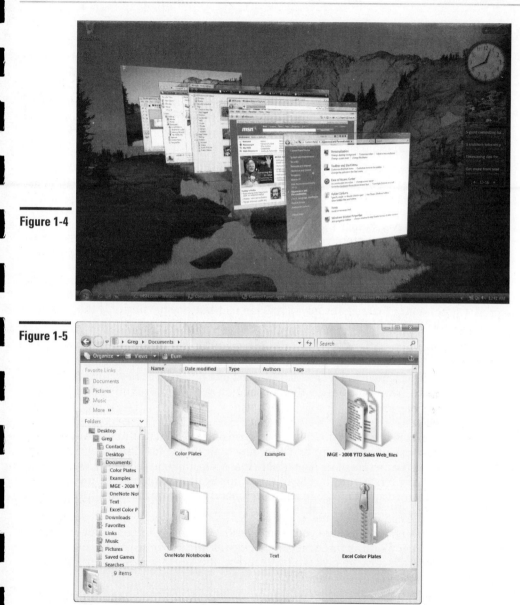

Figure 1-4

Figure 1-5

Ah, That's What They Did with It!

If you're coming to Windows Vista as a user of Windows XP who was completely comfortable with its tried and true ways of doing business, the new Windows Aero Glass desktop may appear to you initially as less open and simple than originally promised. In fact, if your first few minutes with the new and improved Windows graphical user interface are anything like mine, you may feel just a wee bit lost when you first start doing the everyday tasks you seemingly did so effortlessly in the past with Windows XP.

Never fear! You have absolutely no reason to panic: In no time at all, I can set you straight on the new, *more efficient* ways of finding all the stuff on your computer system that you used in the past, while at the same time pointing out what they did with some of your more familiar Windows elements such as the much-beloved My Documents and the underrated Run command.

Start is a very good place to begin

The first thing to note is that the Start button on the Vista taskbar is no longer a rectangular green button that says Start and sports the four-color Microsoft Office banner. Instead, it's now a real circular button sporting only the four-color Microsoft Office banner icon.

Clicking the Start button on the Vista taskbar (or pressing the Start key on your keyboard, if it's so equipped) still opens the Start menu in a two-column format. However, as shown in Figure 1-6, this Start menu has some new buttons and a whole new way of displaying the information about the stuff on your computer.

The new elements located along the bottom of the Vista Start menu include

- ✔ **Start Search** text box, where you can enter search text to find any folder or document on your computer or any topic on the Internet by typing the first few characters of its name. Note that Vista immediately starts matching the characters in the Start Search text box against the contents on your computer (displaying the results in left-hand column of the Start menu) as you type them.

- ✔ **Sleep** button to save your work session and put your computer into a low power mode so that you can quickly resume working with the current desktop arrangement simply by pressing a key (such as Shift or Enter) or by clicking the mouse button.

- ✔ **Lock This Computer** button to lock up your computer when you're away from your desk so that nobody else can use it — keep in mind that you must be able to accurately produce your user password in the text box at the startup screen with your login and picture in order to unlock the computer so you can use it once again (assuming that you've been assigned a password).

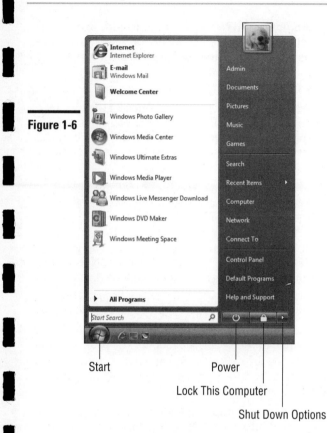

Figure 1-6

Start

Power

Lock This Computer

Shut Down Options

✔ **Shut Down Options** button to open a pop-up menu containing the following options: Switch User to enable you to log onto the computer with a different user account, Log Off to close down your work session and select a different user account, Lock to lock your computer (see the previous bullet "Lock This Computer"), Restart to completely reboot the computer, Sleep to put the computer into a low-power state (see "Sleep" earlier in this list), Hibernate (if you're running Vista on a laptop computer) to save any work in memory to your hard drive and shut your machine down, and Shut Down to close all windows and shut down all power to the computer.

The left-hand column of the Start menu still contains the icons for Windows programs you recently used (which you can fix to this part of the Start menu by right-clicking it and then clicking Pin to Start on the shortcut menu). The right-hand column, although vaguely familiar, lacks all of your accustomed "My" windows (from My Document to My Network Places). All of its items (from Documents to Help and Support) are arranged under the icon you selected for your user account and your username (see the dog icon above Admin in Figure 1-6). As you mouse over the items in this column, you'll notice that a new icon representing the type of item replaces your user account picture at the top of the right-hand column.

TIP Documents, Pictures, Music, Computer, and Network on the Windows Vista Start menu respectively take the place of My Documents, My Pictures, My Music, My Computer, and My Network Places on the Windows XP Start menu.

Using the All Programs item

The All Programs item on the Windows Vista Start menu performs the exact same function as it did in Windows XP — opening menus that you can use to launch Windows utilities and applications programs installed on your computer. Here, however, Vista has it all over XP because it performs this in a much tidier and more efficient manner.

Instead of opening sprawling menus and submenus that can take over pretty much your entire desktop (depending upon how many programs you've installed), Vista keeps all the All Programs menu action restricted to the left-hand column of the Start menu. When you click its All Programs button, Vista displays a list of all the application programs and Windows utilities on your computer (with a vertical scroll bar if there are too many items to display on the left-hand column) and the button changes from an All Programs to Back.

To launch a program or utility, simply click its item in the left-hand column. If the item sports a folder icon (such as Microsoft Office or Accessories), clicking the icon causes an indented submenu to appear (still within the left-hand column of the Start menu) and you can then click the icon for the program you want to launch.

The role of Start Search

You may have noticed the Search item that appeared on the right side of the Windows XP Start menu has changed into a Start Search text box at the very bottom of the Start menu in Windows Vista. This Start Search text box is part of the Search feature that permeates the Vista operating system (you find a similar Search text box in most of the utility windows such as Documents, Pictures, Music, and so on).

Unlike the old clunky search feature in Windows XP that simply opened a dialog box where you had to specify the type of search before you entered the search text and then started the search operation, Quick Search in Vista is always ready to go. All you have to do to initiate a search is to start typing the first few characters of the item you're looking for. Vista starts displaying matching items in the open window (or on the left-hand side of the Start menu when using Start Search) as you type.

For example, if I want to open Microsoft Word to create a new document on my computer, I simply type **wo** in the Start Search text box. Doing this almost immediately displays Microsoft Office Word 2007 (among other items such as WordPad and folders and files whose names contain the letters "wo" as part of their names) above the Start Search text box in the left-hand column of the Start menu (see Figure 1-7). Then all I have to do is click this Microsoft Office Word 2007 link to launch this application in its own program window. (Note that to display the link for launching Excel, I only have to type **e**, which also gives me access to Windows and Internet Explorer.)

In the same vein, on the rare occasion that I need to open the Run dialog box to do something like enter a setup command to install a new program, I only type **r** in the Start Search text box (no need even to type the u to display the Run icon) and then click the Run item. To display the Command Prompt link to open the Command Prompt window where I can access the system directly by typing weird old DOS commands, I only have to type **c** in the Start Search text box (of course, doing this also enables me to open the Media Center, the Calculator utility, and my personal contact list).

TIP   The key to living happily ever after with Windows Vista is to stop worrying about where the items you want to use are actually located on your computer system and just start finding them with Search. Use Start Search on the Start menu to find application programs, Windows components, folders, and files just by entering a few characters in their names.

Figure 1-7

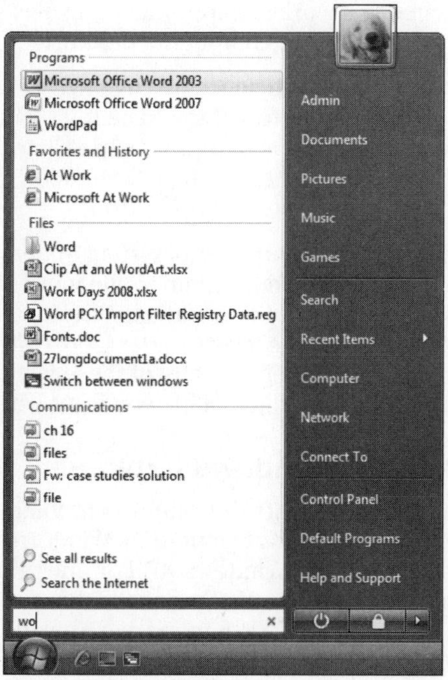

Programs
W Microsoft Office Word 2003
W Microsoft Office Word 2007
WordPad
Favorites and History
At Work
Microsoft At Work
Files
Word
Clip Art and WordArt.xlsx
Work Days 2008.xlsx
Word PCX Import Filter Registry Data.reg
Fonts.doc
27longdocument1a.docx
Switch between windows
Communications
ch 16
files
Fw: case studies solution
file

See all results
Search the Internet

wo

Admin
Documents
Pictures
Music
Games
Search
Recent Items
Computer
Network
Connect To
Control Panel
Default Programs
Help and Support

Looking at virtual folders with Windows Explorer

Windows Vista, like all versions of Windows before it, relies on a structure of Explorer windows that display all the document files and subfolders stored within it. The big difference in Windows Vista is the appearance of an entirely new type of folder called a *virtual folder* that can appear in these windows.

Virtual folders are quite a bit different from the ones you create manually by actually moving and copying particular document files and subfolders into them. Instead, virtual folders are created from some type of search. Because of this, they can contain files that are not actually stored in the same folder (directory) and their contents are dynamically updated (as you add new files that fit a virtual folder's search criteria, they automatically appear in that virtual folder).

The best examples of virtual folders are found in the Documents window (opened by clicking the Documents link in the right-hand column of the Start menu). When this window opens, you see a list of Favorite Links in the Navigation pane on the left side of the window that includes links to two virtual folders: Recently Changed and Searches.

If you click the Recently Changed link, Windows displays the Recently Changed virtual folder containing a listing of all the various files on your computer that you've modified during the current day's work session (including files you've created, edited, or copied or moved onto your computer's hard drive).

You can then filter this list of folders and files by clicking Organize ▶ Layout ▶ Search Pane to display the Search pane at the top of the Recently Changed window, where you can click the particular type of files you want listed. Note that the Search pane contains the filtering buttons E-mail, Document, Picture, Music, and Other to the right of the already selected All button.

If you click the Searches link, Vista displays a number of virtual folders from Attachments through Unread E-mail in the Name column to the immediate right of the Navigation pane. To open the contents of one of these virtual folders such as the Recent E-mail or Unread E-mail, double-click its folder icon. Note that you can also use the Search pane to filter the contents of any of these virtual folders by selecting the button representing just the kinds of file you want listed.

Notable differences in the Vista Windows Explorer

When you first open a folder such as Documents or Computer in Vista, you immediately notice a big difference between the layout of its Windows Explorer and that of earlier Windows versions such as Windows XP. For one thing, in Vista, the Navigation pane on the left contains only Favorite Links in place of the usual File and Folder and Other Places links of XP. For another, the address bar in Vista now appears on top of the Standard Buttons toolbar (which doesn't contain any of the standard buttons!). You also don't see a menu bar in any of the windows unless you click Organize ▶ Layout ▶ Menu Bar or press the Alt key.

Finally, in Vista, Windows Explorer contains a fourth pane, the Details pane, that appears at the very bottom of the window.

TIP

Pressing the Alt key when one of these windows is open acts like a toggle switch: The first time you press it, Vista displays the menu bar; the second time you press it, Vista hides the menu bar display.

In addition, you have the option to display two more new panes in Vista: a Search pane, which appears immediately below the address bar and enables you to quickly filter the contents of any open folder, and a Reader pane, which appears on the right side of the Explorer window and shows you a large thumbnail of the currently selected folder or file.

REMEMBER

Don't forget that you can manipulate the size of the Navigation pane and Details pane (when this pane is displayed) in the Vista Windows Explorer by positioning the mouse pointer anywhere on the edge of the pane that abuts the central display of the subfolders and files in the open folder. When the pointer becomes a two-headed arrow, drag the mouse to the left or right (or up and down in the case of the Details pane) to make the pane smaller or larger.

The Navigation pane

When you first open Windows Explorer, the Navigation pane contains only the Favorite Links Documents, Pictures, and Music along with the Recently Changed and Searches links to its virtual folders. To display the contents of any of the three main folders — Documents, Pictures, or Music — you simply click its link in the Favorite Links area. Vista then displays a complete listing of all the folders and files this folder contains to the right of the Navigation pane in the main part of Windows Explorer.

REMEMBER

When, however, you need to display the contents of a folder other than the three main and two virtual listed in Favorite Links section of the Navigation pane, you have to remember to click the Folders button, the one with the triangle pointing upward at the bottom of this pane.

Clicking the Folders button displays a hierarchical listing of all the different components and folders on your computer (see Figure 1-8). You can then switch to a new component on your system such as the Desktop, Control Panel, or Recycle Bin or to open a new folder such as Downloads, Favorites, or Searches by clicking its icon on this list. When you do, Vista displays the contents of the component or folder you selected in the main part of Windows Explorer.

TIP

You can easily expand or collapse this hierarchical list of folders in the Navigation pane. To expand a folder by displaying its subfolders indented and underneath it, click the open triangle pointing to the right in front of the folder's icon and name. To contract a folder by removing the display of all its subfolders, click the black triangle pointing downward to the right at a 45-degree angle.

Figure 1-8

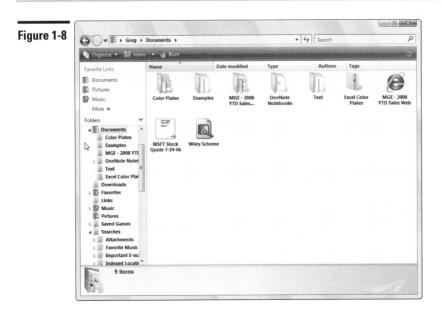

The standard buttons on the toolbar

When you open Windows Explorer either by clicking the Windows Explorer or Documents link on the Start menu, the toolbar may contain a variety of buttons, depending on whether you've selected individual folder or file icons that are displayed in the open Windows Explorer window. These buttons can include

- ✔ **Organize** button opens a drop-down menu with options that perform common folder and file tasks including New Folder, Cut, Copy, or Paste, Select All (to select the items in the current window), Delete, and Rename along with a Layout option that enables you to display the Classic pull-down menus and to control which panes are displayed and hidden in the Explorer. A Properties option opens the Properties dialog box (to turn on and off sharing, revert to earlier versions, and to customize the default appearance of its icons) and a Close item that closes the window (just like clicking the red Close button in the window's upper-right corner).

- ✔ **Views** button changes the way that the file and folders in the current window are displayed by selecting the next view option (Extra Large Icons, Large Icons, Medium Icons, Small Icons, List, Details, and Tiles) — click its drop-down button to display a slider that enables you to try out different sizes in each of these views before selecting the one you want.

- ✔ **Open** button to open the currently selected file with the XPS (XML Paper Specification) Document Viewer or the application program that created it.

- ✔ **Explore** button to open the currently selected folder and display its contents.

✔ **E-mail** button to open a new mail message in the default e-mail program with the selected file or files (if a folder icon is selected) as attachments to the new message.

✔ **Share** button to open the File Sharing dialog box, where you can designate the people on the network with whom you want to share the computer's files.

✔ **Burn** button to copy the items selected in the Explorer to a temporary folder from which you can then burn them to a CD or DVD disc.

When you open Windows Explorer by clicking the Computer link in the Start menu or by clicking Computer in the Folders section of the Navigation pane after opening the Documents Explorer, the toolbar contains the standard Organize and Views buttons. In addition, this toolbar also includes the following buttons when one of the hard drives or a network drive on your system is selected:

✔ **Properties** button to open the General tab of a Properties dialog box for the selected drive. The General tab enables you to change the drive's name, view the amount of used and free space on the drive, compress it, and index the folders and files on it for faster searching. In addition, this dialog box contains tabs with options for customizing and sharing the drive on a network, among other things.

✔ **System Properties** button to open a new System window that displays basic system information about your computer including its microprocessor, the amount of memory, version of Windows Vista installed as well as the computer's name, and its domain or workgroup on a network and the Vista product ID.

✔ **Uninstall or Change a Program** button to replace the Computer Explorer window with the Programs and Features Control Panel window, where you can remove a program you've installed or modify its installation (either by adding components or reinstalling them).

✔ **Map Network Drive** button to open the Map Network Drive dialog box, where you can assign a drive letter to a folder located on a physical drive of a network computer (to which you have access). You can then use the mapped drive letter to open that network folder from the Computer window in Windows Vista.

If you click the icon for a removable storage drive such as a CD or DVD disc drive installed on your computer system, the following three additional buttons appear on the toolbar:

✔ **AutoPlay** button to begin playing the setup or multimedia files on the CD or DVD disc you've inserted into the selected removable drive (on the odd occasion when Vista doesn't automatically start playing them right after inserting the disc).

✔ **Eject This Disk** button to have Vista open the CD or DVD disc drive so that you can either remove the current disc or insert a new disc to play or record to.

✔ **Burn to Disc** button to open the Burn to Disc Wizard, which takes you through the steps of burning selected folders and files to the CD or DVD disc. Note that for this to work, your computer must be equipped with a drive that is capable not only of reading but also of burning files, and a disc of the correct type that is either blank or is re-recordable and has sufficient room for all the files and folders you select.

Remember that a continuation button (>>) automatically appears on the toolbar if the screen resolution is too large and the current size of the Windows Explorer window too small to display all the buttons on the toolbar. In that case, click the continuation button to display a drop-down menu with the missing options that don't currently fit.

Taking a good look at the Views

You have to admit that earlier versions of Windows such as XP did an excellent job of hiding the Views button that you use to change the appearance of the icons of the subfolders and files contained in the folder currently open in Windows Explorer (this unmarked button at the right end of the Standard Buttons toolbar uses a static icon with a dialog box with rows of tiny colored rectangles that just doesn't do a very good job of indicating its function). Contrast this to the Views button in the Vista Windows Explorer that always appears as the second button right after Organize on the toolbar, is clearly marked Views, and dynamically changes its icon to reflect the currently selected view.

In addition, clicking the drop-down button attached to the Vista Views button displays a slider rather than a static drop-down menu of options in XP. You can then use this slider not only to select a new look for your folders and files (in Vista, you have a choice between Extra Large Icons, Large Icons, Medium Icons, Small Icons, List, Details, and Tiles), but also, when settling on one of the Icons selections, you can use the slider to dynamically opt for sizes in between the actual preset Extra Large Icons, Large Icons, Medium Icons, and Small Icons sizes.

Keep in mind that you can cycle through four of the seven preset views (Extra Large Icons, List, Details, and Tiles) by repeatedly clicking the Views button without having to even open the slider. Each time you click the Views button to select the next preset, Vista also updates the icon on the Views button itself to reflect the new view you've selected.

Also, remember that you can sort the subfolders and files displayed in the open folder in Windows Explorer by using any of the column headings listed at the top of the area containing their icons regardless of what view you select (although it's only when you select the Details view that the folder and file info only line up with these column headings). To reorder the icons, click the column heading or field. Click one time to sort the folders and files in ascending order (from A to Z alphabetically, smallest to largest, or least recent to most recent) and a second time to sort them in descending order (Z to A, largest to smallest, or most recent to least recent).

Using the address bar

In Windows Vista, the address bar that keeps you abreast of the path of the folder whose contents is currently displayed in Windows Explorer is not only at the top of the window above the toolbar (in XP, it's located immediately below the Standard Buttons toolbar), but this bar is also flanked on the right by a Search text box with its own More Search Options button and with Back, Forward, and Recent Pages buttons on the left.

In Windows XP, the Back and Forward buttons are part of Standard Buttons toolbar along with an Up button, which is totally absent in Vista. Rather than the Up button (to move up a level in the navigation hierarchy), Vista gives you a Recent Pages drop-down button (the blue triangle pointing downward). When you click this button, Vista displays a drop-down menu showing you all the folders you opened both before and after opening the current folder. To redisplay the contents of a particular you folder you visited, just click its name on this drop-down menu.

One really big difference between the address bar in Vista and that in Windows XP is the way in which the current folder path is displayed on the bar. In place of the backslash (\) separators and the all-squished-together-with-no-spaces pathname, Vista employs black right-pointing triangles (▶) with plenty of space in between the different folder names that make up the path. Moreover, the Vista pathname begins with your username rather than the drive letter.

TIP

If you select the wrong folder as you're building the path by opening subfolders at lower levels in the file hierarchy, you can back up a level and select another folder on that level by clicking the right-pointing triangle immediately in front of the folder you selected by mistake. Vista then displays a drop-down menu with the names of all the folders at that level and you can select the correct one by clicking its name on this list.

REMEMBER

If the path is too long to display all its components on the address bar, a << button appears at the beginning of the pathname. Click this button to display a drop-down menu that lists all individual folders and subfolders in the hierarchical path in the top portion of the menu from the folder immediately above to the Windows desktop. The bottom portion of this drop-down menu lists other folders (from your personal folder to the Recycle Bin) on your computer that you can open by clicking their names.

Just like the address bar in the Windows XP Explorer Window, the one in the Vista Explorer Window contains a drop-down button that that enables you to select the paths of previously opened folders from a drop-down menu. Surprise of surprises, clicking this drop-down button immediately converts the Vista path separated by black triangles into the old backslash-separated and mushed-together pathname of Windows XP. That's the way that all the paths to all the previously opened folders on the drop-down menu appear as well!

However, the moment that you click one of the old-fashioned mushed-together pathnames on this drop-down menu, Vista immediately converts it back into the new-fangled path separated by right-pointing black triangles.

For example, suppose earlier in my work session, I opened the Program Files folder on my computer's local hard drive, given the designation Local Disk (C:), and I now want to reopen it in Windows Explorer. When I click the address bar's drop-down button, this path appears on the drop-down menu:

`C:\Program Files`

However, as soon I click the C:\Program Files item on this pull-down menu, Vista opens this folder and displays the following path on Windows Explorer's address bar following an initial folder icon:

▶ `Computer` ▶ `Local Disk (C:)` ▶ `Program Files` ▶

Note how the new Vista pathname designations with the right-pointing triangles are more accurate than the old ones in describing the actual process you followed to open the current folder. In the previous example, I actually selected the Computer link on the Start menu followed by double-clicking the Local Disk (C:) icon in the Computer window and the Program Files folder icon. The older designations with the backslashes are, however, more accurate in describing the actual location of the folder in the computer's hierarchy of directories and files.

Making the most of the Details pane

The Details pane at the bottom of the window gives you extra information about the folder or file that's currently selected in the main section of Windows Explorer. When a folder is selected, the categories of this information can include the folder name, number of files, and the date the folder was last modified. When a file is selected, the categories of the information can include the filename, size, type, date created, date last modified, and date last accessed, as well as any keywords that you've assigned to the file such as title, authors, and rating. In the case of graphic files and Excel workbook files, Vista also automatically displays a tiny thumbnail of the image or initial worksheet on the left side of the Details pane (see Figure 1-9).

Sometimes you need to enlarge the size of the window to display all the categories and information about the file currently selected in the Details pane. Remember that you can also increase the height of the Details pane by dragging its top border upward.

Figure 1-9

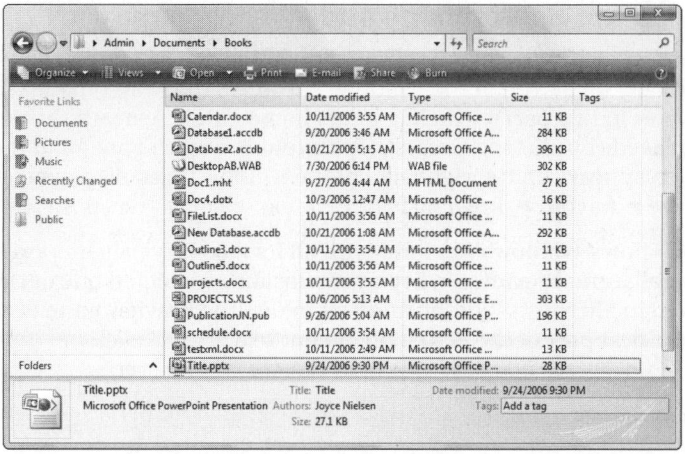

The information displayed in the Details pane can be quite helpful in identifying a folder or file for use. Moreover, the tags, ratings, and keywords assigned to particular files can be used in doing searches for the file. (*See* "Search" later in this part).

TIP

Vista enables you to add tags and edit keywords that you can assign to a file directly from the Details pane. After clicking the file icon in Windows Explorer to select it, you then position the mouse pointer over the category in the Details pane and then, when an outline appears around the current entry and the pointer becomes an I-beam shape, click the insertion point in the field and type the new tag or keyword or edit its contents. Depending upon the type of file (text, graphic image, audio, or video), you are able to edit various fields on this tab.

After you add or edit a tag, you then need to click the Save button that appears the moment you set the insertion point in one of the fields to save the new data as part of the file. Click the Cancel button if you decide not to add the tag or save the editing change.

When you select a music or graphics file, you can give the file a rating between one and five stars by clicking the star (from left to the right) that represents the highest star you want to give it.

Displaying the Search pane and Preview pane

Vista's version of Windows Explorer offers you the use of two extra panes that aren't normally displayed in the window. These are the Search pane (*see* "Search" later in this part), which appears immediately beneath the address bar when displayed (by clicking Organize ▶ Layout ▶ Search Pane) and the Preview pane, which appears on the right side of the window when displayed (by clicking Organize ▶ Layout ▶ Preview Pane).

Figure 1-10 shows Windows Explorer with all its auxiliary panes — Navigation, Search, Details, and Preview — displayed. Because I selected one of the chapter files created in Microsoft Word in an open folder, the Preview pane in this figure displays the first part of the actual document text.

Figure 1-10

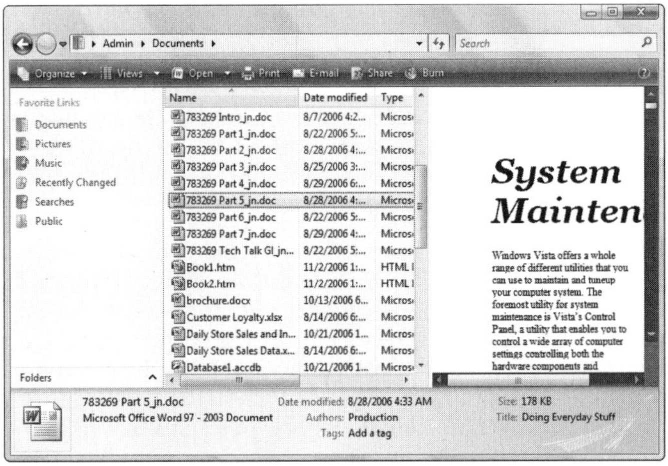

Note that when you select a Microsoft Excel workbook file, the Preview pane displays the first part of the initial worksheet. So too, when you select a graphics file, the Preview pane displays a larger version of the graphic image. When you select a folder rather than a file icon, the Preview pane displays a large semi-open folder on its side with its best representation of the types of documents it contains (assuming the folder's not empty).

Moreover, when you select a video clip or a movie file (perhaps created with Windows Movie Maker — *see* Part 7) in Windows Explorer, the Preview pane displays the first frame of the video file with a video controller beneath complete with Stop, Play/Pause, and Switch to Full Mode buttons that you can use to actually preview the video from start to finish if you so desire.

Likewise, when you select an audio file in Windows Explorer, the Preview pane displays a stock image of a multimedia file (including a music file above the same controller with its Stop, Play/Pause, and Switch to Full Mode buttons). You can then use the Play/Pause button to play the selected audio file from the Preview pane.

 TIP Click the Switch to Full Mode button in the Preview pane if you want to listen to the selected video or audio file in a separate Windows Media Player window. Doing this gives you access to the full array of playback features of this much-improved media player application (*see* "Windows Media Player 11" in Part 7 for details).

Restoring the Classic pull-down menus to Windows Explorer

If you're anything like me, in your time working with earlier versions of Windows such as 98, ME, and XP, you've come to rely upon the so-called Classic pull-down menus in the Explorer Window and, to a lesser extent, the ordering and arrangement of items on the Start menu that you now know so well. Fortunately, you can easily restore some of the good old classic look and feel of bygone Windows versions to Vista anytime you want to.

By far the most important classic element to know how to restore to Vista is the display of the Classic pull-down menus (File, Edit, View, Tools, and Help) in the Windows Explorer windows. To bring back these very valuable (and in rare cases indispensable) menus to all your Explorer windows, click Organize ▶ Folder and Search Options to open the Folder Options dialog box. There, click the View tab and then select the Always Show Menus check box at the top of the Advanced Settings list box before you click OK. After this check box is selected, these pull-down menus automatically appear on their own row between the address bar and the toolbar in every Windows Explorer window you open (including windows opened by clicking the Computer, Network, and Control Panel links on the Start menu).

TIP You can also restore the Classic pull-down menus to your Explorer windows by pressing the Alt key one time. Press the Alt key a second time to once again hide the menus.

Restoring the Classic Windows Start menu

Although I personally do not prefer the rather sloppy cascading submenu arrangement of the Start menu in older Windows versions, preferring instead the tidy new self-contained Start menu of Vista, you can, if you want, return quite readily to the tried-and-true Start menu of your mother's Windows. (After all, the Classic Start menu does include a Run option immediately above the old familiar Shut Down option.)

To make the switch back, right-click the Start button and then click Properties on its shortcut menu to open the Taskbar and Start Menu Properties dialog box with its Start Menu tab selected. On this tab, you click the Classic Start Menu option button and then click OK.

Note, however, that when you first switch back to the Classic Start menu in Vista, this menu does not resemble so much the Windows XP Start menu as it hearkens back to an even earlier vintage, more like the Start menu of Windows 98 (now that takes me back a bit).

You can however, customize the look and feel of the Classic Start menu. One way to do this is to click the Default Programs option that now appears at the very top of the Start menu and then click the Set Your Default Programs link in the Default Programs Control Panel window. You can then select the programs such as Internet Explorer, Windows Mail, and the like that you always want to appear on the Start menu.

The other way to customize the Classic Start menu is to reopen its Properties dialog box and then click its Customize button on the Start Menu tab to open the Customize Classic Start Menu dialog box. There, you can use Add, Remove, and Sort buttons as well as the check boxes in the Advanced Start Menu Options list box to customize what items do and don't appear on the menu and in what order.

Getting rid of the Vista glassiness

Let's face it: You either love the shiny new Aero Glass look of Windows Vista or you find it to be totally distracting and a big waste of your precious computer resources. If you happen to hold the latter opinion, follow these steps to get rid of the ritzy glassy look and go back to the old clunky opaque view of yesteryear:

1. Right-click anywhere on the Vista desktop and then click the Personalize item on its shortcut menu.

2. Click the Window Color and Appearance link in the Personalization Control Panel window.

3. Click the Open Classic Appearance Properties for More Color Options link at the bottom of the Window Color and Appearance Control Panel window.

4. Click the Windows Classic selection in the Color Scheme list box and then click OK.

And that's all there is to it: Vista fades to black. When the screen comes back up, in place of all that glittery, semitransparent taskbar and windows nonsense, every Vista screen now has a thick-as-mud look and feel that would do Windows 95 proud!

TIP Just click the Enable Transparency check box in the Window Color and Appearance Control Panel window to remove its check mark if you're happy with the default Windows Vista color scheme and only want to get rid of the transparency effects.

Adopting a Classic view of the Control Panel

Finally, you may find the default look of the Vista Control Panel (which is, fortunately a little less sparse than the Category View of the Windows XP Control Panel) not to your liking. Switching back to the display of rows of individual Control Panel icons (in alphabetical order from Add Hardware through Windows Update) is really simple.

Click the Control Panel link on the Start menu and then click the Classic View link in its Navigation pane immediately beneath Control Panel Home. Just remember that when the Control Panel is in Classic View, you must double-click the Control Panel icon whose settings you want to modify in order to open its dialog box.

Click the Control Panel Home link in the Navigation pane to return to the default category display.

Things that haven't changed a bit

Although it may seem as though quite a bit of the user interface is radically different, you'll be glad to know that many, many of the ways of doing things in Windows Vista have remained the same. Here's a short list of such things to give you an idea of just how much you already know how to do:

- ✔ You still move a window by dragging it by its title bar (which is a bit easier given the larger size in Vista) and minimize, maximize, and close windows with these buttons in the upper-right corner.

- ✔ You still resize windows by dragging one of their side borders or corners.

- ✔ All items still have shortcut menus associated with them that are opened by right-clicking them.

- ✔ All your common shortcut keystrokes such as Ctrl+C (for Copy), Ctrl+X (for Cut), Ctrl+V (for Paste), Ctrl+Z (Undo) as well as Alt+← for Back, Alt+→ for Forward, Alt+F4 for Close Current Window (or shut down Vista if all windows are closed) still work just as before.

- ✔ You can still modify the desktop by selecting a new desktop background image, screen saver, as well as add standard desktop icons (such as Documents, Computer, and Internet Explorer) if you don't like having to choose them from the Start menu — right-click the desktop and then click Personalize on its shortcut menu to open the Personalization Control Panel window.

✔ You can still map folders located on your network to virtual drive letters (up to Z just as long as they don't duplicate drive letters already assigned to physical devices connected to the machine) that appear each time you log on to the computer — just choose Tools⇨Map Network Drive when the Classic menus are displayed in Windows.

✔ You can still add desktop shortcuts for any item (drive, program, folder, or file) on your computer, network, or the Internet that you can then open by double-clicking — **see** "Displaying additional desktop icons" later in this part for details.

Flip and Flip 3D

When you have many windows open in Vista, the Flip and Flip 3D (also known as the Window Switcher) features provide you with two quick methods for activating the window you want to work by displaying it on the top of the others.

To use the Flip feature, hold down Alt+Tab. Vista displays a band in the middle of the desktop showing thumbnails of each open window in the order in which they were opened (refer to Figure 1-3). To activate a new window, press Alt+Tab (or hold down the Alt key as you press → or ←) until the thumbnail of that window is highlighted and its name appears centered above in the band. Then release the Alt key along with Tab or the left or right arrow key. To minimize all the open windows as buttons on the Vista taskbar, highlight the Desktop, Windows Explorer thumbnail that appears as the last image on the right of the group.

 To use the Flip 3D feature (refer to Figure 1-4), click the Switch between Windows button (shown in left margin) on the Quick Launch toolbar. Vista then dims the background of the desktop and displays all open windows in 3-D cascading arrangement. If your mouse is equipped with a center wheel, you can then zip (and I mean zip) through the 3-D stack by turning the wheel (forward to flip backward through the stack and backward to flip forward).

As soon as you've brought the image of the window you want to activate to the front of the 3-D stack, click anywhere on the image. Vista then returns the desktop to normal, collapsing the 3-D stack while at the same time activating the window you clicked by placing it on top. If your mouse doesn't have a center wheel, you can still select a window to activate by clicking the part of it that is exposed in the 3-D stack.

When all the open windows in Vista are minimized as buttons on the taskbar — as after clicking the Show Desktop button (shown in left margin) on the Quick Launch toolbar — remember that you only need to position the mouse pointer over each button to display a thumbnail of its window. Then when you see the image of the window you want to activate, click its button on the taskbar to display it on the Vista desktop either full-screen or in its previous position and size.

Personalize

Vista makes it easy for you to personalize your computer by selecting a new desktop background image, a color scheme for the various Windows elements, a screen saver to use when the computer has been idle for a certain period, as well as the sound effects to play when different events take place.

The easiest way to open the Personalization window (see Figure 1-11) for changing these settings is by right-clicking anywhere on the desktop background and then clicking Personalize at the bottom of the desktop's shortcut menu.

Figure 1-11

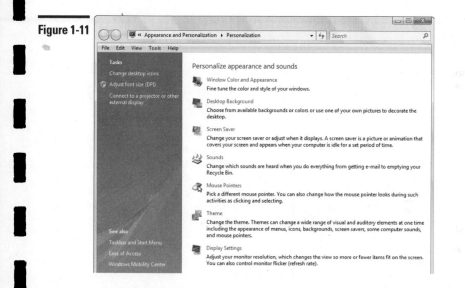

Note that you can also open this dialog box through the Control Panel (Start ▶ Control Panel) by first selecting the Appearance and Personalization link followed by the Personalization link, but this method requires a whole lot more steps to do the same thing.

The options for customizing Vista in the Personalization window include

✔ **Window Color and Appearance** to replace the Personalization window with the Window Color and Appearance window (see Figure 1-12), where you can select a new color and the amount of glassiness for the title bars of windows, the Start menu, and taskbar. To select a Windows XP color scheme, click the Open Classic Appearance Properties for More Options link to open the Appearance Settings dialog box, where you then select or customize one of its ready-made schemes.

Figure 1-12

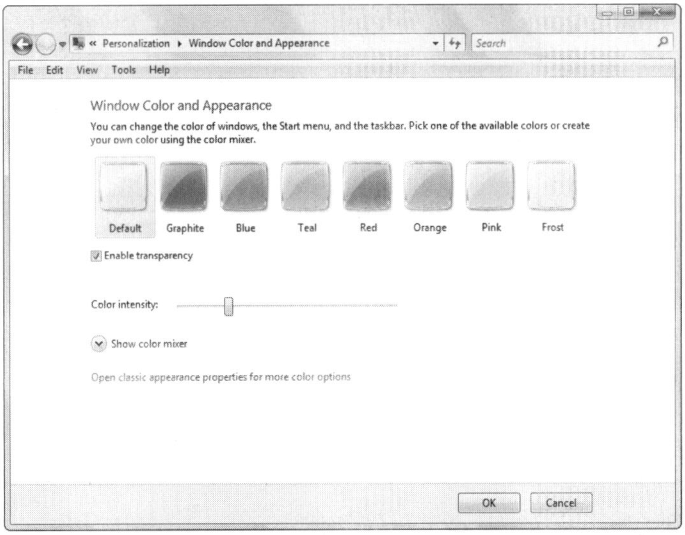

✔ **Desktop Background** to replace the Personalization window with the Desktop Background window (see Figure 1-13), where you can select a new ready-made wallpaper image, select your own photo image as the wallpaper (with the Browse button), change how the wallpaper image is displayed on the desktop (Fit to Screen, Tile, or Center), or select a new solid color for the background by clicking Solid Colors on the Picture Location drop-down list.

✔ **Screen Saver** to open the Screen Saver Settings dialog box, where you can select a new screen saver to use, customize the amount of idle time before the screen saver kicks in, and adjust your monitor and hard drive power settings (by clicking the Change Power Settings link).

✔ **Sounds** to open the Sounds dialog box, where you can assign new sounds to different program events and save your new choices as a custom sound scheme to reuse.

✔ **Mouse Pointers** to open the Mouse Properties dialog box with the Pointers tab selected, where you can select a new mouse pointer scheme (very helpful if you suffer a vision impairment that makes it difficult to track the normal mouse pointer), as well as customize what icons are used in various pointing situations.

✔ **Theme** to open the Theme Settings dialog box, where you can select a new ready-made theme to use or save the changes you've made to the color scheme, desktop background, screen saver, and sound effects (as described below) as a new theme to reuse.

✔ **Display Settings** to open the Display Settings dialog box, where you can select a new monitor (if you have more than one connected to your computer) as well as new screen resolution and color-depth settings for the monitor or monitors you have attached to your computer. Note that the range of the resolution and color settings you have to choose from depends on the capabilities of the monitor or monitors you have.

Figure 1-13

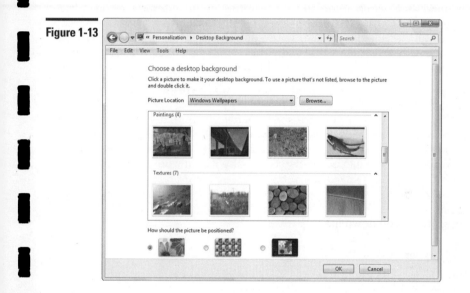

Search

The Search feature provides you an extremely efficient way to locate any program, folder, or file on your computer system. A Search text box appears in the upper-right corner of all the major Explorer windows — Computer, Documents, Network, Control Panel, Pictures, Music, and the like — where it's labeled *Search,* and at the bottom of the Start menu, where it's labeled *Start Search.*

Search immediately starts searching your computer system for matches to any characters you enter into one of its search text boxes the moment you type them. The feature not only automatically searches for matches in the names of programs, drives, folders, files, and so on on your computer, but in the metadata in files (that is, keywords you assign and statistics such as author, date modified, and so on that Windows and other programs automatically assign), and even in text contained in document files.

Keep in mind that Search automatically searches all the indexed files on your computer system for the characters you type into a search text box. If you only want to search a particular drive or folder on your computer system, you need to perform an advanced search by using the Search pane (*see* "Doing advanced searches with the Search pane" later in this part).

Figure 1-14 illustrates this point. This figure shows the results in a Search Results in Indexed Locations window (opened by clicking Search on the Start menu) after conducting a search for the term *blue*. Note that Vista not only finds all the files whose filenames contain the word *blue,* but also several Excel workbook files whose spreadsheets contain references to blueberry muffins. It even finds a Word document named Hidden Gems of Wisdom whose text contains a reference to a precious blue gem.

Figure 1-14

Name	Date modified	Type	Folder	Authors	Tag
Hidden Gems of Wisdom	8/27/2006 3:07 PM	Microsoft Office W...	Text (C:\Users\Gre...	Greg Har...	
037377 Ch07	8/27/2006 2:01 PM	Microsoft Office W...	Text (C:\Users\Gre...	Greg Har...	Mu
OAM's Blues	8/26/2006 1:06 PM	Windows Media A...	Sample Music (C:\...		
04 Sunday Mornin'	8/16/2006 11:29 AM	Windows Media A...	20th Century Mast...		
05 Like To Get To Kno...	8/16/2006 11:26 AM	Windows Media A...	20th Century Mast...		
01 Sunday Will Never B...	8/16/2006 11:26 AM	Windows Media A...	20th Century Mast...		
03 Lazy Day	8/16/2006 11:26 AM	Windows Media A...	20th Century Mast...		
Chris Cookies - Jan08 S...	7/11/2006 7:59 AM	Microsoft Office E...	Examples (C:\User...	Greg Har...	
037377 Ch12	6/21/2006 3:43 PM	Microsoft Office W...	Text (C:\Users\Gre...	IDG BOOKS	
037377 Ch10	6/21/2006 9:59 AM	Microsoft Office W...	Text (C:\Users\Gre...	Default	

Search Results in Indexed Locations • blue

Show only: All   E-mail   Document   Picture   Music   Other   Advanced Search

Organize •   Views •   Save Search   Search Tools •   Burn

Favorite Links
Documents
Pictures
Music
More »

Folders
Desktop
Search Results in Inde
Greg
Public
Computer
Network
Control Panel
Recycle Bin

Did you find what you were searching for?
Advanced Search

10 items

Adding tags for searches

Because Search automatically searches the metadata added to your files, you can make these searches much more effective by adding your own tags, including key-words and other types of search data, whenever possible.

When creating documents with application programs such as Microsoft Word or Excel, you can add all kind of your own metadata tags including subject, category, keywords, and comments by opening the document in the program and then selecting the Summary tab of its Properties dialog box (File⇨Properties). In a program such as Adobe Reader 7, you can add keywords by opening the PDF file and then selecting the Description tab of the Document Properties dialog box (File⇨Document Properties).

For media files on your computer (music, video, and photos and other graphic images), Vista actually enables you to add tags in the Preview pane that appears along the bottom of Music, Videos, and Pictures Explorer windows. To add tags to one of these media files, all you have to do is select the file in its Explorer window, and then add the desired tags to the appropriate fields on the Details tab pane.

TIP Music, video, and graphic media files also enable you to specify other metadata tags on the Details tab of their Properties dialog boxes such as titles, dates and time taken, and a rating between one and five stars (by clicking the appropriate star).

Doing advanced searches with the Search pane

Most of the time, you only need to perform simple searches in order to find the item you're looking for. Vista does, however, provide an Advanced Search button on the right side of the Search pane that you can display in any Windows Explorer window (Organize ▶ Layout ▶ Search pane). When you click the Advanced Search button, Vista expands the Search pane (see Figure 1-15) by adding the following options you can use in a search:

✔ **Location** drop-down list box to select a particular drive on your computer to search

✔ **Date** drop-down list box to search for documents by the Date Modified, Date Created, or Date Accessed (selected on the Date drop-down list) that you specify in its text box, using the criteria you select on its Any drop-down list box (Is, Is Before, or Is After)

✔ **Size (KB)** drop-down list box to search for documents by the file size that you enter in the text box, using the criteria you select on its Any drop-down list box (Equals, Is Less Than, or Is Greater Than)

✔ **Name** text box to search for a document by its filename by entering all or part of the filename in this text box — you can use the asterisk (*) to stand for one or more wild-card characters in the filename and a question mark (?) to stand for individual wild-card characters

✔ **Tags** text box to search for a document by the tags assigned to it by entering one or more of them into this text box

✔ **Authors** text box to search for documents by a particular author whose name is entered in this text box

Figure 1-15

When creating searches in the Advanced Search pane, keep in mind that all the conditions you specify with the Location, Date, Size (KB), Filename, Tags, and Authors options are inclusive so that all their conditions must be met in order for the types of files you've specified to be returned to your Search Results window.

Saving search results in a search folder

Instead of having to go through the whole rigmarole of reentering the same search criteria each time you want to find the same types of items on your computer, you can save the results of your search as a search folder. That way, you have access to the items simply by opening the search folder after selecting the Searches link in a Windows Explorer window.

To save your search results as search folder, follow these steps:

1. Click the Save Search button on Windows Explorer or Search window's toolbar.

   Vista opens a Save As dialog box where you specify the name and description for your new virtual folder.

2. (Optional) Add additional author names to the folder by clicking Authors and entering them, or add tags that identify the search folder and can be used in searching for it by clicking the Add a Tag text in the Tags field.

3. Click the Save button to create your search folder and close the Save As dialog box.

After saving your search results as a search folder, Vista automatically re-creates the search criteria, performs the Search, and then displays the same results each time you select the folder in a Windows Explorer window.

 Vista automatically saves your search folder as part of the Searches virtual folder so that all you have to do to find your search folder and open up it up again is to click the Searches link near the top of the Navigation pane in your Windows Explorer window and then double-click its search folder icon.

Sidebar and Gadgets

Sidebar and gadgets are the names given to a new Vista's desktop feature that gives you instant access to volatile information such as the current time, weather, stock quotes, and the like. The *Sidebar* is the name of the pane — appearing either on the right or left side of your computer's desktop — that contains the *gadgets*, the name given to the specialized miniapplications that give you the up-to-date information.

Figure 1-16 shows you my desktop with the Search All Gadgets window displayed (*see* "Adding new gadgets to your Sidebar" later in this part) and the Sidebar itself appearing on the right side of the computer's desktop (its default position). This Sidebar is running the three default gadgets that automatically install with Windows Vista:

✔ **Clock,** which shows an analog clock with the current time for any time zone you select.

✔ **Slide Show,** which displays a continuous slideshow of the images that you have stored in your Pictures folder.

✔ **Feed Headlines,** which shows you headlines for the RSS you select. (*See* "Internet Explorer 7" in Part 4 for details on RSS feeds and how to subscribe to them.)

Figure 1-16

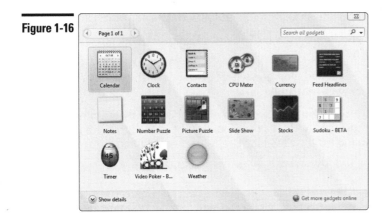

Changing where and how the Sidebar appears

To display the Sidebar on the left side of your computer's desktop or to make sure that it always appears on the top of other windows you have open on the desktop, you need to open the Windows Sidebar Properties dialog box. The easiest way to do this is by right-clicking somewhere in the Sidebar area on the right side of the screen (but outside any of the gadgets) and then clicking Properties on the Sidebar's shortcut menu.

To have Vista display the Sidebar on the left side of the screen, click the Left option button — just keep in mind that opening of the Start menu may overlap some of the gadgets when the Sidebar is displayed on the left side of the screen.

To have Vista display the Sidebar on top of all open windows on the desktop, click the Sidebar is Always on Top of Other Windows check box before clicking OK.

Note that when you do elect to have Vista display the Sidebar on the left side of the screen *and* display the Sidebar on top of all other windows, Vista makes sure that none of its gadgets obscure the Recycle Bin (and any other desktop icons you add) by automatically offsetting such desktop icons to the right, out of the way of the Sidebar. Vista also ensures that none of its gadgets obscure any items on the Start menu by always displaying the Start menu on top of the Sidebar when the Sidebar appears on the left side of the screen.

If you have more than one monitor connected to your computer, you can select the monitor on which the Sidebar is displayed as well. To switch the Sidebar to a new monitor, open the Windows Sidebar Properties dialog box and then select the number of the monitor in the Display Sidebar on Monitor drop-down list box.

If you don't know the number of the monitor on which you want the Sidebar displayed, right-click the desktop. On the shortcut menu that appears, click Personalize, followed by the Display Settings link in the Personalization Control Panel window to open the Display Settings dialog box. Then click the Identify Monitors button to find out the number of each monitor connected to your computer.

Hiding or eliminating the Sidebar

If you want to temporarily hide the Sidebar and all its gadgets, right-click anywhere on the Sidebar outside of its gadgets and then click Close Sidebar on the shortcut menu.

To redisplay the hidden Sidebar, click the Windows Sidebar icon (the blue icon that at first glance looks like an old TV set) in the Notification area of the Windows taskbar.

If you want to get rid of the Sidebar on a more-or-less permanent basis, open the Windows Sidebar Properties dialog box by right-clicking somewhere on the Sidebar (outside of the gadgets) and then click Properties on its shortcut menu. Then click the Start Sidebar When Windows Starts check box to remove its check mark before you click OK. Doing this prevents Vista from starting up the hidden Sidebar the next time you boot up your computer.

You can also open the Windows Sidebar Properties dialog box by clicking Start ▶ Control Panel ▶ Appearance and Personalization ▶ Windows Sidebar Properties.

Adding new gadgets to your Sidebar

You can easily add gadgets to the few that are initially displayed on the Sidebar when you first install Windows Vista. Not only can you select new gadgets from among those that are automatically shipped with the Vista operating system (but just not displayed on the Sidebar), but you can always download gadgets from an ever-expanding online library.

To add gadgets to the Sidebar from among those that are included with Windows Vista, follow these steps:

1. Click the plus sign (+) that appears at the top of the Sidebar or right-click somewhere on the Sidebar outside of any gadgets, and then click Add Gadgets on the shortcut menu.

   Vista opens the Gadget Gallery window that displays all the gadgets on your computer similar to the one shown in Figure 1-16.

2. Click the Show Details link to expand the dialog box before you click the thumbnail of the gadget you're interested in adding to the Sidebar.

   The Details pane of the Gadgets Gallery window displays a brief description of the purpose of the gadget whose thumbnail you click.

3. When you locate a gadget you want to add to the Sidebar, drag its thumbnail to the Sidebar or double-click its thumbnail or right-click it and then click Add on its shortcut menu.

When you double-click the thumbnail or right-click and click Add, Vista then immediately adds the gadget you selected to the top of the Sidebar, moving all the existing gadgets down one. Note, however, that you can reorder any of the gadgets displayed on the Sidebar by dragging them to a new position.

To download more gadgets from the Internet, open the Gadgets Gallery window as outlined in the previous steps and then click the Get More Gadgets Online link. Vista then opens the Microsoft Gadgets Web page in the Internet Explorer. This page offers not only gadget news and instructions on how to download new gadgets, but also information how to build your own gadgets, if you're so inclined.

To remove a gadget from the Sidebar, position the mouse pointer in the upper-right corner of the gadget you want to remove and then click the X that appears. Note that removing a gadget from the Sidebar does not delete it from your computer — to do that, you need to open the Search All Gadgets window, and then right-click the gadget's thumbnail and click Uninstall on its shortcut menu. To restore a gadget that you've removed from the Sidebar, just repeat the previous steps for adding a new gadget.

Customizing the contents of a gadget

Many of the gadgets you add to the Sidebar are generic and need to be customized. For example, you can customize the Clock gadget by selecting a new clock face, giving it a name, and selecting a time zone other than your own (this analog clock automatically displays the same time as the digital time display in the Notification area of the Vista taskbar). You also need to customize the Feed Headlines gadget so that it displays headlines for a particular RSS feed to which you've subscribed (*see* "Internet Explorer 7" in Part 4 for details on how to subscribe to an RSS feed).

To customize the contents of a gadget, position the mouse pointer in the upper-right corner of the gadget and then click the wrench icon that appears immediately beneath the X. Alternatively, you can also right-click its icon on the Sidebar and then click Options on the gadget's shortcut menu. Vista then opens a dialog box specific to the gadget that enables you to customize its display.

For example, if you open the settings dialog box for the Clock gadget, you can then select a new clock face by clicking the button with ▶ symbol, and entering a clock name (such as London or Beijing that then appears on the face of the clock) in the Clock Name text box. Next, select the appropriate time zone for the clock in the Time Zone drop-down list box. In addition, this dialog box contains a Show the Second Hand check box that you select if you want the Clock gadget to display a moving red second hand.

Changing the opacity of a gadget

In addition to customizing what information appears in the gadget (as in the RSS feed headlines shown in the Feed Headlines gadget), you can also customize the overall opacity of the gadget. Any gadget you add to the Sidebar is automatically displayed at 100% opacity (making it as opaque and non-see-through as possible). You can, however, lighten up any of your gadgets, thereby making them more see-through by changing the gadget's opacity.

To modify the opacity of a gadget, right-click the gadget and then highlight Opacity on its shortcut menu. Doing this displays a submenu where you click the new opacity percentage you want to use (20%, 40%, 60%, or 80%). The lower the percentage, the more transparent the gadget is.

Detaching a gadget from the Sidebar and freely moving it around the desktop

Finally, Vista enables you to customize any gadget on the Sidebar by completely detaching it from the Sidebar. This makes it possible for you to then drag the gadget to any position you want on the entire desktop (to move a detached gadget, you just drag its icon around the desktop like you would any other desktop icon or title bar of any open window).

To detach a gadget, position the mouse pointer in the upper-right corner of the gadget and then drag the gadget off of the Sidebar to a new position on the desktop by using the handle that appears beneath the wrench. (This handle looks like eight tiny white dots in two columns.)

You can also detach a gadget by right-clicking the gadget and then clicking Detach from Sidebar on its shortcut menu. Vista then immediately redisplays the gadget on the desktop off to the side of the Sidebar. You are then free to drag the gadget to a new position on the desktop.

If you decide you no longer want a gadget to be free-floating on the desktop, you can easily reattach it to the Sidebar by dragging it to the Sidebar and then dropping it into the position where you want it to appear.

 TIP Note that if you add a new gadget when the Sidebar is hidden, Vista automatically adds it as a detached gadget that you can immediately drag to the desired position on the desktop.

Vista Desktop

The Vista desktop consists of the taskbar (*see* "Vista Taskbar" immediately following) that appears along the bottom of the screen, a background image (or color) that fills the rest of the screen (*see* "Personalize" earlier in this part), the Sidebar with its gadgets on the right side of the screen (*see* "Sidebar and Gadgets" earlier in this part), and whatever desktop icons and desktop shortcuts you then choose to place on this background.

In keeping with Vista's open and spacious Aero Glass design (*see* "Aero Glass Interface" earlier in this part), the Windows desktop starts out with just a single Recycle Bin desktop icon (where you drop any files, folders, and desktop shortcuts you want delete from the system).

Displaying additional desktop icons

In addition to the Recycle Bin icon, you can add the following icons to your Vista desktop:

- **Computer** to open your Computer window (same as choosing Start ▶ Computer from the taskbar), which shows all the drives and components connected to your computer (including virtual drives that you've mapped onto a drive letter).

- **User's Files** to open your Documents window (same as choosing Start ▶ Documents from the taskbar), which shows all the document files on your computer. (*See* "Windows Explorer" in Part 2.)

- **Network** to open the Network window (same as choosing Start ▶ Network), which shows all the computers on your local area network. (*See* Part 3.)

- **Internet Explorer** to launch the Internet Explorer 7 (same as choosing Start ▶ Internet Explorer), which you use to browse the Web. (*See* "Internet Explorer 7" in Part 4.)

- **Control Panel** to open the Control Panel window (same as Start ▶ Control Panel), which enables you to customize all sorts of computer settings. (*See* "Control Panel" in Part 5.)

To add any or all of these desktop icons, follow these steps:

1. Right-click somewhere on the desktop background (outside of any icon) and then click Personalize on the shortcut menu.

2. Click the Change Desktop Icons link in the Navigation pane of the Personalization window to open the Desktop Icon Settings dialog box.

3. Click the check boxes for all the desktop icons (Computer through Control Panel) you want to appear on the Vista desktop.

4. Click OK to close the Desktop Icon Settings dialog box and then click the Close button in the upper-right corner of the Personalization window.

After adding a desktop icon to the Vista desktop, you can open its window by double-clicking the icon or right-clicking it and then selecting Open on its shortcut menu.

Creating desktop shortcuts

You can create desktop shortcuts to launch application programs you've installed as well as to open drives, folders, and documents on your computer system, and Web pages on the Internet.

To create a desktop shortcut, you need to do just two things:

✔ Locate the icon for the program, drive, folder, or document for which you want to create the shortcut on the Start menu or in the Computer, Network, or Documents window. (To create a shortcut to a Web page, open the page in the Internet Explorer.)

✔ Right-click the program, drive, folder, or document icon and then select Send To ▶ Desktop (Create Shortcut) on the icon's shortcut menu. (In the case of a Web page, choose File ▶ Send ▶ Shortcut to Desktop on the Internet Explorer's pull-down menu when the Classic menus are displayed.)

Note that to create a desktop shortcut to a drive on your computer system, you must choose the Create Shortcut item on its shortcut menu (there is no Send To item).

You can also use a Wizard to create a desktop shortcut by following these few steps:

1. Right-click anywhere on the desktop outside of an existing desktop item and then choose New ▶ Shortcut on the shortcut menu.

2. Enter the location of the item to which you want to create the shortcut either by entering its path and filename or URL (Web) address or by clicking

the Browse button and locating the item in the Browse for Files or Folders dialog box before you click OK.

3. Click the Next button and then, if you want, edit the name for the shortcut in the Type a Name for This Shortcut text box before you click Finish.

After creating a desktop shortcut, you can open the program, drive, folder, document, or Web page associated with it by double-clicking the shortcut icon or by right-clicking it and then clicking Open on its shortcut menu.

 Use the options on the View desktop shortcut menu to change the size of all desktop icons, to remove automatic arrangement of the icons and alignment to an invisible grid, as well as to temporarily remove the display of all icons. Use the options (Name, Size, Type, and Date Modified) on the Sort By desktop shortcut menu to change the order in which your desktop shortcuts appear in columns across the desktop.

Vista Taskbar

The taskbar is your constant companion in Windows Vista. No matter where you go or what you do, the taskbar and the buttons of the various toolbars continue to be displayed along the bottom of the screen. That way, you have access to all those features no matter whether you're writing a letter in your favorite word processor, surfing the Web with Internet Explorer 7, or perusing your favorite graphic images in the Windows Photo Gallery or Media Center.

The taskbar forms the base of the Windows desktop. Running along the bottom of the complete width of the screen, the taskbar is divided into three sections:

- **The Start button,** with the accompanying Start menu at the far left

- **Buttons for open toolbars and minimized windows** in the center area

- **The Notification area** (at the far right; also called the system tray), with current time and icons showing the current status of computer components and programs and processes that are running in the background

When you open an Explorer window or program window on the Vista desktop, Windows adds a button representing that window to the center section of the taskbar. When you have multiple windows open at a time, you can bring a window to the top of the stack by clicking that button on the taskbar or with the Flip or Flip 3D features (*see* "Flip and Flip 3D" earlier in this part).

Whenever you minimize a window by clicking the Minimize button, Windows reduces it to just a button on the taskbar. When you click this button on the taskbar, Windows restores the window to the previous size and position on the Windows desktop.

The Start menu

The Start button that opens the Start menu (shown in the left margin) always appears as the first button on the taskbar. The Start menu is the most basic menu in Windows, giving you access to all the stuff on your computer.

To open the Start menu, simply click the Start button icon in the lower-left corner of the taskbar or press Ctrl+Esc or press the Windows button on your keyboard (if your keyboard has this button).

The Start menu is divided into two columns, and your user picture and name appears at the top of the second column on the right. The options appearing on this right column of the Start menu are fixed and never change. In the left column, only the All Programs button and Start Search button at the bottom and the Internet Explorer options at the top are fixed. All the other icons that appear in the area in between change over time as they represent icons of the programs that you launch most frequently.

TIP

To fix a particular item on the Start menu, open the menu and then right-click the item before you click Pin to Start Menu on its shortcut menu.

To open an Explorer window, such as Documents or Network, to connect to the Internet, or to run one of the recently used programs, you simply click that icon in the right column of the Start menu. To launch a program or open a Windows component that does not appear in the right column, click the All Programs item and then click the desired item in the left-hand column.

To lock your computer when you're away from it so that nobody else in the office can go messing with your files (unless you're naïve enough to give them your password), click the Lock button (the one with the padlock icon). Vista then displays a screen containing your username and personal icon below which you find a Password text box. In order to get back to your desktop and resume work, you must then correctly enter your password into this text box and then press Enter or click the Arrow button to the right of the Password text box.

To give your computer a much-needed nap during lunch or when you're on break, you can put it to sleep (a lower-power mode in which all your work is kept in memory for quick startup when you return) by clicking the Sleep button (the one with the vertical bar in the middle of a circle) to the immediate left of the Lock button.

To log off the computer, switch users, or to lock, restart, or shut it down, click the pop-up button that appears to the immediate right of the Lock button (the one with padlock — refer to Figure 1-6) and then click the desired item on its pop-up menu.

To locate a program or Windows component on your computer, type the first characters of the item's name in the Start Search text box.

See "Customizing the Start menu" later in this part for details on how you can change the look and contents of the Start menu.

Customizing the taskbar

The Taskbar and Start Menu Properties dialog box enables you to customize the settings for the taskbar and the Start menu. To open this dialog box, right-click the Start button or any open area (with no buttons) on the taskbar and then click Properties on the taskbar shortcut menu. Click the Taskbar tab in the Taskbar and Start Menu Properties dialog box that appears.

The check boxes in the Taskbar Appearance section at the top of the Taskbar tab do the following:

- ✔ **Lock the Taskbar:** Locks all the bars so that you can't adjust the size of the different areas of the taskbar, such as the Quick Launch toolbar.

- ✔ **Auto-hide the Taskbar:** Hides the taskbar until you roll the mouse pointer somewhere over that position. This way, the taskbar appears only when you need it.

- ✔ **Keep the Taskbar on Top of Other Windows:** Always places the taskbar in front of any window that you move down so far that they overlap it.

- ✔ **Group Similar Taskbar Buttons:** Displays buttons for files opened by the same program in the same area of the taskbar. Moreover, if the taskbar becomes so crowded with buttons that become too small to display, Windows collapses the buttons for a particular program into one button that, when clicked, displays a pop-up menu from which you can select the file you want to display on the desktop.

- ✔ **Show Quick Launch:** Displays the Quick Launch toolbar on the Windows taskbar immediately following the Start button.

- ✔ **Show Window Previews (Thumbnails):** Displays a thumbnail of each open window that's minimized on the taskbar when you position the mouse over its button.

Customizing the Start menu

To customize the appearance of the Start menu, you need to click the Start Menu tab in the Taskbar and Start Menu Properties dialog box. This tab gives you a choice between the Start menu as it now appears in two columns and the old single-column classic method used in previous versions of Windows. To switch to this single-column view, click the Classic Start Menu option button. Should you later decide to switch back to the default two-column arrangement, you can do so by clicking the Start Menu option button.

Both option buttons are accompanied by Customize buttons that open dialog boxes in which you can change what icons appear on the Start menu. Figure 1-17 shows the Customize Start Menu dialog box, which appears when you click the Customize button associated with the Start Menu option button that controls the default two-column Start menu arrangement.

Figure 1-17

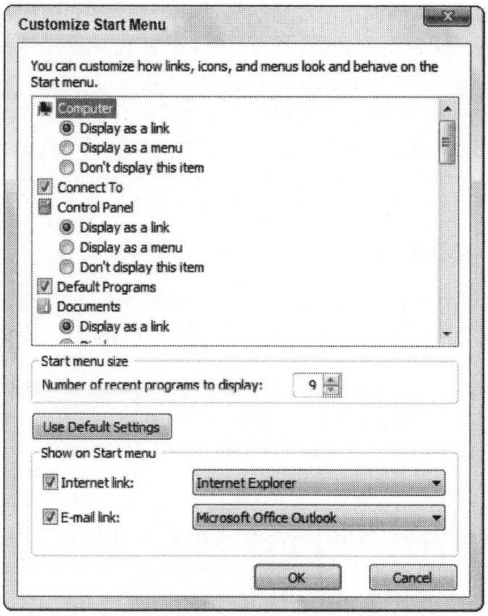

Use the check boxes in the list box of this dialog box to control which items appear in the right-hand column of the Start menu. For example, to add a Printers item that opens the Printers window (where you can add new printers), click the Printers check box to put a check mark in it. Likewise, to remove the Default Programs item that opens the Default Programs dialog box (where you can configure what default programs to use for tasks such as Web browsing and reading e-mail), click the Default Programs check box to remove its check mark.

To change the way fixed icons, such as Computer, Control Panel, Documents, and the like, are displayed, click one of the following option buttons:

- ✔ **Display As a Link:** This option button is the default setting for all fixed items. It causes Windows to open a folder window showing the item folders and files.

- ✔ **Display As a Menu:** Select this option button when you want Vista to display the item folders and files as menu items on a continuation menu that you can select and open from the Start menu.

- ✔ **Don't Display This Item:** Select this option button to remove the display of the fixed item, such as Network Places.

After changing items in the Customize Start Menu dialog box, click its OK button and then click the Apply button in the Taskbar and Start Menu Properties dialog box. This enables you to open the Start menu to check that the modifications you want on the Start menu have been put into place before you click OK in the Taskbar and Start Menu Properties dialog box to close it.

By default, at the top of the Start menu, Vista displays the Internet Explorer as the Internet link and Windows Mail as the e-mail link. If you have another Web browser and e-mail program installed on your computer and you want to use them, you can change these Start menu links by selecting the desired browser and e-mail program in the Internet Link and E-mail Link drop-down list boxes, respectively, that appear near the bottom of the Customize Start Menu dialog box.

Using the Quick Launch toolbar

The Quick Launch toolbar adds a group of buttons to the Windows taskbar that you can use to start commonly used modules to get back to the desktop. These buttons may include

- ✔ **Internet Explorer:** Starts Internet Explorer 7 for browsing Web pages — note that this button does not appear until after your first use of the Internet Explorer.

- ✔ **Show Desktop:** Minimizes all open windows in order to obtain immediate access to the Windows desktop and all the desktop icons and shortcuts it contains.

- ✔ **Switch between Windows:** Displays all open windows in a 3-D stack that you can flip through by using the center wheel on your mouse (*see* "Flip and Flip 3D" earlier in this part).

- ✔ **Windows Media Player:** Starts Windows Media Player 11 so that you can play music or video on your computer (*see* "Windows Media Player 11" in Part 7).

In addition to these standard buttons, you can add your own custom buttons to the Quick Launch toolbar by dragging a desktop shortcut to the desired position on the Quick Launch toolbar. The mouse pointer indicates where the new button will be inserted with a dark I-beam cursor at the tip of the pointer. A button for the shortcut then appears at the position of the I-beam in the Quick Launch toolbar.

You can delete any of the buttons from the Quick Launch toolbar by right-clicking the button, clicking the Delete command on the shortcut menu, and then clicking the Yes button in the alert dialog box that asks you to confirm the deletion.

As you continue to add new buttons to the Quick Launch toolbar, some of the existing buttons at the end of the bar become hidden from view when the Lock the Taskbar option is selected (as it is by default). Vista then adds a continuation button (>>) to the end of the Quick Launch toolbar, which you can click to display a pop-up menu with the other options you add.

Adding other toolbars to the taskbar

Vista also includes the following toolbars that you can display on the taskbar:

- ✓ **Address** toolbar where you can directly enter pathnames for folders and files you want to open or URL addresses for Web pages you want to visit.

- ✓ **Windows Media Player** to display the Windows Media Player as a button on the taskbar when you minimize its window.

- ✓ **Links** toolbar that enables you to add links to Web pages you visit regularly by dragging the Web page icon to the immediate left of the page's URL address to a place on the toolbar.

- ✓ **Tablet PC Input Panel** toolbar (button, really) that opens the Input Panel on the Vista desktop where you can write rather than type your entries (assuming that you're running Vista on a Tablet PC laptop computer).

- ✓ **Desktop** toolbar that gives you access to all the desktop items on your computer.

To add any (or all) of these toolbars to your taskbar, right-click the bar at a place where there isn't already a toolbar and then click Toolbars on the pop-up menu followed by the name of the toolbar to add.

Creating new toolbars

You can add your own custom toolbars to the Vista taskbar from the folders that you keep on your computer. When you create a custom toolbar from an existing folder, Windows creates buttons for each of the shortcuts and icons that the folder contains.

To create a custom toolbar from a folder, follow these steps:

1. Right-click the taskbar (without clicking any of the buttons or icons it contains) and then choose the Toolbars ▶ New Toolbar command on the shortcut menu that appears.

   Windows opens the New Toolbar dialog box, where you select the folder to be used in creating the new toolbar.

2. Select the folder whose contents are to be used in creating the new toolbar by clicking the folder icon in the navigation list box.

3. Click the Select Folder button to close the New Toolbar dialog box.

   As soon as you close the New Toolbar dialog box, Windows adds the new toolbar, indicated by the folder's name followed by a continuation button (>>). When you click this continuation button, Vista displays a pop-up menu showing all the subfolders and documents that it contains.

All custom toolbars that you create are automatically deleted the moment you remove their display from the Vista taskbar (by right-clicking the taskbar and then choosing Toolbars followed by the name of the custom toolbar).

The Notification area

The Notification area (or system tray) displays the current time and icons that indicate the active status of various components such as the status of your network connection, Active Sync connection to your hand-held device, PCMCIA cards inserted into a laptop computer, or the printer queue. In addition, the Notification area displays icons representing various programs or processes that run in the background, such as the Windows Sidebar for hiding and redisplaying the Sidebar, the Language Bar for using Voice Recognition and Handwriting Recognition in Microsoft Office programs, the Windows Clipboard when it contains multiple items, and Windows Messenger.

This is also the place from which the Windows Update feature displays its Update Reminder message telling you that new updates for the system are available; *see* "Windows Update" in Part 5.

To identify an icon that appears in the status area, position the mouse pointer over it until the ScreenTip appears. To change the status of an icon, right-click it to display the pop-up menu and then click the appropriate menu option. For example, to open the Volume Control dialog box to adjust the volume of your speakers, you right-click the speaker icon in the Notification area and then click Open Volume Mixer on the pop-up menu.

To temporarily expand the Notification area so that all of its icons are displayed, click the Show Hidden Icons button (the one to the left of the first displayed icon in this area with an arrowhead pointing to the left). Note that you can also customize the Notification area as part of customizing the taskbar and Start menu properties. *See* the upcoming section, "Customizing the Notification area" for more information.

Customizing the Notification area

You can also customize the settings for the Notification area of the taskbar by altering the settings on the Notification tab of the Taskbar and Start Menu Properties dialog box.

By default, all the system icons and Hide Inactive Icons check boxes are selected. To remove a system icon from the Notification area, click its check box to remove the check mark. To display all the Notification icons, even when the processes they represent are inactive, click the Hide Inactive Icons check box to remove the check mark. Note that when the Hide Inactive Icons setting is active, Windows adds a Show Hidden Icons button that you can click to temporarily display all the Notification icons.

In addition to changing these two settings for the Notification area, you can change the circumstances under which particular notification icons are displayed in the Notification area. To do this, click the Customize button near the bottom of the taskbar to open the Customize Icons dialog box.

The Customize Notification Icons dialog box contains a list box that is divided into Current Items and Past Items sections. You can change the display status for any icon listed in either section. To do this, click the icon and then click the drop-down button that appears next to the current status (Hide when Inactive is the default setting for all the icons). To always have the icon displayed in the Notification area, click Show in this pop-up menu. To never have the icon appear in this area, click Hide instead.

Switching between open windows

The Vista taskbar makes switching between programs and other open windows as easy as clicking its minimized button. Doing this immediately activates the program by restoring its window on the desktop.

Don't forget that you can preview the contents of a window by positioning the mouse over its minimized button on the taskbar. Also, you can quickly flip through all the minimized windows to find the one you want to activate by using the Flip and Flip 3D features (**see** "Flip and Flip 3D" earlier in this part).

Arranging windows on the desktop

Normally when you open multiple windows on the desktop, they overlap one another, with only the most recently opened window fully displayed on top. As you open more windows, it becomes increasingly difficult to arrange them so that the information you need is displayed on-screen (this is especially true when copying or moving files and folders between open windows).

To help you organize the windows you have open, Vista offers several arrangement options. To rearrange the open windows with one of these options, you need to right-click the taskbar at a place that isn't occupied by a window button and then click one of the following options:

- ✔ **Cascade Windows** to overlap the open windows so that the title bars are all displayed one above the other in a cascade

- ✔ **Show Windows Stacked** to place the windows vertically one on top of the other

> ✔ **Show Windows Side by Side** to place the windows horizontally side by side

> ✔ **Show the Desktop** to reduce all the windows open on the desktop to minimized buttons on the taskbar

Using the Task Manager

Windows Task Manager keeps tabs on your system and how it's running. You can use Task Manager to get an overview of what programs and processes are running on your computer. You can also use it to switch to programs and to end programs that have stopped responding (in other words, programs that have frozen up on you).

To open Windows Task Manager, right-click the taskbar at a place where there are no buttons and then click Task Manager on the shortcut menu. Figure 1-18 shows you Windows Task Manager when running three different applications.

Figure 1-18

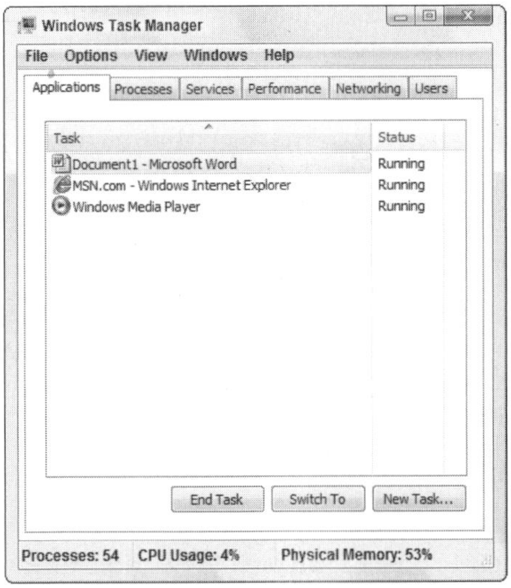

To switch to another program or window from Windows Task Manager, click it in the list box on the Applications tab and then click the Switch To button. Windows then minimizes Task Manager and displays the selected window on the desktop.

To end a process or program that has frozen up on you, click it in the list box on the Applications tab and then click the End Task command button. Note that you will probably get an alert dialog box indicating that the program has stopped responding. Click the End command button in this dialog box (as many times as you have to) to get Vista to kill the process.

The status bar of Windows Task Manager shows you statistics on the number of processes running under the program, the percentage of the CPU (Central Processing Unit, the big chip at the heart of the computer), and the memory usage of the program. If you like to look at schematics, click the Performance tab in this window to see a dynamic charting of the total CPU and memory usage on your computer (and to find really useful stuff like the number of handles, threads, and processes that are being run).

Welcome Center

The Vista Welcome Center (similar to the one shown in Figure 1-19, except that it has your name and picture rather than mine) automatically opens on the desktop when you first start your computer — and every time thereafter until you remove the check mark in the Run at Startup check box in the lower-left corner).

Figure 1-19

The top section of the Welcome Center window (Welcome) displays statistics on your computer including its name, processing chip, and total amount of memory, and the like. (To open the System Control Panel, where you can change a few settings such as the computer name, click the Show More Details link in this top section.)

The center section of the Welcome Center window (Getting Started with Windows) displays icons that enable you to become more familiar with Windows Vista as well as customize your computer. (To display a complete list of icons, click the Show All 14 Items link in this section.)

The bottom section of the Welcome Center window (Offers from Microsoft) displays icons that you can click to get even more stuff for your Windows Vista, including Microsoft's new Windows Live programs. (To display a complete list of icons, click the Show All 7 Items link in this section.)

To display information about the function of a particular icon in the top section of the Welcome Center window, click the icon. To open a new information window or start a new process (such as installing a new printer for use with Windows), double-click its icon in the Getting Started with Windows section.

Windows Help and Support

Vista has an extensive help system that you can use not only to get general and detailed information on how to use Windows, but also to get answers from Microsoft on specific problems that you're experiencing. To open the Windows Help and Support window (see Figure 1-20), click Start ▶ Help and Support.

The Windows Help and Support window contains six main links in the Find An Answer section at the top:

✔ **Windows Basics** to display a list of basic topics ranging from Introduction to Computers to What Accessibility Features Does Windows Offer?

✔ **Security and Maintenance** to display a page of information on Vista's various maintenance features including Security Center (*see* Part 6) and Windows Update (*see* Part 5)

✔ **Windows Online Help** to open the Windows Vista Help and Support Web page in your computer's Web browser (probably Windows Internet Explorer 7)

✔ **Table of Contents** to display a table of contents with links to the help topics ranging from Getting Started to Mobile PC

✔ **Troubleshooting** to open a page of troubleshooting tips with links to help you identify particular problems in the areas of networking, surfing the Web, using e-mail, and getting the correct drivers for your computer hardware

✔ **What's New?** to display a page with an article on all the new and cool features in Windows Vista

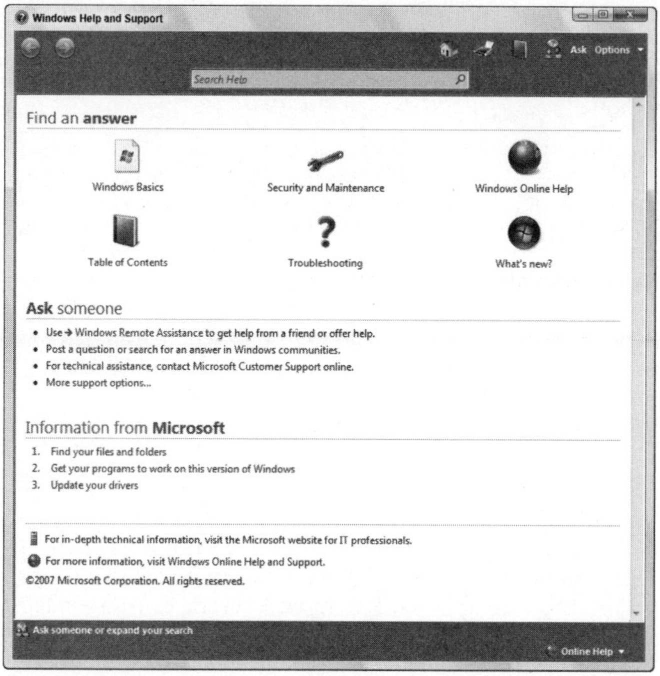

Figure 1-20

In addition to these links, the Windows Help and Support window contains a Search Help text box that you can use to search for particular topics. This text box works just like any other Search text box in Windows Vista: Simply type the name of the feature you need help on (such as **printing** or **searching files**) and then click the Search Help button (the one with the magnifying glass icon) to display links to all related topics in the Windows Help and Support window.

Part 2

Computer Management

Computer processing is really not much more than managing the application programs and data files on your computer. In order to do this with Windows Vista, you also need to know about the physical media on which they're stored (hard drives, CD-ROMs, and the like), as well as the structure of the folders in which they're arranged. In this part, you get the lowdown on disk, file, folder, and program management. For good measure, I throw in info on how to use Windows Explorer to keep tabs on this stuff.

In this part . . .

- ✔ **Accessing hard drives and all kinds of removable media**
- ✔ **Creating new files and folders**
- ✔ **Copying and moving files and folders**
- ✔ **Deleting files and folders**
- ✔ **Navigating your computer with Windows Explorer**

Disk Management

In Vista, the Computer window (Start ▶ Computer) is the place to go when you need access or information about all the drives (including virtual drives mapped to network folders) and disks connected to your computer system.

Figure 2-1 shows the Computer window for my laptop computer running Windows Vista. As you can see, Vista automatically separates the various drive icons into the following three categories:

✔ **Hard Disk Drives,** of which there are four: Local Disk (C):, RECOVERY (D:), Local Disk (E:), and the USB-connected BUSLINK (G:)

✔ **Devices with Removable Storage,** of which there are currently four connected to the computer: DVD-RW Drive F: and three Removable Disks named H:, I:, and J:

✔ **Network Location,** which contains a single network drive named Dilbert mapped to drive Z:

Figure 2-1

Note that the Preview pane gives you valuable statistics about any drive that you select in the Computer window, including the total size, the amount of free space (which is also shown visually in the Space Used indicator), and the type of file system (the older FAT32 supported by Windows 95, 98, and ME or the newer NTFS supported by Windows XP, 2000, and Vista).

Opening folders on drives in the Computer window

To open any of the drives or disks that appear in your Computer window and display the folders and files they contain, double-click its drive icon in the central area of the Computer window.

To collapse a category in the Computer window to temporarily hide its drive icons, click the collapse button (the one with the black triangle pointing upward at the far right of the category name). To later expand a collapsed category to once again display its hidden drive icons, click the expand button for the hidden category. (The expand button automatically replaces the collapse button.)

Formatting a disk

In this day and age, when floppy disk drives are almost never included in new computer systems, most of you will never experience the "joy" of formatting a floppy disk. Almost all the disks that you purchase today, including CDs and DVDs, are preformatted (this is done as part of the automated process that checks the disks for errors). From time to time, you may want to reformat a prepared disk that has become corrupted or that contains data that you no longer need. In very rare situations, you may even have to reformat a hard drive on your computer.

To format a disk or computer drive, follow these steps:

1. When formatting a floppy, CD, or DVD disc, insert the blank disk or a disk that holds files and folders that you don't give a hoot about.

2. Open the Computer window (Start ▶ Computer) and then right-click the icon of the drive that holds the disk (or that you want to reformat).

3. Select the Format command from the drive shortcut menu to open the Format dialog box.

   In order to format any hard drive on your computer, your user account must be an administrator type. You cannot, however, reformat the drive that contains the Windows Vista operating system.

4. (Optional) Select the Capacity for the size of the disk that you're formatting.

   When formatting a floppy disk, choose the lesser (double-density) capacity 3.5", 720KB, 512 bytes/sector if you inserted that kind of disk into your floppy drive.

5. (Optional) By default, Windows XP selects NTFS (supported by Windows XP, 2000, and Vista) in the File System drop-down list box as the file system for which to format the disk. If you're formatting a floppy disk for an older system running Windows 95, 98, or ME, select FAT on the File System drop-down list.

6. (Optional) Type a label in the Volume Label text box if you want to attach a name to the floppy, hard, or flash disk that you can use to identify it.

When you format by using the FAT system, you're restricted to 11 characters; when you're using the NTFS system, you're limited to a maximum of 32 characters.

7. (Optional) Click the Quick Format check box in the Format Options (if you're reformatting a disk that contains files and folders that you no longer need). If you're formatting a brand-new disk, leave this check box empty.

8. (Optional) If you're formatting a floppy or CD as a startup disk for a MS-DOS computer, click the Create an MS-DOS Startup Disk check box.

9. Click the Start button to begin formatting the disk and then click OK in the alert dialog box warning you that formatting erases all data currently on the disk.

After you click Start and then OK, Windows keeps you informed of the progress in the Formatting box at the bottom of the Format dialog box. If you need to stop the process before it's complete, click the Cancel button.

Mapping a network folder as a local drive

If your computer is part of a local area network and you use files that are stored in folders on another networked computer, you will find it helpful to map a drive letter to that network folder so that you can access it directly from the Computer window.

In order to be able to map a network folder to a local drive, the folder must be shared and you must have permission to access it on the other computer.

To map a network folder to a drive letter on your computer, follow these steps:

1. Open the Computer window by clicking Start ▶ Computer.

2. Click the Map Network Drive button on the toolbar to open the Map Network Drive dialog box (see Figure 2-2).

3. Select an unused drive letter for the network folder in the Drive drop-down list box.

4. In the Folder text box, enter the network share pathname (following the \\server\share example shown beneath the Folder text box), click the drop-down button to the immediate right of the text box and select its previously entered pathname from the list, or click the Browse button and locate the shared network folder in the Browse For Folder dialog box. Click OK.

5. (Optional) If you want Vista to re-create this network drive by mapping the network folder to the same drive letter each time you start the computer, click the Reconnect at Logon check box.

6. Click the Finish button.

Figure 2-2

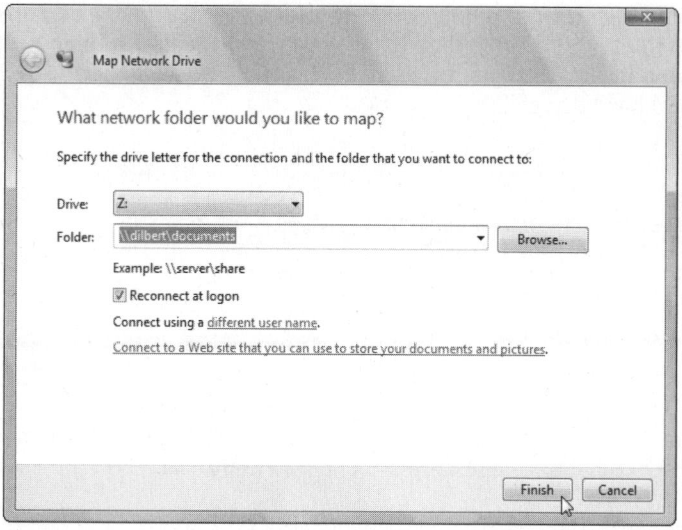

> **Map Network Drive**
>
> What network folder would you like to map?
>
> Specify the drive letter for the connection and the folder that you want to connect to:
>
> Drive: Z:
>
> Folder: \\dilbert\documents   Browse...
>
> Example: \\server\share
>
> ☑ Reconnect at logon
>
> Connect using a different user name.
>
> Connect to a Web site that you can use to store your documents and pictures.
>
>   Finish   Cancel

When you click Finish, Vista creates the network drive and automatically opens it in Windows Explorer. After that, you can access any of the folder's subfolders and files by simply opening the network drive in the Computer Explorer window.

TIP Note that Vista indicates a mapped network drive by automatically assigning it to the Network Location category in the Computer window. A special network icon is also added to the normal drive icon.

File and Folder Management

Files contain all the precious data that you create with those sophisticated Windows-based programs. Files occupy a certain amount of space rated either in kilobytes (KB, or thousands of bytes) or megabytes (MB, or millions of bytes) on a particular disk, be it your hard drive, a CD-ROM, DVD disc, or even, in very rare cases, a removable floppy disk.

Folders are the data containers in Windows Vista. They can contain files or other folders, or a combination of files and folders. Like files, folders occupy a certain amount of space (rated in KB or MB) on the particular drive.

As you open folders and subfolders to get to the file you want to use in one of the Explorer windows, Vista keeps track of the path in the address bar at the top of the window. This path starts with the disk or folder icon followed by the names of drives, folders, and subfolders in succession separated by the ▶ symbol (indicating a new sublevel).

For example, the address bar in the Computer window shown in Figure 2-3 shows you the path for finding an Excel worksheet file named Invoice 021507 that is stored in a Payables subfolder within an Accounts folder on my computer's local hard drive (C:).

Figure 2-3

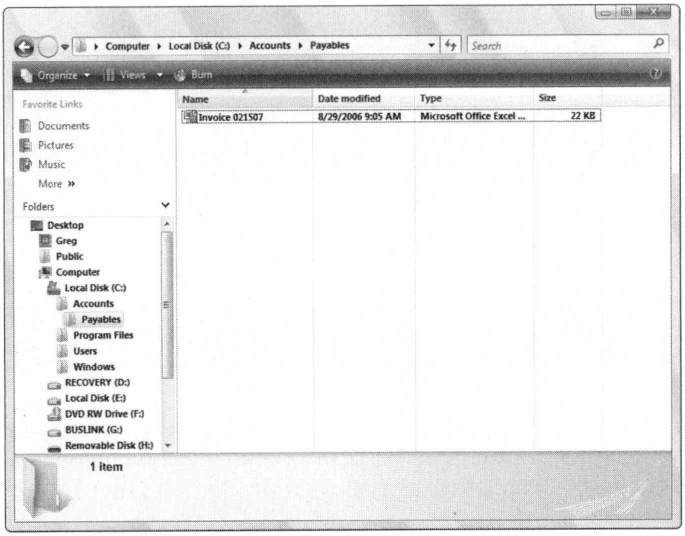
Computer ▸ Local Disk (C:) ▸ Accounts ▸ Payables
Search
Organize
Views
Burn
Favorite Links
Documents
Pictures
Music
More »
Folders
Desktop
Greg
Public
Computer
Local Disk (C:)
Accounts
Payables
Program Files
Users
Windows
RECOVERY (D:)
Local Disk (E:)
DVD RW Drive (F:)
BUSLINK (G:)
Removable Disk (H:)
Name
Date modified
Type
Size
Invoice 021507
8/29/2006 9:05 AM
Microsoft Office Excel ...
22 KB
1 item

If you click the drop-down button at the right end of the address bar (or anywhere outside path list), Vista converts the path on the address bar into the more traditional form of a pathname separated by backslashes that is used exclusively in the previous versions of Windows. For example, after clicking the address bar's drop-down button in the Computer window shown in Figure 2-3, its path immediately changed to:

```
C:\Accounts\Payables\
```

REMEMBER

This more traditional pathname format is what you see when open a drop-down menu in an address bar in an Explorer window or the Address toolbar on the taskbar (***see*** "Adding other toolbars to the taskbar" in Part 1). When specifying the pathname for a file by using this format, you simply append the filename to the path, as in:

```
C:\Accounts\Payables\Invoice 021507
```

Assigning filenames

Each filename in Windows consists of two parts: a main filename and a file extension. The file extension, which identifies the type of file and what program created it, is traditionally three characters, although extensions for newer apps such as Microsoft Office Word 2007 (.docx) and Excel 2007 (.xlsx), as well as .html for Web pages, are four characters. File extensions are automatically assigned by the creating agent or program and Vista does not normally display extensions as part of filenames that appear in Windows Explorer. For information on how to display file extensions as part of the filename, *see* "Customizing a window's Folder Options" later in this part.

Whereas the creating program normally assigns the file extension, Windows Vista enables you to call the main part of the filename whatever the heck you want, up to a maximum of 255 characters (including spaces!). Keep in mind, however, that all pre-Windows 95 programs, and even some that run on Windows 98, don't support long filenames. These programs allow a maximum of only eight characters, with no spaces.

In Vista, files are assigned distinctive file icons indicating the type of file along with the filenames. These icons help you quickly identify the type of file when you're browsing the files in your folders with Windows Explorer. This also enables you to launch the appropriate program while at the same time opening the file by simply double-clicking its file icon.

TIP

You can change what program opens a particular file. Right-click its file icon and then click Properties to open its Properties dialog box. Then click the Change button that appears to the immediate right of the program that currently opens the file. Select the new program in the Open With dialog box. Note that if you can't locate the program you want to assign to the file in the Open With list box, click the Browse button and use the Navigation pane to open the Program Files folder and locate the application there (*see* "Program Management" later in this part).

Creating new files and folders

You can create new files to hold new data and new folders to hold your files right within Windows Vista.

To create a new, empty folder, follow these steps:

1. Open Windows Explorer window (such as Documents or Computer) in which the new folder is to appear.

2. Click the Organize button on the window's toolbar and then click New Folder.

  If the Classic menus are displayed in the Explorer window, you can also choose File⇨New⇨Folder or, if not, press Alt+F+W+F.

3. Replace the temporary folder name (New Folder) by typing a name of your choosing and pressing Enter.

To create an empty file that holds a certain type of information, follow these steps:

1. Open Windows Explorer window where the new file is required.

2. Right-click a blank area in the folder's display area and then highlight New on the shortcut menu.

If the Classic menus are displayed in the Explorer window, you can also choose File⇨New from the menu bar or, if not, press Alt+F+W.

3. Choose the type of file you want to create (such as Microsoft Office Word Document, Microsoft Office Excel Worksheet, Text Document, Briefcase, and so on) from the New submenu.

4. Replace the temporary filename (such as New Microsoft Word Document) by typing a name of your choosing and pressing Enter.

Create a new folder when you need to have a new place to store your files and other folders. Create an empty file when you want to create an empty file in a particular folder before you put something in it — remember that you can always launch the associated program and open the blank file in it by double-clicking its file icon.

Customizing a window's Folder Options

Vista enables you to customize many aspects of a folder's appearance and behavior in an open window by using the controls in the Folder Options dialog box (see Figure 2-4). To open this dialog box, click the Organize button (the first button on a window's toolbar) and then click Folder and Search Options on its drop-down menu.

If the Classic menus are displayed in the window, you can also open Folder Options by choosing Tools⇨Folder Options. If they aren't displayed, press Alt+T+O.

The Folder Options dialog box contains three tabs:

- ✔ **General** controls whether Explorer windows display Classic pull-down menus (the Use Windows Classic Folders options button) or the toolbar with the Organize button, Views button, and so on (the default Show Preview and Filters option button). The General tab also controls whether folders open in the same or a new window, as well as how you select items in an open window and how you select and open folders and files.

- ✔ **View** controls how files and folders appear in an open window.

- ✔ **Search** to control how searches are conducted in Explorer windows and whether the searches use nonindexed locations for searching the contents of files or just their filenames.

Figure 2-4

Changing how you select and open items

Normally, you click to select an item in an open window (indicated by highlighting its name and/or icon) and double-click to open the item. If you're more of the Web surfing type, you can change this scheme by clicking the Single-Click to Open an Item (Point to Select) option button on the General tab of the Folder Options dialog box. After selecting this option, you have only have to point to an item in a folder to select and click it once to open it.

 When you choose the Single-Click to Open an Item (Point to Select) option button on the General tab, Vista automatically activates and selects the Underline Icon Titles Only When I Point at Them option button as well. When this option is in effect, you only see the underlining (akin to a hyperlink on a Web page) when you actually position the mouse pointer over the item. If you want this hyperlink-type underlining to always appear beneath items you open in a window (making windows even more like your typical Web page), click the Underline Icon Titles Consistent with My Browser option button instead.

Changing how items are displayed in a folder

The View tab of the Folder Options dialog box (see Figure 2-5) contains a wide variety of check boxes and option buttons for controlling the appearance of the items in the Explorer windows you open. Among the most important options on this tab, you find the following:

  ✔ **Always Show Menus** check box to ensure that each window displays a bar of pull-down menus, File through Help (not selected by default)

✔ **Hidden Files and Folders** option with its two option buttons: Do Not Show Hidden Files and Folders (selected by default) to hide the display of certain system-type files and folders, and Show Hidden Files and Folders to display them

✔ **Hide Extensions for Known File Types** check box (not selected by default) to suppress the display of the filename extensions such as .doc, .xlsx, and .html

✔ **Remember Each Folder's View Settings** check box (selected by default) to have Vista retain a folder's individual arrangement of menus and panes

✔ **Restore Previous Folder Windows at Logon** check box (not selected by default) to have Vista open at start-up all the Explorer windows you had open when you last shut the machine down

Figure 2-5

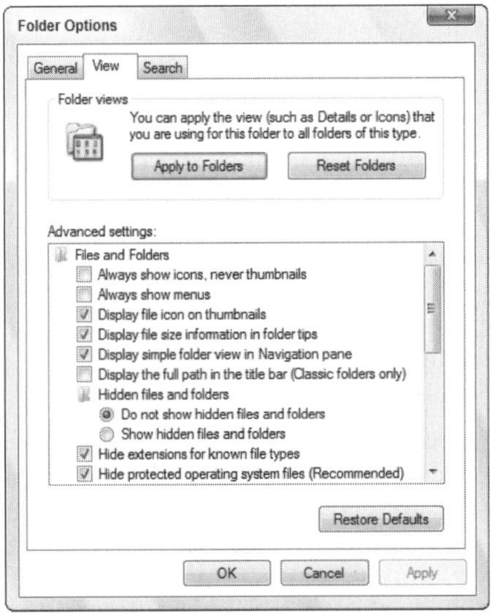

Folder Options

General | View | Search

Folder views

You can apply the view (such as Details or Icons) that you are using for this folder to all folders of this type.

Apply to Folders   Reset Folders

Advanced settings:

Files and Folders
  ☐ Always show icons, never thumbnails
  ☐ Always show menus
  ☑ Display file icon on thumbnails
  ☑ Display file size information in folder tips
  ☑ Display simple folder view in Navigation pane
  ☐ Display the full path in the title bar (Classic folders only)
  Hidden files and folders
    ⦿ Do not show hidden files and folders
    ○ Show hidden files and folders
  ☑ Hide extensions for known file types
  ☑ Hide protected operating system files (Recommended)

Restore Defaults

OK   Cancel   Apply

 Click the Restore Defaults button at the bottom of the View tab of the Folder Options dialog box whenever you want to restore all the Windows Vista original view settings.

Creating compressed (zipped) folders

If you're running short on disk space, you can conserve precious free space by creating compressed folders that automatically compress every file and subfolder that you put into them. To create a blank compressed folder, follow these steps:

1. In Windows Explorer, navigate to where you want the new compressed folder to be.

2. Right-click in a blank area anywhere in the central part folder's display area and then highlight New on the shortcut menu. Click Compressed (Zipped) Folder on its continuation menu.

    If the Classic menus are displayed in the Explorer window, you can also choose File➪New➪Compressed (Zipped) Folder. If not, press Alt+F+W and then click Compressed (Zipped) folder on the continuation menu.

    Windows creates a new folder icon (sporting a zipper to indicate its special zip-type compression abilities) that sports the temporary filename New Compressed (Zipped) Folder.

3. Replace the temporary filename, New Compressed (Zipped) Folder, by typing your own filename; press Enter.

After creating a compressed folder, you can copy or move files and folders into it just as you would a regular file folder. As you copy or move files or folders, Vista compresses their contents. You can then copy compressed folders to removable media, such as CD-ROMs and flash drives. You can also attach them to e-mail messages.

Microsoft has even gone so far as to make the compression schemes that compressed folders use compatible with other compression programs. This means that you can send compressed folders to people who don't even use Windows (if you know any), and they can extract (decompress) their contents by using their favorite compression/decompression program.

Note that Windows Vista automatically appends the name you give a compressed folder with the .zip file extension to help identify the folder as containing zipped-up files. Of course, you must make sure the Hide Extensions For Known File Types check box on the View tab of the Folder Options dialog box is unselected in order for this filename extension to be displayed in Windows Explorer.

You can run program files from within compressed folders simply by double-clicking their program icons, provided that the program doesn't depend upon any other files (such as those pesky .DLL files or some sort of data files). If the programs in the compressed folder do depend upon these kinds of auxiliary files, you must extract them before you can run the program. Also, be aware that when you open text or graphic documents stored in a compressed folder, they open in read-only mode. Before you or anyone else can edit such documents, they must be extracted from the folder as described in the following section.

Extracting files from a compressed folder

Because the files placed in a compressed folder automatically open in read-only mode, you may need to extract them (that is, decompress them) so that you can again edit their contents. To extract files from a compressed folder, you follow these steps:

1. Open the window in Windows Explorer that contains the compressed folder whose files you want to extract.

2. Right-click the compressed folder (remember, its icon should sport a zipper down the front) and then click Extract All on its shortcut menu.

   If the Classic menus are displayed in the Explorer window, you can perform this step by clicking the compressed folder's icon and then choosing File➪Extract All on the pull-down menus. If not, press Alt+F+T.

   Vista then opens an Extract Compressed (Zipped) Folders dialog box, where you designate the folder into which the extracted files are to be copied.

3. (Optional) Replace the path and the filename of the compressed folder in the Files Will Be Extracted to This Folder text box with the pathname of the folder in which you want to store the extracted (decompressed) files.

   To browse to the folder in which you want the extracted files copied, click the Browse button; select the (destination) folder in the outline of your computer system, and click OK. To extract the files in their original compressed folder, don't replace the path and filename for the compressed folder that appears in this text box. Just be aware that the only way to recompress the files that you extract in the compressed folder is to first move them out of the folder and then move them back in!

4. Click the Extract button at the bottom of the Select a Destination and Extract Files dialog box to begin extracting the files.

   As soon as Windows finishes extracting the files, Vista opens the destination folder displaying the uncompressed files.

Selecting files and folders

To select the files and folders to which you want to do stuff like copy, move, open, or print, you select the file or folder icons (the small pictures identifying the folder or file). Most of the time, you click the file and folder icons in the windows to select them. Windows lets you know when an icon is selected by highlighting it in a different color (normally, a light blue unless you change the Windows appearance settings).

If you change the click options in the Folder Options dialog box so that single-clicking opens an item (*see* "Changing how you select and open items" earlier in this part for details), remember that instead of clicking a folder or file icon to select it (which succeeds only in opening the item), you just hover the mouse pointer over it.

When you need to select more than one file or folder in a window, you have a choice of things to do:

✔ To select all the items in an Explorer window (this includes all drive, file, and folder icons located within it), press Ctrl+A or click the Organize button on the window's toolbar and then click Select All on its drop-down menu.

If the Classic menus are displayed in the Explorer window, you also choose Edit⇨Select All on the window menu bar. If not, press Alt+E+A.

✔ To select multiple folder or file icons that are located all over the place in the window, hold down the Ctrl key as you click each folder or file icon (the Ctrl key adds individual icons to the selection) — if you use single-clicking to open items, you need to hover over each item as you hold down the Ctrl key (no easy feat).

✔ To select a series of folder or file icons that are all next to each other in the window, click the first one in the series and then hold the Shift key as you click the last icon in the series (the Shift key adds all the icons in between the first and last one you click to the selection). If you use single-clicking to open items, you need to hover over the first item until it's selected and then hold the Shift key as you hover over the last icon in the series (and if you think Ctrl+hovering is hard, wait till you try Shift+hovering).

✔ If the Classic menus are displayed, you can reverse the icon selection in a window so that all the icons that aren't currently selected become selected, and all those that are currently selected become deselected by choosing Edit⇨Invert Selection. If not, you can press Alt+E+I.

Note that the Invert Selection menu command is really useful when you want to select all but a few folders or files in a window: First, use one of the aforementioned methods to select the icons of the files you do *not* want selected; then choose Edit⇨Invert Selection (Alt+E+I). Voilà! All the files in the window are selected except for those few you selected in the first place.

Copying (and moving) files and folders

Windows Vista provides two basic methods for copying files and folders from one disk to another or from one folder to another on the same disk:

✔ **Drag-and-drop,** whereby you select items in one open Explorer window and then drag them to another open Explorer window (on the same or different disk) where you drop them into place.

✔ **Cut-and-paste,** whereby you copy or cut selected items to the Windows clipboard and then paste them into another folder (on the same or different disk).

The technique of moving files and folders with drag-and-drop is really straight-forward:

1. Open two separate Explorer windows and arrange them on the Vista desk-top with as little overlap as possible: the first is the source Explorer window that contains the item(s) you want to move and the second is the destina-tion Explorer window where these items are to be moved.

TIP

To eliminate all overlap between the source and destination Explorer window and thereby make it easy to drag from one to the other, use Vista's Show Windows Side by Side or Show Windows Stacked option on the taskbar's shortcut menu before proceeding to Step 2.

2. Select the item(s) you want to move in the first source Explorer window.

   See "Selecting files and folders" earlier in this part for the techniques Vista provides for selecting folders and files.

3. While continuing to hold down the mouse button, drag the folder/docu-ment icon representing the selected items (and showing the number of items selected) to the destination Explorer window.

4. Vista shows you where selected items are to be inserted in the destination window by using either a vertical or horizontal I-beam (depending upon which View option the destination window uses) along with a ScreenTip that says, "Move to *such and such folder*" (where *such and such a folder* is the actual name of the destination folder). When you've positioned the I-beam pointer at the place in the destination Explorer window where you want the items to appear, release the mouse button to drop and insert the moved items there (see Figure 2-6).

To copy files with drag-and-drop, you only have to vary these foregoing steps by remembering to hold down the Ctrl key as you drag the selected items from the source Explorer window to the destination window. Vista lets you know that you're copying rather than moving the selected items by displaying a + (plus) sign under the folder/document icon and displaying a "Copy to *such and such folder*" ScreenTip when you reach a place in the destination folder where the items being copied can be dropped.

TIP

If you don't care where the items you move or copy with drag-and-drop are posi-tioned in the destination folder, you don't even have to bother opening the desti-nation folder in its own window: Just drag the folder/document icon representing the selected items from the source Explorer window to the destination folder's icon and then drop it on this icon. Note that this drop-directly-on-the-destination-icon method works on shortcuts of other drives (both local and on your net-work), folders, and printers (to print the selected documents) on the Vista desktop (*see* "Creating desktop shortcuts" in Part 1).

Figure 2-6

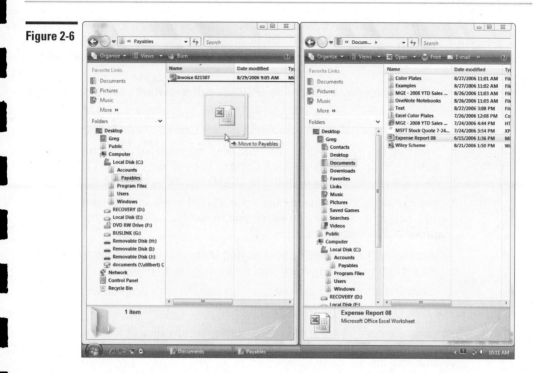

Keep in mind that when you drag files or folders from one drive to another, Windows Vista automatically copies the files and folders, instead of moving them. This means that you don't have to hold down the Ctrl key when you intend to copy them from one disk to another. This also means that you must still delete them from their original disk after making the copies if you need to free up the disk space.

Drag-and-drop moving from folder to folder is great because it's really fast. This method does have a major drawback, however: It's pretty easy to drop your file icons into the wrong folder. If you forget to undo your last action (Ctrl+Z), instead of panicking when you open what you thought was the destination folder and find that your files aren't there, locate them by using the Search feature; *see* "Search" in Part 1.

Instead of turning to drag-and-drop, you can use the cut-and-paste method, the oldest way of moving and copying items in Windows. Cut-and-paste, as the name implies, involves two distinct processes. In the first, you cut or copy the selected files or folders to a special area of the computer memory known as the Windows Clipboard. In the second, you paste the item(s) saved on the Clipboard into the new folder.

You can perform the cut, copy, and paste commands by selecting the Cut, Copy, and Paste commands on the Organize button on the Explorer window's toolbar, or by using standard Ctrl+X (Cut), Ctrl+C (Copy), and Ctrl+V (Paste) keyboard shortcuts.

To move or copy files with cut-and-paste (using either method), follow these steps:

1. Open the folder with Windows Explorer (Documents, Computer, or Network) that holds the subfolders or files that you're moving or copying.

2. Select all the items to be copied and then press Ctrl+C or on the Organize button's drop-down menu, click Copy to copy them, or press Ctrl+X or click Cut on the Organize button's drop-down menu to move them.

3. Use the Navigation pane in the Explorer window to open the destination folder (that is, the one into which you're moving or copying the selected folder or file items).

   Don't forget to click the Folders button in the Navigation pane to display the hierarchy of components and folders on your computer.

4. Press Ctrl+V or click Paste on the Organize button's drop-down menu to paste them into the destination folder.

When using the cut-and-paste method to move or copy files or folders, keep in mind that you don't have to keep open the folder with the files or folders you're moving or copying during the paste part of the procedure. You can close this folder, open the folder to which you're moving or copying them, and then do the paste command. Just be sure that you don't use the Copy or Cut commands again in Windows Vista until after you've pasted these files and folders in their new location.

 If the Classic menus are displayed in the Explorer window, you can also access the Cut, Copy, and Paste commands by choosing Edit⇨Cut, Edit⇨Copy, and Edit⇨Paste respectively from the source and destination Explorer window's drop-down menus. If not, you can press Alt+E+T to cut, Alt+E+C to copy, and Alt+E+P to paste.

 In addition, when the Classic menus are displayed, you have access to the special Edit⇨Copy to Folder and Edit⇨Move to Folder commands (or if they're not displayed, you can press Alt+E+F for Copy to Folder and Alt+E+V for Move to Folder). When you choose either of these menu commands (after selecting the items to be moved or copied), Vista displays a Copy Items or a Move Items dialog box (depending upon which you command you choose). You then select the icon of the destination folder in the outline map of your system before clicking the Move or Copy button to perform the move or copy operation.

 Keep in mind that if all you want to do is back up some files from your hard drive to a CD or DVD disc in your computer's CD-ROM/DVD drive (D:, E: or some other letter), you can do so with the Send To shortcut menu command. After

selecting the files to copy, just right-click to open the shortcut menu attached
to one of the file icons and then choose the correct drive on the Send To menu
such as DVD-RW Drive (E:). Oh, and one thing more: Don't forget to insert a
blank CD-ROM or DVD disc or one to which you can append new files before
you start this little operation.

Deleting files and folders

Because the whole purpose of working on computers is to create junk, you need
to know how to get rid of unneeded files and folders to free space on your hard
drive. To delete files, folders, or shortcuts, follow these steps:

1. Open the window in Windows Explorer that holds the files or folders that
   need to be given the old heave-ho.

2. Select all the files, folders, or shortcuts to be deleted.

3. Press the Delete key on your keyboard or choose Delete on the Organize
   button's drop-down menu on the window's toolbar.

   If the Classic menus are displayed in the Explorer window, you can also
   choose File⇨Delete or, if not, press Alt+F+D. If you're really motivated, you
   can drag the selected items and drop them on the Recycle Bin desktop icon.

4. Click the Yes button in the Delete File or Delete Multiple File dialog box
   that asks whether you want to send the selected items to the Recycle Bin.

Windows Vista puts all items that you delete in the Recycle Bin. The Recycle Bin
is the trash can for Vista. Anything you delete anywhere in Windows goes into
the Recycle Bin and stays there until you either retrieve the deleted item or
empty the Recycle Bin.

Note that the Recycle Bin icon (shown in the left margin) is the one permanent item on the Windows desktop. To open the Recycle Bin window (see
Figure 2-7), you simply double-click the icon on the desktop.

Use the following tips to work efficiently with the Recycle Bin:

✔ **To fill the Recycle Bin:** Select the folders or files you no longer need, drag
   their icons to the Recycle Bin icon on the desktop, and drop them in.

✔ **To rescue stuff from the Recycle Bin:** Open the Recycle Bin and then select
   the icons for the items you want to restore. Next, click the Restore This
   Item button (if only one item is selected) or the Restore the Selected Items
   button (if multiple items are selected) on the Recycle Bin window's toolbar.

   If the Classic menus are displayed, you can also select File⇨Restore on the
   pull-down menu to remove the selected item or items (if not, you can press
   Alt+F+E. Also, you can always drag the icons for the files and folders you
   want to save out of the Recycle Bin and drop them in the desired location.

✔ **To rescue all the stuff in the Recycle Bin:** Open the Recycle Bin and click the Restore All Items button on the Recycle Bin window's toolbar. Note that this button is replaced by the Restore This Item or Restore the Selected Items button when you select one or more items.

✔ **To empty the Recycle Bin:** Open the Recycle Bin and click the Empty the Recycle Bin button on Recycle Bin window's toolbar.

If the Classic Menus are displayed, you can also choose File⇨Empty Recycle Bin from the menu bar. If the menus are not displayed, press Alt+F+B.

Figure 2-7

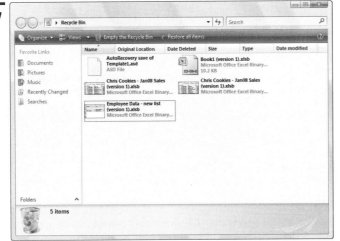

Keep in mind that choosing the Empty Recycle Bin command immediately gets rid of everything in the Recycle Bin window. Don't ever empty the Recycle Bin until after you examine the contents and are absolutely sure that you'll never need to use any of those items ever again. Delete items in the Recycle Bin only when you're sure that you're never going to need them again (or you've backed up the files on disks or some other media, such as CD-ROM or DVD discs).

If you hold down the Shift key when you press the Delete key, Windows displays a Delete File dialog box that asks you to confirm the permanent deletion of the selected items. Click the Yes button or press Enter *only* when you want to kiss these babies goodbye forever! They won't be placed in the Recycle Bin.

Renaming files and folders

You can rename file and folder icons directly in Windows Vista by typing over or editing the existing file or folder name, as I outline in these steps:

1. Open the window that contains the folder or file you want to rename.

2. Right-click the file or folder icon, and select Rename on the shortcut menu.

3. Type the new name that you want to give the folder (up to 255 characters) or edit the existing name. You can use the Delete key to remove characters and the → or ← key to move the cursor without deleting characters.

4. When you finish editing the file or folder name, press the Enter key to complete the renaming procedure.

TIP

When the file or folder name is selected for editing, typing anything entirely replaces the current name. If you want to edit the file or folder name rather than replace it, you need to click the insertion point at the place in the name that needs editing before you begin typing.

Sharing files

You can share your files with all the users across your network or with selected users on the same computer. To share files on a network, you copy or move the files you want to share into your Public folder. To access the Public folder on your computer, follow these two steps:

1. Open the Documents window (Start ▶ Documents). If only the Favorite Links are displayed, click the Folders button.

2. Scroll way down to almost the bottom of the list of components and folders and then click the Public folder icon in the Navigation pane to display all subfolders within the Public folder on your computer (see Figure 2-8).

Figure 2-8

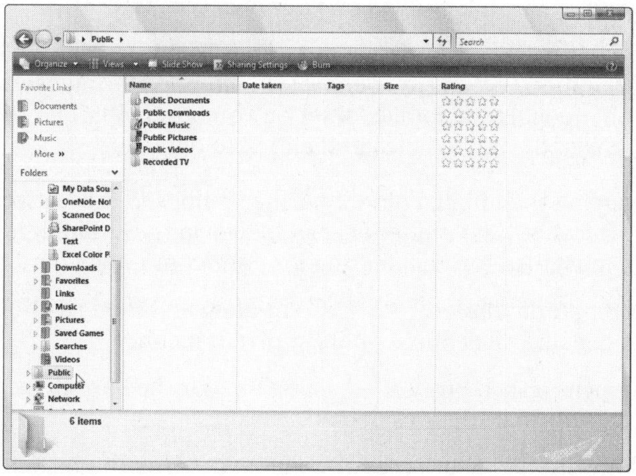

Vista automatically creates six subfolders within your Public folder: Public Documents, Public Downloads, Public Music, Public Pictures, Public Videos and Recorded TV. The operating system can also create Public subfolders for particular types of media files unique to your computer.

If your user account status is that of an administrator (*see* "User Account Control" in Part 6 for details), you can add your own subfolders to the Public folder in which you want to store certain types of files you want to share with everybody on the network.

Changing the settings for the Public folder

You can easily change the settings for the shared files you place in your Public folder. To do this, click the Sharing Settings button on Public window's toolbar (after selecting Public in the Navigation pane of the Documents window) to open the Network and Sharing Center Control Panel window.

In the Sharing and Discovery section of this Control Panel window, click the expand button to the right of Public Folder Sharing to display the following three options:

- ✔ **Turn On Sharing So Anyone with Network Access Can Open Files** option button, which enables all network users to open your shared files as read-only files but does not enable them to make any changes in your Public folder (including creating and deleting Public subfolders).

- ✔ **Turn On Sharing So That Anyone with Network Access Can Open, Change, and Create Files** option button, which enables all network users to open all shared files as well as to make any necessary changes in your Public folder. (You must select this option before you can create new subfolders in your Public folder even on your own computer.)

- ✔ **Turn Off Sharing (People Logged On to This Computer Can Still Access This Folder)** option button (the default), which prevents all users on the network from opening the Public folder on your computer and therefore displaying any of the shared files in their subfolders.

In addition to changing the Public Folder Sharing settings in the Network and Sharing Center to allow at least reader access to files in the subfolders of your Public folder, you must also turn on sharing for your computer's hard drive (C:):

1. Open the Computer window (Start⇨Computer) and then right-click the hard drive icon and click Share on its shortcut menu.

   Vista then opens a Disk Properties dialog box for the hard drive you selected with the Sharing tab selected.

2. Click the Network and Sharing Center link in the Disk Properties dialog box to open the Network and Sharing Center Control Panel window.

3. Select the File Sharing , Public Folder Sharing, Printer Sharing, Password Protected Sharing, and Media Sharing options you want used when sharing your computer's file in the Sharing and Discovery section Public Folder of the Network and Sharing Center Control Panel window and then click the Close button.

   To grant access to anyone who can connect to your network rather than just those who have a user account and password for the computer, click the Turn Off Password Protection Sharing option button in the Password Protected Sharing subsection.

   To grant reader access to the files in your public folders, click the Turn On Sharing So Anyone with Network Access Can Open Files option button in the Public Folder Sharing subsection. To give complete access to the files (not usually recommended), click the Turn On Sharing So Anyone with Network Access Can Open, Change and Create Files option button instead.

   To enable the users who have access to your computer to use the printer(s) installed on it, click the Turn On Printer Sharing option button in the Printer Sharing subsection.

   To enable users who have access to your computer to share the music, pictures, and videos that you place in your public folders, click the Change button in the Media Sharing subsection and then click the Share My Media option button. Next click OK in the Media Sharing dialog box and Continue in the User Account Control dialog box.

4. Click the Advanced Sharing button in the Disk Properties dialog box, and then click the Continue button in the User Account Control dialog box to open the Advanced Sharing dialog box.

5. Click the Share This Folder option button.

6. Enter a descriptive name for the shared drive in the Share Name text box.

   Note that this share name can contain spaces.

7. (Optional) If you want to restrict the maximum number of users who can access the share, click the Limit The Number of Simultaneous Users To option button and then enter the number (or select it with the spinner buttons) in its text box.

8. (Optional) To set read and write permissions for individual users, click the Permissions command button and then make the necessary changes in the Permissions dialog box before you click OK. To determine whether the files and programs on the shared drive are available offline and how they are cached on the other computers, click the Caching command button and then make your changes in the Offline Settings dialog box and click OK.

9. Click the OK button in the Advanced Sharing dialog box.

   Vista then closes the Advanced Sharing dialog box and returns you to the drive's Properties dialog box where the word Shared now appears beneath the hard drive's letter at the top of the Sharing tab.

10. Click the OK button in the drive's Properties dialog box to close it and start sharing the hard disk drive.

After closing the Properties dialog box, you'll notice that the hard drive icon in the Computer window now sports the picture of two people to indicate that the drive is now being shared with others on the network.

Keep in mind that after you move or copy a file or folder to one of the subfolders in the Public Explorer window, all the network users who have access to your computer can use its files by opening the Public folder on your computer (the path to which is C:\Users\Public).

Although you can restrict network users from making changes to the contents of the Public folder on your computer, keep in mind that Vista provides no way for you to limit the display of the files you place in any of its subfolders. Therefore, don't ever put any files there to which not every single soul on the network should have access.

To stop sharing a drive, right-click the drive icon and click Share to once again open the drive's Properties dialog box. Click the Advanced Sharing command button and then click the Continue button in the User Account Control dialog box. Click the Share This Folder check box to remove its check mark. Click OK to close the Advanced Settings dialog box and then Close to close the drive's Properties dialog box.

Sharing folders and files with other users on the same computer

If you share your computer with other co-workers, you can share any of your files with them provided that you (or your computer's administrator) have set up a user account and password on your computer (*see* "User Account Control" in Part 6 for details).

To share a file with a networked co-worker who has a user account and password on your computer, you follow these simple steps:

1. Open the Explorer window with the folder(s) and/or file(s) you need to share.

2. Select the folder(s) and file(s) and then click the Share button on the window's toolbar.

   Vista opens a File Sharing dialog box listing the names of all the users who have accounts on your computer (see Figure 2-9).

3. Select the names of the user accounts to add in the Choose People to Share With drop-down list box and then click the Add button to add the names to the Sharing list box below.

   If a particular user's name is not listed, click the Create a New User item at the bottom of the drop-down list to open the User Accounts Control Panel, where you can set up a new user account for the person (*see* "User Accounts Control" in Part 6).

4. (Optional) By default, Vista assigns the Reader permission level to all new user accounts that you add to the Choose People to Share With list box. If you want to grant other permissions, click Contributor or Co-owner in the Permission Level drop-down list.

   The levels of permission are

   - **Reader,** to restrict the user to viewing the files in the folder

   - **Contributor,** to allow the user to add as well as view the folder and delete only those files that they add to it

   - **Co-owner,** to give full permission to the user to make any editing changes to the files in the folder, including adding, deleting, and modifying them

5. After adding the accounts of all the users who need to share the selected folder(s) and file(s) and setting their permission levels, click the Share button to close the File Sharing dialog box.

Figure 2-9

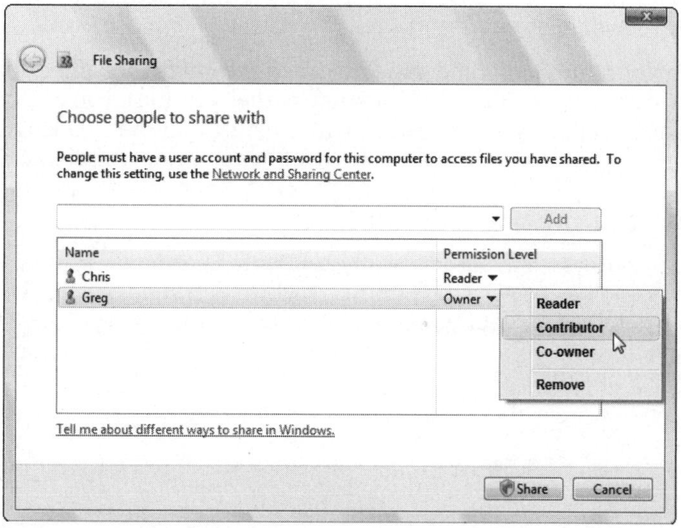

Program Management

All application programs that you purchase out of the box have their own setup programs that lead you through the entire installation procedure. Most of these setup programs launch automatically as soon as you place their program CD-ROMs or DVDs in your computer's CD-ROM/DVD drive.

 On the rare occasion that a setup program does not start running on its own, you can jump-start the procedure by opening the Run window from the Start menu (just type **ru** in the Start Search text box if Run doesn't appear on the Start menu and then click its hyperlink) and then typing **setup.exe** in its Open text box before you click OK or press Enter.

After you've installed your application programs on your Vista computer, you can use its Installed Programs Control Panel window to monitor these programs as well as to repair or remove them.

Removing or repairing a program

To remove a program installed on your computer, you need to open the Programs and Features Control Panel window. To do this, click Start ▶ Control Panel and then click the Uninstall a Program link under Programs in the Control Panel Home window. Next, select the application name in the list and then click the Uninstall (sometimes called Uninstall/Change) button on the Programs and Features Control Panel window's toolbar. Next, Vista may open a User Account Control dialog box when you do to this, in which case you need to click the Continue button. Then click the Yes button on the alert dialog box that appears asking you if you're sure that you want to remove the program and all its components from your computer.

 If you're having trouble running one or more of the Microsoft Office application programs (in Microsoft Office 2003 or some earlier version), you can try fixing the programs by clicking the Microsoft Office listing and then clicking the Repair button on the Programs and Features Control Panel window's toolbar.

Changing the program defaults

By default, Windows Vista automatically configures particular programs to do certain tasks such as browse the Internet, receive and send e-mail, and play audio and video files on your computer. You can, if you desire, change these program associations on your computer by opening the Set Program Access and Computer Defaults dialog box.

You open the Set Program Access and Computer Defaults dialog box by clicking Start ▶ Default Programs. Next click the Set Programs Access and Computer Defaults link in the Default Programs Control Panel window followed by the Continue button in the Permission dialog box.

The Set Program Access and Computer Defaults dialog box contains three Configuration option buttons:

- ✔ **Microsoft Windows** to select all Microsoft programs for your Internet and media playing needs

- ✔ **Non-Microsoft** to select all the non-Microsoft programs that you've installed on your computer for your Internet and media playing needs

- ✔ **Custom** (the default) to use whatever Internet or media-playing program that you're currently using on the computer but still retain access to Microsoft's Internet and media software (just in case you one day see the light and decide that you want to junk your non-Microsoft browser, e-mail client, or media player in favor of Internet Explorer, Windows Mail, Windows Media Center, and Windows Media Player)

To completely change a new configuration, simply click its option button in the Set Program Access and Computer Defaults dialog box and then click OK. To change only certain program associations within a configuration (especially the Custom configuration), click its expand button (the one with two >> pointing downward) and then modify individual settings within that configuration before you click OK.

Figure 2-10 shows you the Set Program Access and Computer Defaults dialog box on my computer after expanding its Custom section to display the default Web browser and default E-mail program settings.

Figure 2-10

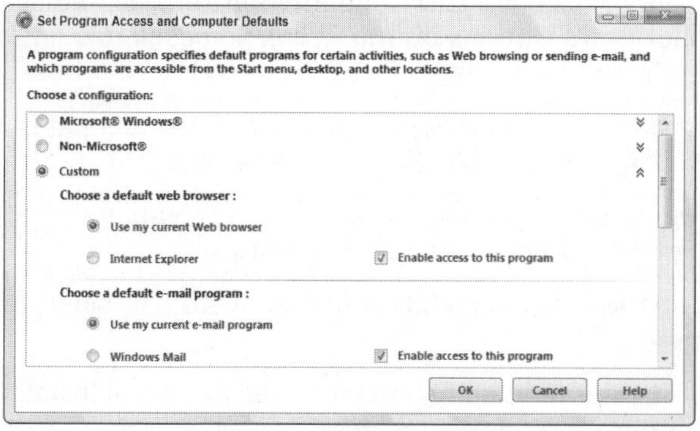

Set Program Access and Computer Defaults

A program configuration specifies default programs for certain activities, such as Web browsing or sending e-mail, and which programs are accessible from the Start menu, desktop, and other locations.

Choose a configuration:

○ Microsoft® Windows®

○ Non-Microsoft®

◉ Custom

   Choose a default web browser :

      ◉ Use my current Web browser

      ○ Internet Explorer   ☑ Enable access to this program

   Choose a default e-mail program :

      ◉ Use my current e-mail program

      ○ Windows Mail   ☑ Enable access to this program

OK   Cancel   Help

Restart, Sleep/Hibernate, Lock, Log Off, and Shut Down

After you press the computer's power button to power up the machine and start the Windows Vista operating system, the Vista Start menu contains all the other controls you need in order to switch between users, reboot the system, and, at the end of the day, power down and shut the machine off.

To the immediate right of the Start Search text box at the bottom of the Start menu, you find a brown button (with a vertical bar in the middle of a circle). On a desktop computer, this is the Power button that, when clicked, saves all open files and programs to the computer's hard drive before putting the machine in a low-power state for quick start-up. If you're running Vista on a laptop computer, the Power button functions as a sleep button that keeps all your open windows and programs in the computer's memory before going into a low-power mode for even quicker start-up.

 You can change the function of the Power button. Open the System Settings Control Panel window (Start ▶ Control Panel ▶ Hardware and Sound ▶ Change What the Power Buttons Do) and then click the When I Press the Power Button drop-down button and select an option (Do Nothing, Sleep, Hibernate) on its drop-down list. If you're changing the settings for the Power button on a laptop, you can select different settings for the Power button when the laptop is on battery power and when it's plugged in.

To the immediate right of the Power button, you find the Lock This Computer button (with a picture of a padlock). When you click this button, Vista locks up the computer so that no one can use it again without first correctly entering your password at your start-up screen. This mode is very useful when you're going to be away from your computer (as when on break or lunch) and want to make sure that no unauthorized person can access your files.

To the immediate right of the Lock This Computer button, you find a pop-up button called the Shut Down Options button. When you click this button, a menu with the following items appears:

- ✔ **Switch User** to switch to another user account on the computer without closing your open programs and Windows processes

- ✔ **Log Off** to switch to another user account on the computer after closing all of your open programs and Windows processes

- ✔ **Lock** to lock up the computer while you're away from it (same as clicking the Lock button)

- ✔ **Restart** to reboot the computer (often required as part of installing new software programs or Windows updates)

- ✔ **Sleep** to put the computer into a low-power mode that retains all running programs and open windows in computer memory for super-quick restart

✔ **Hibernate** (found only on laptop computers) to put the computer into a low-power mode after saving all running programs and open windows on the machine's hard drive for quick restart

✔ **Shut Down** to quit all programs you have running and close all open windows before completely powering down the computer

 TIP Vista shows its old DOS roots by still honoring the good old three-finger salute — Ctrl+Alt+Del. When you press these keys in unison in Vista, the screen blacks out for a moment before presenting you with a blue-green screen containing the following text options: Lock This Computer, Switch User, Log Off, Change a Password, and Start Task Manager.

In addition to these text options, this screen contains the following buttons:

✔ **Cancel** button to return to the Vista desktop along with all of your open program windows.

✔ **Ease of Access** button — the blue button in the lower-left corner of the screen — to open the Ease of Access dialog box where you can select among various accessibility settings for making the computer easier to use for those visual and other physical impairments.

✔ **Power** button — the red button — to shut down the computer equipped with its own pop-up button in the lower-right corner of the screen — note that the items on the menu attached to this pop-up button include Restart, Sleep, Hibernate (on a laptop), and Shut Down.

Windows Explorer

Windows Explorer (not to be confused with Internet Explorer, its Internet equivalent) provides you the means for navigating your computer system by giving you access to all aspects of your computer system from your user files (simply called documents) to the Control Panel.

You can access Windows Explorer by clicking any of the following links that appear in the right column of the Start menu:

✔ **Documents** typically contains the text and data type files (also known as document files) you create — this is the default location for saving document files for programs such as Microsoft Word and Excel and is the Vista equivalent of My Documents in Windows XP.

✔ **Pictures** typically contains the digital photographs and other types of graphic files you store on your computer — this is the Vista equivalent of My Pictures in Windows XP.

✔ **Music** typically contains the music audio files (in all different audio formats such as MP3, WMA, and WAV) you store on your computer — this is the Vista equivalent of My Music in Windows XP.

✔ **Games** contains all the games that come installed with Windows Vista (*see* "Games" in Part 7).

✔ **Search** to open a window where you can quickly search the entire contents of your computer (*see* "Search" in Part 1).

✔ **Computer** displays all the local and mapped network drives on your computer as well as all peripheral devices currently connected to it (*see* "Disk Management" earlier in this part).

✔ **Network** displays all the computers currently a part of your local area network (*see* "Network and Sharing Center" in Part 3).

✔ **Control Panel** displays all the settings you can change on your computer system (*see* "Control Panel" in Part 5).

Changing the display of an Explorer window

You can control how the information returned to any Explorer window is displayed through the use of the Layout item on the Organize button's drop-down menu and the View buttons on its toolbar.

The Layout menu item on the Organize button's drop-down menu contains the following submenu:

✔ **Menu Bar** to turn on and off the display of the pull-down menus File through Help.

✔ **Search Pane** to turn on and off the display of the Search pane, where you can perform a quick or advanced search for particular folders or files. (*See* "Search" in Part 1.)

✔ **Details Pane** to turn on and off the display of the Details pane along the bottom of the window that gives you information about the currently selected item in the window and often enables you to add searchable information through the use of its Edit link.

✔ **Preview Pane** to turn on and off the display of the Preview pane on the right side of the window that displays a live view of whatever folder or file is currently selected in the window.

✔ **Navigation Pane** to turn on and off the display of the Navigation pane on the left side of the window that you use to open new folders on your computer system.

The pop-up slider attached to the Views button contains the following view options (you can also select Large Icons, List, Details, and Tile options in succession by repeatedly clicking the Views button):

- ✓ **Extra Large Icons** to display the folders and files in the window as really huge icons with their name displayed as a caption beneath the icons.

- ✓ **Large Icons** to display the folders and files in the window as fairly larger icons with their name displayed beneath the icons.

- ✓ **Medium Icons** to display the folders and files in the window as medium-sized icons with their name displayed beneath the icons.

- ✓ **Small Icons** to display the folders and files in the window as fairly small icons with their name displayed as a caption to the right side of the icons.

- ✓ **List** to display icons followed by the folder and file names in a single-column list.

- ✓ **Details** to display information about the folders and files in the window in a strict columnar format that includes Name, Date Modified, Type, Authors, and Tags — note that you can widen and narrow these columns as needed by dragging the borders of their labels to the left and right.

- ✓ **Tiles** to display the folders and files in the window as icons with text giving their names and file size arranged in one or two vertical columns.

Keep in mind that when selecting any one of the Icons options, you can use the Views slider to select sizes in between the preset sizes utilized by selecting the Extra Large Icons, Large Icons, Medium Icons, or Small Icons option.

Sorting and filtering items in an Explorer window

Regardless of which view you use in an Explorer window, the Name, Date Modified, Type, Authors, and Tags buttons continue to appear at the top of the display area (although they only function as column headings when you select Details as the Views option).

You can use any of these buttons to sort or filter the current contents of any Explorer window. To sort the contents, simply click the button that you want to use in sorting: once to sort the list of folders and files in descending order (Z to A for text and most recent to least recent for dates) indicated by a triangle pointing downward in the middle above the name of the column, and a second time to return the files to their original ascending order (A to Z for text and least recent to most recent for dates) indicated by a triangle pointing upward.

When using a view other than Details, all these buttons also enable you to rearrange the folder and file contents of the current window into different related bundles by using the Stack option that appears at the bottom of the button's drop-down menu. Figure 2-11 illustrates this kind of stacked arrangement. Here, I have selected the Stack by Name option on the Name columns' drop-down menu (with the Large Icons view selected). Vista then opens a Search Results window that arranges all the documents on my computer into five different stacks: Other for files whose names begin with symbols, 0-9 for files whose names begin with numbers, A-H, I-P, and Q-Z for files whose names begin with those groups of letters. To open an Explorer window listing of all the files in any one of these different stacks, all I have to do is to double-click its stack icon.

Figure 2-11

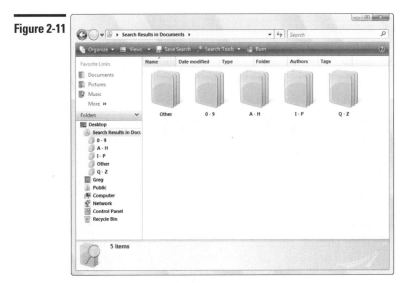

All the buttons (Name through Tags) enable you to rearrange their contents into related groups, using a Group search option on the button's drop-down menu. Figure 2-12 shows an example of this kind of arrangement. Here, you see the Search Results windows after I've selected the Group option on Type column's drop-down menu when the Details view is selected. As you can see, Vista provides both expand (the downward-pointing > symbol) and collapse (the upward-pointing > symbol) buttons for each kind of folder and file group it creates so that you can easily hide and display its individual listings.

TIP — To return the contents of an Explorer window to its normal display after using a button's Stack or Group option, all you need to do is click the Sort option on that column's drop-down menu (to the immediate left of the Group option).

In addition to being able to sort and rearrange the items in an Explorer window, Vista also enables you to filter their contents to just those types of folders and files you want to see. All you have to do to filter the contents by using any of the different buttons (Name through Tags) is to open its drop-down menu and then click the check boxes for all the types of folders and files you want displayed.

Figure 2-12

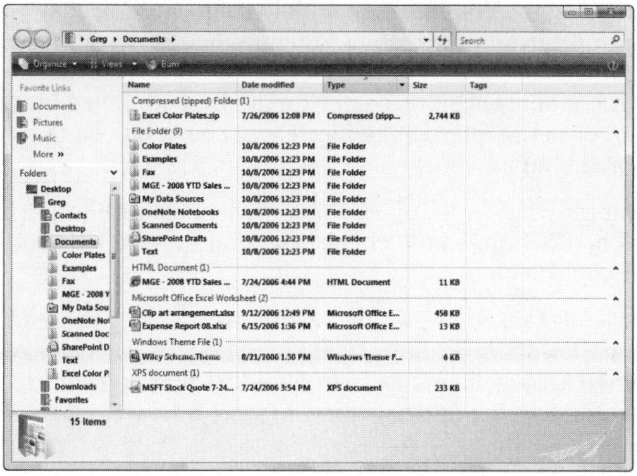

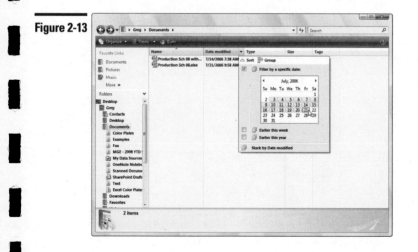

For example, Figure 2-13 shows you my Documents window after filtering its contents by selecting the July 3 through July 21, 2006, by dragging through these dates on the Date Modified column's Filter by a Specific Date calendar. As soon as I do this, Vista filters out all folders and files except for those that I worked with sometime during these three work weeks in July, 2006.

Figure 2-13

Note that when filtering the contents of a window, you can select settings from more than one button's drop-down menu to refine the results. For example, if I want to see only the Excel workbook files I modified during the first week of May, 2006, I would not only select the dates on the Date Modified button's drop-down calendar but click the Microsoft Office Excel check box on the Type button's drop-down menu as well.

TIP

To restore an Explorer window to its previous contents after filtering it, simply remove the check marks from all the check boxes on the different buttons' drop-down menus that you selected.

REMEMBER

You can always filter a stacked or grouped list to display only those folders and files you want to work with. In addition, keep in mind that you can save these stacked and grouped arrangements as search folders that you can redisplay simply by opening them in the Search window (Start ▶ Search). *See* "Search" in Part 1 for details.

Part 3

Networking

Windows Vista is right at home with all types of private networking currently in use, everything from peer-to-peer or ad hoc networks in the home to small-scale local area networks (LANs) and wide-area networks (WANs) in business. Networks like the one shown in this figure enable the computers you have to share resources such as network printers, scanners, and, most important, broadband connections to the Internet.

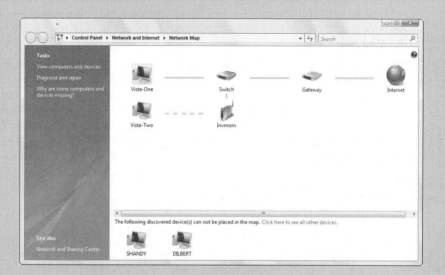

In this part . . .

- ✔ **Connecting to a dialup, VPN, or wireless network**
- ✔ **Viewing and exploring the computers on the network**
- ✔ **Managing network connections for wired and wireless networks**
- ✔ **Viewing a map of the network**
- ✔ **Managing and setting up your network connections**

Connect to a Network

Types of connections to such private networks include the more traditional Ethernet connection, with its network adapters and cabling, along with the newer, and ever increasingly popular, wireless connection (commonly referred to as Wi-Fi), with its wireless network adapters and access points (also known as hotspots).

Fortunately, during installation, Vista is super at detecting existing private networks and often requires little or no additional network setup. The topics covered in this part of the book pinpoint the networking features in Vista and how you use them to create networking connections as well as how to maintain them.

If your computer running the Vista operating system connects to your network via a dialup, VPN (virtual private network), or wireless connection, you can click the Connect To item on the Start menu either to disconnect from a current connection or to make a new connection.

When you click Start ▶ Connect To, Vista opens a Connect to a Network dialog box similar to the one shown in Figure 3-1. By default, Vista shows all the networks to which your computer is or can be connected. To limit this listing to just those wireless networks that are in range, click the Wireless option on the Show drop-down list. To limit the network connection listing to just those dialup or VPN networks to which you can connect, click the Dial-up and VPN item on the Show drop-down list.

Figure 3-1

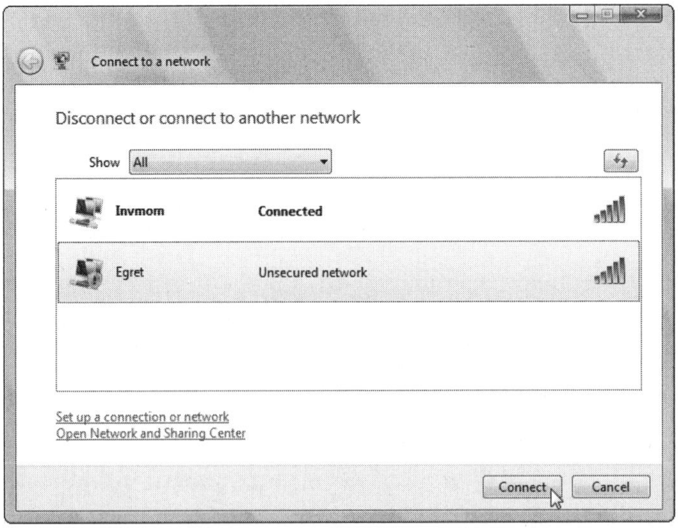

To connect to a listed network, click its name and then click the Connect button. If the network requires you to supply a key, Vista then prompts you to enter your network security key in the Connect to a Network dialog box, assuming that your wireless connection requires some type of authentication — click the Show Characters check box to have the characters you type displayed in the Encryption text box. After you successfully enter your security key, click the Connect button to have Vista use the key in establishing the connection.

To disconnect from the network to which you're currently connected, click it and then click the Disconnect button. Vista then prompts you to confirm your disconnection in the Connect to a Network dialog box by clicking the Disconnect link, after which you can click the Close button.

Manage Network Connections

You can use the Network Connections window to manage any of the Ethernet and wireless connections you use to connect your computer to the company's network or the Internet. To open this window, click the Manage Networks Connections link that appears in the Navigation pane of your computer's Network and Sharing Center Control Panel (opened by clicking Start ▶ Network and then clicking the Network and Sharing Center button, or by clicking Start ▶ Control Panel ▶ View Network Status and Tasks).

When you click the Manage Network Connections link, Vista opens a Network Connections Control Panel window similar to the one shown in Figure 3-2. This windows shows all the wired and wireless networks that your computer attempts to automatically access when you turn on your computer.

Figure 3-2

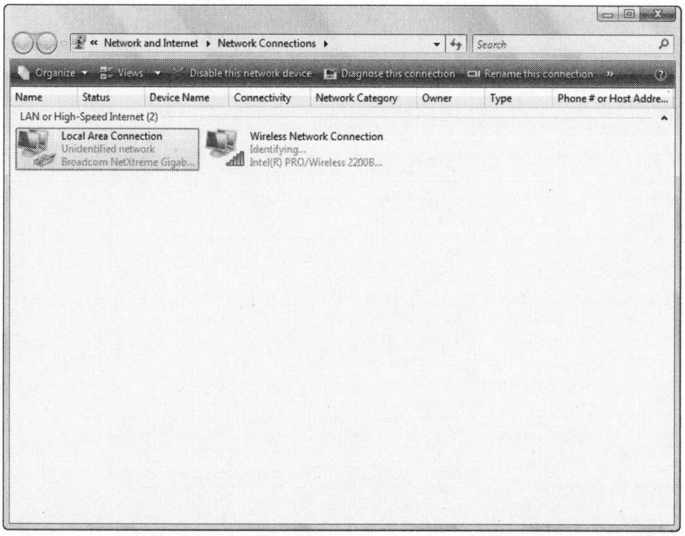

To change any of the settings for a particular network connection displayed in this window, right-click the Connection icon and then click the appropriate option on its shortcut menu. Click the Diagnose option when you're having trouble using a particular connection to get online and you want to see if Windows can suggest ways to fix the problem. Click the Properties option when you need to view or change any of the networking or sharing settings. Note, however, that you must have administrator user status in order to open up the properties dialog box for any of your computer's network connections.

Manage Wireless Networks

If your computer uses a Wi-Fi adapter to connect to your company's network as well as to the Internet, you can use the Manage Wireless Networks link that appears in the Navigation pane of your computer's Network and Sharing Center Control Panel (opened by clicking Start ▶ Network and then clicking the Network and Sharing Center button, or by clicking Start ▶ Control Panel ▶ View Network Status and Tasks).

When you click the Manage Wireless Networks link, Vista opens a Manage Wireless Networks Control Panel window similar to the one shown in Figure 3-3. This windows shows all the wireless networks that your computer attempts to automatically access when the computer (assuming it's a laptop) is in range of the network, along with the type of security it uses.

Figure 3-3

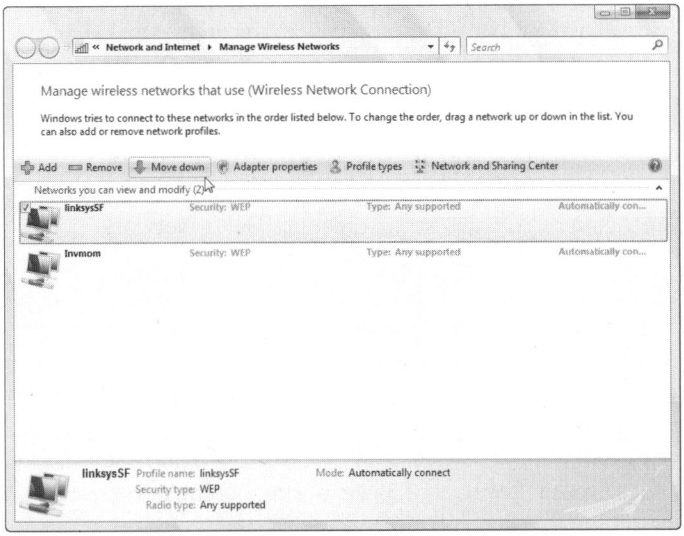

Modifying the order in which Vista automatically connects to wireless networks

To modify the order in which your computer tries to connect to one of the wireless networks listed in the Manage Wireless Networks Control Panel window, all you have to do is drag its network icon to a new position in the list (up to the top of the list to promote it as the first network to try to connect to, and down to the bottom to demote it as the last network to try to connect to).

You can also change the order of a wireless connection by clicking it in the Manage Wireless Networks window and then clicking either the Move Up or Move Down buttons that appear on the toolbar above the list of the connections as needed.

Manually adding a new wireless network

Sometimes, you will want to manually add a wireless network to the list in the Manage Wireless Networks Control Panel window for which you're currently out of range, but to which you want Vista to automatically connect whenever you do come in range.

To add a new wireless network to the Manage Wireless Networks Control Panel window, follow these steps:

1. Open the Network and Sharing Center Control Panel either by clicking Start ▶ Network and then clicking the Network and Sharing Center button, or by clicking Start ▶ Control Panel ▶ View Network Status and Tasks.

2. Click the Manage Wireless Networks link in the Navigation pane of the Network and Sharing Center Control Panel window.

3. Click the Add button on the Manage Wireless Networks window toolbar to open the How Do You Want to Add a Network? dialog box.

4. Click the Manually Create a Network Profile option to open the Manually Connect to a Wireless Network dialog box.

5. Enter the name of the wireless network in the Network Name text box.

6. If the wireless network is secured, select the type of security used (WEP, WPA-Personal, WPA2-Personal, WPA-Enterprise, WPA2-Enterprise, or 802.11x) in the Security Type drop-down list box that currently contains No Authentication (Open).

   WEP (Wired Equivalent Privacy) and WPA (Wi-Fi Protected Access) are two security standards currently in use. Of the two, WEP is older and less reliable. WPA2 (also known as 802.11i) is the latest version of WPA security for wireless networks. Personal mode is the one most often used by home and small business wireless networks.

7. If you select WPA2-Personal or WPA2-Enterprise as the Security Type and your wireless network uses TKIP rather than AES type encryption, click TKIP in the Encryption Type drop-down list box.

   AES (Advanced Encryption Standard) is a block-type cipher adopted by the U.S. government. TKIP (Temporary Key Integrity Protocol) is an older security protocol created to correct deficiencies in the WEP security standard.

8. Click the Security Key/Passphrase text box and there enter the security key or passphrase assigned to the type of security and encryption used by your wireless network.

   WEP security keys are normally from either 5 to 13 case-sensitive characters or 10 to 26 hexadecimal case-sensitive characters. WPA and WPA2 security keys contain between 8 to 63 case-sensitive characters. To display the characters in the Security Key/Passphrase text box as you type them, click the Display Characters check box.

9. (Optional) By default, Vista automatically connects to the network when the computer comes into range. If you want to manually connect to the network each time the computer's in range (using Start ▶ Connect To), click the Start Connection Automatically check box to remove its check mark.

10. (Optional) To have Vista connect to the in-range network even when it's not broadcasting, click the Connect Even If the Network Is Not Broadcasting check box.

    Vista opens a version of the Manually Connect to a Network dialog box displaying a Successfully Added message along with a Connect To and Change Connection Settings option.

11. Click the Connect To option if you now want to connect by using the new wireless connection. Click the Change Connection Settings to open the Wireless Network Properties dialog box for the new connection (where you make modifications to the Connection or Security settings). Otherwise, click the Close button.

After you close the Manually Connect to a Wireless Network dialog box, Vista displays the name of the new wireless network connection at the top of the list in the Manage Wireless Networks Control Panel window. You can then adjust the order in which Vista uses this connection by dragging it down or demoting it by clicking the Move Down button on the toolbar.

Removing an unused network from the list

To remove a wireless network that you no longer use from the list, click its network icon in the Manage Wireless Networks Control Panel window and then click the Remove button on the window's toolbar. Vista then displays a Warning dialog box cautioning you that if you proceed by clicking OK, you will no longer be able to connect to the wireless network automatically.

Network Access

Clicking Start ▶ Network opens a Network window similar to the one shown in Figure 3-4. This Network window displays all the computers currently connected to the network and gives you access to their files (assuming that the network file and Discovery and Sharing has been turned on).

Figure 3-4

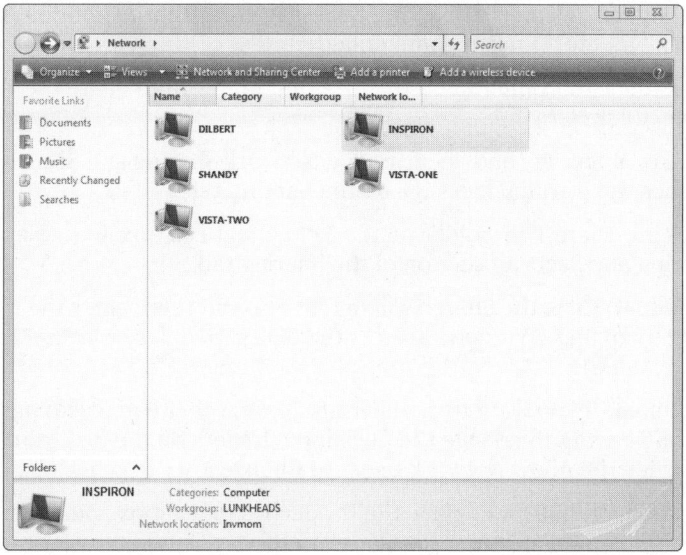

Figure 3-4 shows you the shared computers currently connected to my local area network. Note that all five of these computers (including Vista-Two, the computer on which this screenshot was taken) are a part of the same workgroup called LUNKHEADS, indicated by the group heading (of which DILBERT happens to be the name of the network server). (To create this arrangement by workgroup, I simply clicked the Group option on the menu opened by clicking the Domain field's drop-down button.)

> **WARNING**
>
> Icons for the computers connected to your network for which File Sharing (in computers running pre-Vista Windows) or Discovery and Sharing has not been turned on do *not* show up in the Network window even when the computers are turned on and connected to the network.

Turning on File Sharing or Discovery and Sharing

When a computer on the network is running an earlier version of Windows such as Windows XP, the Sharing and Security settings for the hard drive whose files you want to share must be enabled in order to allow sharing and for the computer's icon to appear in Vista's Network window. To turn on file sharing for the computer's hard drive or a folder, follow these steps:

1. Click Start→My Computer to open the My Computer window.

2. Right-click the hard drive icon for the drive whose files you want to share and then click Sharing and Security on the drive's shortcut menu.

   Windows opens the Properties dialog box for the selected drive with the Sharing tab selected displaying a message that sharing the root drive of your computer is not recommended.

3. Click the If You Understand the Risk but Still Want to Share the Root of the Drive, Click Here link.

   The Local Sharing and Security and Network Sharing and Security options replace the warning message on the Sharing tab.

4. Click the Share This Folder on the Network check box in the Network Sharing and Security section of the Sharing tab.

5. (Optional) Click the Shared Name text box and there enter the name you want to appear (Windows selects the disk's drive letter as the default share name).

6. (Optional) If you want to give permission to other users who have access to the network to change the files in the folders on the disk you're sharing, click the Allow Network Users to Change My Files check box.

7. Click the OK button to close the Properties dialog box and begin sharing the drive on the network (indicated in the My Computer window by the appearance of the hand underneath the drive icon).

Windows closes the Properties dialog box and the next time you open the My Computer window, the icon for the drive you've just shared will have a hand holding the disk indicating that it's now being shared.

When a computer on the network is running Windows Vista, the Network Discovery and File Sharing settings for that computer must be enabled in order for that computer's icon to appear in the Network window. To do this, assuming that your user account has administrator status, follow these steps:

1. Open the Network window by clicking Start ▶ Network.

2. Click the Network and Sharing Center button on the Network window toolbar to open the Network and Sharing Center window.

3. Click the downward pointing > to the right of Network Discovery in the Sharing and Discovery section of the window, and then click the Turn On Network Discovery option button and click the Apply command button.

4. Click the Continue button in the User Account Control dialog box that appears.

   Windows replaces the Off after Network Discovery to On, indicating that this setting is now enabled.

5. Repeat Steps 3 and 4, this time for the File Sharing listing immediately below Network Discovery in the Sharing and Discovery section of the Network and Sharing Center Window.

   After clicking the Turn On File Sharing option button and the Continue button in User Account Control dialog box, On now appears after File Sharing in the Sharing and Discovery list.

6. Click the Close button to close the Network and Sharing Center window.

Opening and exploring shared computers on the network

You can open any of the computers displayed in the Network window and access their files in whatever drives and folders are shared on that computer. To do this, double-click the computer's icon in the Network window, or right-click it and then click the Open (or Explore) item on the shortcut menu.

Vista then opens a window showing all the shared drives, folders, and devices such as shared printers (which you can then open by double-clicking their icons). Figure 3-5 shows you the window that opens when I double-click the INSPIRON computer icon shown in the Network window in Figure 3-4. As you can see, this window contains a folder for shared C: drive on this computer, its SharedDocs folder, and a bunch of printers.

Figure 3-5

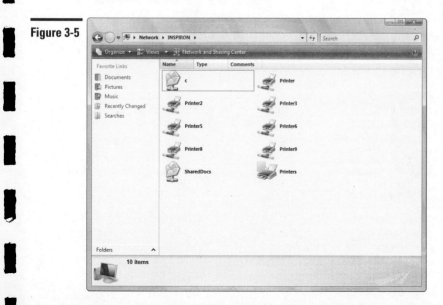

TIP If you find yourself accessing the same files in a particular folder on a network computer or network server on a regular basis, consider mapping that folder as a local drive on your computer. That way, instead of having to open the folder via the Network window, you can access the folder quickly and directly from the Computer window (Start ▶ Computer), where it appears as though it were a local drive. The best part is that you can have Vista map this folder as a local drive in the Computer window each and every time that you boot the computer so that you only have to perform the actual mapping procedure one time. *See* "Mapping a network folder as a local drive" in Part 2 for details.

Network and Sharing Center

Vista's Network and Sharing Center enables you to view at a glance the status of your networks as well as the connections they utilize. To open a Network and Sharing Center Control Panel window similar to the one shown in Figure 3-6, either click the Network and Sharing Center button on the Network window's toolbar (Start ▶ Network), or open it via the Control Panel by clicking Start ▶ Control Panel ▶ View Network Status and Tasks.

Figure 3-6

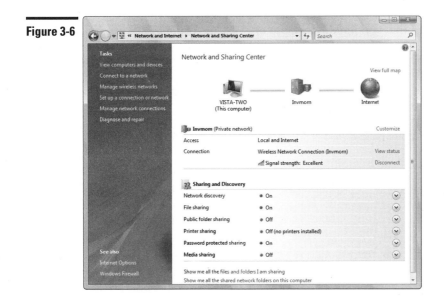

The Network and Sharing Center window contains three sections:

- ✔ **Network and Sharing Center,** which contains a simple schematic showing how your computer (marked This Computer) is connected to the network and the Internet — questionable connections are indicated in the map by exclamation points in a yellow triangle, whereas breaks in the connections are indicated by red Xs.

- ✔ **Private or Public Network,** which shows how your computer is connected as well as the category of the network connection. (*Private* indicates home or business networks that are not open to the general public; *Public* stands for networks that broadcast in public places such as cafes and airports.)

- ✔ **Sharing and Discovery,** which displays a list showing the current status of the various sharing settings on your computer (either On for enabled or Off for disabled — *see* "Turning on File Sharing or Discovery and Sharing" earlier in this chapter for details).

If you find some sort of trouble with your computer's connection to the network or to the Internet in the schematic displayed in the Status area, click the yellow triangle with the exclamation point or the red X in the map to have Vista diagnose the particular problem and, in some cases, even repair the connection.

Network Map

In addition to the simple schematic that Vista displays in the Status area of the Network and Sharing Center Control Panel window (showing your computer's basic connection to the network and Internet), you can have Vista display a more detailed network map. To do this, click the View Full Map link that appears in the upper-right corner of the Status area in the Network and Sharing Center window.

Figure 3-7 shows you the complete Network Map that Vista created in a Network Map Control Panel window when I clicked the View Full Map link in the Network and Sharing Center window shown in Figure 3-6. As shown in Figure 3-7, this detailed map traces all the intermediary steps followed by the two computers in my office that run Windows Vista.

According to the detailed map in Figure 3-7, the computer named Vista-One connects directly to the network Gateway through the Ethernet switch, whereas the computer named Vista-Two connects to the network via a wireless connection (indicated by the dashes in the schematic) to a wireless access point connection called Invmom, which, in turn, connects directly to the Ethernet switch. All traffic routed by the Ethernet switch then goes directly to file server (DILBERT, not included in the schematic), which connects to the Gateway (a broadband cable modem), which provides the Internet access to the network.

Figure 3-7

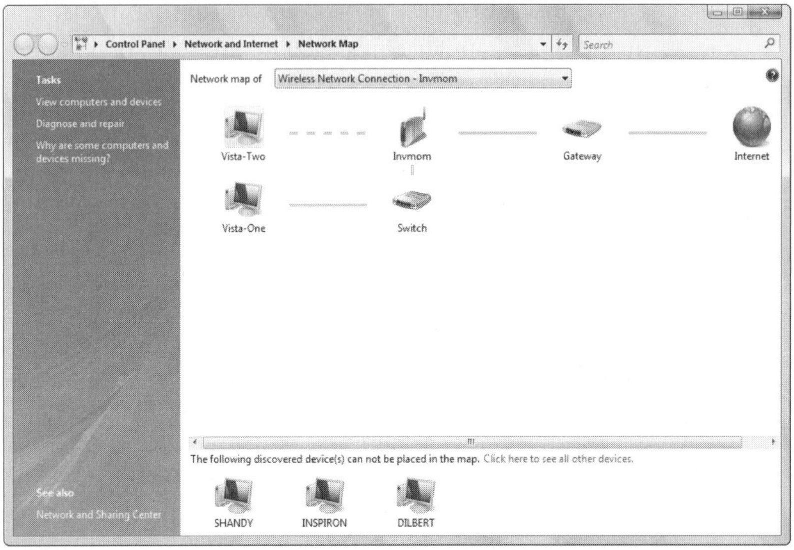

Keep in mind that Vista does not include network computers running non-Vista versions of Windows in the full map created in the Network Map Control Panel window. Icons for network computers not running Vista are orphaned to the Preview pane at the bottom of the Network Map Control Panel window (in the example shown in Figure 3-7, this includes SHANDY and INSPIRON, both running Windows XP, and DILBERT, the network file server running Microsoft Windows Server 2003).

Just as with the simple map shown in the Status area of the Network Center window, if you find some sort of trouble is indicated in the connections shown in the full Network Map, simply click the yellow triangle with the exclamation point or the red X in the full map to have Vista diagnose the particular problem and, hopefully, even repair the connection.

Set Up a Connection or Network

Vista makes it easy to set up a connection to an existing network as well as to a new peer-to-peer or ad hoc network so that you can share files, peripherals such as printers and scanners, and even the Internet.

To set up a network connection, click Set Up a Connection or Network link in the Navigation pane of the Network and Sharing Center Control Panel window

(Start ▶ Control Panel ▶ View Network Status and Tasks). Vista then opens the Set Up a Connection or Network dialog box, shown in Figure 3-8, where you select the type of connection to create before selecting the Next button:

✔ **Connect to the Internet** to open the Connect to the Internet dialog box where you select the type of connection (wireless, broadband (PPPoE) or dialup) to use. Next, specify the information required for you to log onto the Internet Service Provider (ISP) or wireless network for the type of connection you select.

✔ **Set Up a Wireless Router or Access Point** to start a wizard that walks you through the steps of configuring a new wireless router or access point.

✔ **Set Up a Dial-Up Connection** to open the Set Up a Dial-Up Connection dialog box, where you enter the dialup information for your Internet Service Provider (ISP) including the dialup phone number, username, and password.

✔ **Connect to a Workplace** to open the Connect to a Workplace dialog box, where you choose between using a VPN or dialup connection for connecting. If you click Use My Internet Connection (VPN) button, a Connect to a Workplace dialog box opens, where you enter the Internet address and destination name you use to log onto the network at your workplace as provided by the network's administrator or your company's IT department. If you click the Dial Directly button, a Connect to Workplace dialog box opens, where you enter the dialup information for your Internet Service Provider (ISP) including the dialup phone number, username, and password.

Figure 3-8

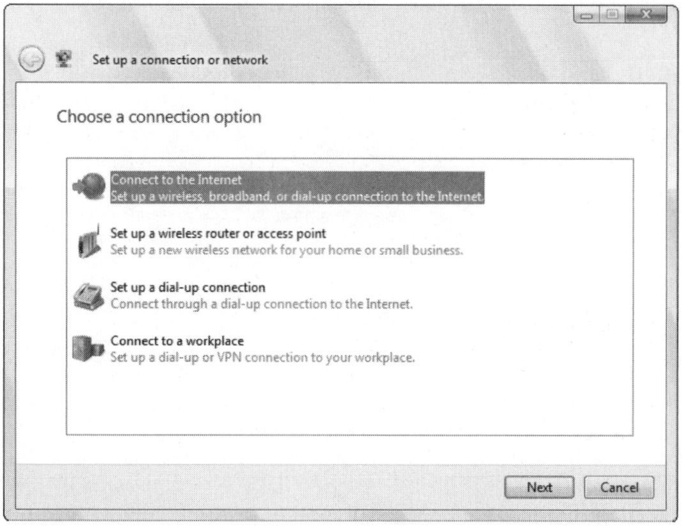

If you're running Vista on a laptop computer equipped with wireless networking, the Set Up a Connection or Network dialog box also contains the following two options:

- ✔ **Manually Connect to a Wireless Network** that enables you to select a hidden network or create a new wireless connection by using a different wireless network adapter installed in your computer.

- ✔ **Set Up a Wireless Ad Hoc (Computer to Computer) Network** that you can use to create a temporary network connection between two wireless laptop computers for sharing files, peripherals, and the Internet (note that the laptops must be within 30 feet of one another).

Part 4

Communications

Windows Vista offers you some pretty exciting communication features in the form of a brand new version of its award-winning Internet Explorer, shown in the following figure, plus a whole new e-mail program simply called Windows Mail. You can also use the new Windows Collaboration feature to share files and programs, and even your Vista desktop, with other computers on your network.

In this part . . .

- ✔ Browsing the Web with Internet Explorer 7
- ✔ Using Vista's speech recognition and text-to-speech features
- ✔ Faxing and scanning documents with Windows Fax and Scan
- ✔ Doing e-mail with Windows Mail
- ✔ Collaborating with other Vista PCs on the network

Internet Explorer 7

Windows Vista includes Windows Internet Explorer 7, which enables you to browse Web pages anywhere on the Internet. This most recent version of the Microsoft Web browser is equipped with all the latest and greatest features for helping you find, visit, and retrieve any online information that might interest you.

Two basic steps are involved in browsing Web pages with the Internet Explorer 7 browser:

> ✔ Connecting to the Internet

> ✔ Going to the Web page

 You can also launch Internet Explorer 7 from a folder window, such as Documents or Computer. When you select a Web page in one of these windows, either by typing the URL in the address bar or selecting a bookmarked Web page on the Favorites menu (when Classic Menus are displayed), Windows launches Internet Explorer 7 and opens the specified page.

Connecting to the Internet

You connect to the Internet either with a dialup modem or a cable or DSL modem connection (all of which use a modem directly connected to your computer), or with a connection to a LAN that's connected to the Internet through some sort of high-speed telephone line, such as a T1 or T3.

When you connect to the Internet via a dialup connection (as you might still have do at home), your modem must call up an Internet service provider (ISP), such as America Online (AOL), whose high-speed telephone lines and fancy switching equipment provide you (for a fee) with access to the Internet and all the online services.

When you connect to the Internet via a cable or DSL modem or a LAN (as is becoming more and more common from home as well as from work), you don't have to do anything special to get connected to the Internet: You have Internet access any time you turn on your computer and launch Internet Explorer.

 To configure a connection to the Internet, click Start ▶ Control Panel ▶ View Network Status and Tasks (under Network and Internet) to open the Network Center window. There, click the Set Up a Connection or Network link to open the Set Up a Connection or Network dialog box, where you click the link for the type of connection. **See** "Set Up a Connection or Network" in Part 3 for more information.

Launching Internet Explorer 7

 To launch Internet Explorer 7, click the Start button on the Windows taskbar and then click the Internet option at the very top of the Start menu. Alternatively, click the Launch Internet Explorer Browser icon (the one with the blue *e* shown in the left margin) in the Quick Launch toolbar that appears on the Windows Vista taskbar.

The first time you launch Internet Explorer 7, Vista displays a Customize Your Settings page, where you specify your language and region before clicking the Save Your Settings button. After doing that, the program displays a Tour of New Features page that you can use to become familiar with the new features. From then on, when you launch Internet Explorer, the program connects to Windows Live home page, which enables you to search for stuff on the Web or customize what content is displayed on this page (see Figure 4-1).

Figure 4-1

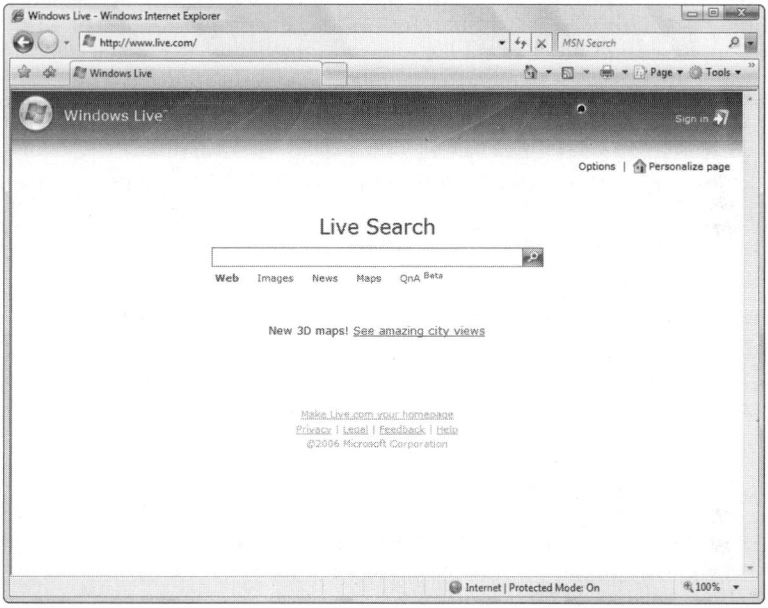

When first installed, Internet Explorer 7 displays neither the menu bar with the pull-down menus (File through Help) nor the Links toolbar to its right (as was the case in all earlier versions of this Web browser). To temporarily bring back the menu bar so you can perform a particular menu command, press the Alt key (you can then complete the command sequence by typing the hot key letters assigned to the other menu items). To permanently bring the menu bar, click the Tools button and then click Menu Bar on the drop-down menu. To display a Links button with its own continuation button (>>) to the right, click the Links option on the Tools ▶ Toolbars menu. After that, you can add new Web pages to the Links continuation menu by simply dragging the current page's icon (that appears to the immediate left of the page's URL in the address bar) and dropping it on the Links button. You can then easily go to the page by selecting its name on this continuation menu.

Adding and changing home pages

When you click the Home button or press Alt+M in Internet Explorer 7, the browser immediately opens whatever page's URL address is listed at the very

top of the Home button's drop-down menu. To change this home page, navigate
to the Web page you want to use as your new home page. Click the drop-down
button attached to the Home button followed by Add or Change Home Page item
on this drop-down menu. Doing this opens the Add or Change Home Page dialog
box. Then click the Use This Webpage as Your Only Home Page option button
before you click the Yes button to close this dialog box.

TIP

In Internet Explorer 7, you can have more than one Web page designated as a
home page and therefore assigned to the additional Home page tabs. If you want
to add another home page, open the Web page you want to add as a home page in
Internet Explorer and click the Add This Webpage to Your Home Page Tabs option
button in the Add or Change Home Page dialog box. Then click the Yes button.

After you create an additional home page, when you next click the Home button,
Internet Explorer 7 then adds a tab for this additional home page that automatically appears to the right of the first home tab each time you launch this Web
browser. Then all you have to do to open one of the home pages is click its tab
or select the page with the Quick Tabs button (*see* "Using Internet Explorer 7
tabs" later in this part).

REMEMBER

Keep in mind that if you ever want to remove a home page and its tab from
Internet Explorer 7, you can do so by clicking Remove on the Home button's
drop-down menu, and then clicking the page to remove — Home Page, Home
Page (2), Home Page (3), and so on — from the submenu. Finally, click Yes in the
Delete Home Page dialog box to confirm its removal.

Navigating the Web

After your connection to the Internet is made and the home page appears in the
browsing window, you're free to begin browsing other pages on the World Wide
Web by doing any of the following:

- ✔ Entering the Uniform Resource Locator (URL) of the Web page in the
  address bar and pressing Enter or clicking the Go To button (the one with
  the right-pointing arrowhead that appears as soon as you begin typing the
  URL in the Address Bar).

- ✔ Clicking hyperlinks on the currently displayed Web page that take you to
  other Web pages, either on the same Web site or on another Web site.

- ✔ Selecting a bookmarked Web page that appears in the Favorites Center or
  the Favorites Explorer bar (Ctrl+I), or one that you've recently visited on
  the History Explorer bar (Ctrl+H). *See* "Adding Web Favorites" later in this
  part for details on how to add Web pages to the Favorites menu.

- ✔ Using the MSN Search text box to the right of the Address bar to display
  hyperlinks for the home pages of Web sites that might possibly fit some
  search criteria, such as "IRA investments" or, better yet, "Hawaiian vacations." *See* "Web search" later in this part for details on searching.

Note that Internet Explorer 7 automatically displays the title of the Web page you're visiting in the current tab as well as on the Windows Internet Explorer program's title bar. *See* "Using Internet Explorer 7 tabs" later in this part for information on adding tabs for the pages you visit.

After you start exploring different Web pages, you can start clicking the Back button to the left of the address bar to return to any of the previously viewed pages. Each time you click Back (or press Alt+←), Internet Explorer goes back to the very last page you viewed. If you've visited several pages during the same browsing session, you can jump to a particular page that you viewed by clicking the Recent Pages drop-down button that appears to the immediate right of the Forward button and then clicking the page you want to revisit from the drop-down list.

You can clear the list of recently browsed Web pages at any time by clicking Tools ▶ Delete Browsing History. Vista then opens the Delete Browsing History dialog box, where you click the Delete History command button followed by the Yes button in the alert dialog box that appears. You can also delete all copies of Web pages, images, and other media cached on your computer for faster viewing from this Delete Browsing History dialog box by clicking its Temporary Internet Files command button and then clicking Yes in its alert dialog box.

You can also revisit the list of pages that are in the browser's history (that is, the pages you've visited in the last 20 days unless you've changed the History option) by clicking the address bar's drop-down button and then clicking the URL of the page you want to revisit from the drop-down list.

After using the Back button to revisit one or more previously viewed pages, the Forward button (right next door) becomes active. Click the Forward button (or press Alt+→) to step forward through each of the pages that you've viewed with the Back button, or select a page to jump to in the Forward button drop-down list.

If you come upon a page that doesn't seem to want to load for some reason (including a broken hyperlink or too much Web traffic), click the Stop button (with the red X to the immediate left of the MSN Search text box) or press Esc to stop the process; then select a new Web site to visit. When revisiting a page, you can make sure that the content currently displayed by Internet Explorer is completely up-to-date by clicking the Refresh button (with the two arrows pointing down and up to the immediate left of the Stop Loading button).

Zooming in on page

If the text on the Web page you're visiting is too small for you to read comfortably on your screen, click the 100% button on the Status bar at the bottom of the Internet Explorer 7 window to zoom in on the page: Click once to zoom up to 125% magnification and a second time to zoom up to a 150% magnification. Clicking this button a third time returns you to 100%. Note that you can also zoom in by using the keyboard and pressing the Ctrl key and the plus key (+).

If you need to boost the magnification of a Web page beyond 150%, you can select the percentage from the Zoom drop-down menu, which you access by positioning the mouse pointer over or clicking the Page button and then highlighting or clicking Zoom. The Zoom menu percentage selections include 50%, 75%, 100%, 125%, 150%, 200%, 400%, and Custom. You can also do this by clicking the Change Zoom Level button (the drop-down button to the immediate right of the 100% button on the Status bar) and clicking the percentage item from its pop-up menu.

If none of these presets work for you, click Custom to open the Custom Zoom dialog box, where you can type any whole percentage number between 1 and 1,000 in the Percentage Zoom text box, or select it with the up and down spinner buttons before you click OK.

You can also use the shortcut keys Ctrl+plus sign (+) and Ctrl+minus sign (–) to zoom the Web page up and down, respectively, in 10% increments.

Using the Panning Hand to scroll the Web page

The Panning Hand button (the one with the right-hand icon to the immediate right of the Home drop-down button) provides a really cool alternative to using Internet Explorer's vertical and horizontal scroll bars to bring new Web page information into view in the Internet Explorer window when all the info won't fit in the window display.

When you click the Panning Hand button (or press Alt+G) to select it, your mouse pointer assumes the hand shape, and you can then use this pointer to drag new, unseen parts of the current Web page into view. Drag to the left to bring hidden information on the right-hand side of the page into view. Drag upward to bring hidden information on lower parts of the page into view.

Be careful to differentiate the hand mouse pointer for selecting hyperlinks on a Web page from the hand mouse pointer for panning up and down and across the page. The hand shape for selecting hyperlinks is a right hand with the thumb and index fingers extended. The hand shape for panning the Web page is a right hand with all the fingers bent and only the thumb extended.

Before you click the mouse to begin dragging across or down a Web page after clicking the Panning Hand button, be sure that you're not over a hyperlink (in which case, the mouse pointer assumes the shape of a hand with the thumb and index fingers extended). Otherwise, you end up selecting the link and jumping to a new page rather than panning the current page.

When you're finished using the Panning Hand mouse pointer to scroll through the information on the page, click the Panning Hand button again to return the mouse pointer to its original arrowhead shape.

Address AutoComplete

Of all the methods for browsing pages on the Web that I mention in the list in the preceding section, none is quite as bad as having to type URL addresses with the **http://** and the **www.** something or other **.com** in the address bar. To help eliminate errors in typing and speed this tedious process, Windows employs a feature called AutoComplete. This nifty feature looks at the first few characters of the URL address you type in the address bar and, based on that, attempts to match them to one of the complete addresses that is stored in the address bar drop-down list.

For example, if you click the cursor in the address bar, select all the characters in the current Web address that follow http://www (the standard beginning for most Web addresses), and then replace the last part of the current address with the letter *h*, AutoComplete opens the address bar drop-down list, displaying all the Web sites that you've visited recently whose URL (after the standard http:// www. stuff) begins with *h*.

To visit any one of the pages listed in the address bar drop-down list, click that name in the drop-down list. Internet Explorer then enters the complete URL address of the Web site you clicked in the address bar and automatically displays the page.

The AutoComplete feature also works when you browse folders on a local or network disk. To display a list of recently viewed documents on your hard drive, click the address bar, and then type the letter of your hard drive (**c**, in most cases); next click the document you want to open in the Address Bar drop-down list.

Adding Web Favorites

You keep bookmarks for all of your preferred Web pages for easy revisiting. You can access your Favorite bookmarks from the Favorites Center, opened by clicking the Favorites Center button (with the star) or pressing Alt+C.

If you display the pull-down menus in Internet Explorer 7 (by clicking Tools ▶ Menu Bar), you can access your bookmarks directly from the Favorites drop-down menu.

When you first start adding to the Favorites Center, you'll find that it already contains folders such as Links and Microsoft. In addition, the Favorites folder may contain a folder with your computer manufacturer's favorite Web sites (called something like "XYZ" Corporation Recommended Sites), Mobile Favorites (if you connect a hand-held device to the computer), and a folder called Imported Bookmarks, if you imported bookmarks from the address book created with another Web browser e-mail program into Windows Mail.

To add a bookmark to the Favorites Center for a favorite Web page on the Internet, follow these steps:

1. Launch Internet Explorer 7 (Start ▶ Internet) and visit the Web page for which you want to add a bookmark in your Favorites folder.

   See "Navigating the Web" earlier in this part for details on how to open a Web page.

2. Click the Add to Favorites button (the star with the plus sign) and then click Add to Favorites on its pop-up menu to open the Add a Favorite dialog box similar to the one shown in Figure 4-2.

   You can also open the Add a Favorite dialog box by right-clicking anywhere on the Web page itself and then clicking Add to Favorites on its shortcut menu.

3. (Optional) If you want a different bookmark description to appear on the Favorites menu, edit the name that currently appears in the Name text box.

4. (Optional) To add the bookmark in a subfolder of the Favorites folder, click the Create In drop-down button to display a list of subfolders and then click the icon of the subfolder in which to add the bookmark. To add the bookmark to a new folder, click the New Folder button, enter the folder name in Folder Name text box in the Create a Folder dialog box, and click Create.

5. Click the Add button to close the Favorites Center dialog box and add the bookmark to the Favorites Center.

Figure 4-2

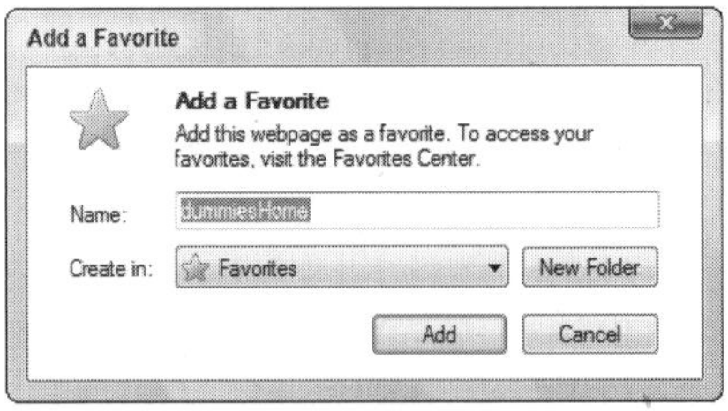

Opening Favorites

After you add a Web page to your Favorites folder (or one of the subfolders), you can open the page simply by selecting the bookmark, either from the Favorites Center or from the Favorites pull-down menu (if the Classic menus are displayed or press Alt+A, if the menus are hidden).

To open the Favorites Center list in a temporary pane, click the Favorites Center button (the one with the star) or press Alt+C. To visit a favorite listed on the pane, click its link in the Favorites Center and then, when the content of the page is loaded in Internet Explorer, click anywhere outside the Favorites Center pane to close it. If the favorite you want to visit is saved in a subfolder, click that folder's icon in the Favorites Center pane to expand and display a list of the favorite links it contains, which you can click to display the page.

To open the Favorites Center list in an Explorer bar that stays open until you close it, press Ctrl+I or click Tools ▶ Toolbars ▶ Favorites. When you are finished browsing your favorite Web pages, you can close the Favorites Center Explorer bar by clicking its Close the Favorites Center button (the one with the X).

You can also keep the Favorites Center open by clicking the Pin the Favorites Center button (the one with the green arrow pointing to the left in the right-hand corner of the Favorites Center list).

To select a bookmark from the Favorites pull-down menu when the classic menus are displayed in Internet Explorer, choose Favorites on the menu bar and then select the name of the bookmark on the Favorites menu. If the bookmark is located in a subfolder of the Favorites, you need to drill down to the subfolder icon to open the submenu, where you can click the desired bookmark.

Organizing Favorites

Many times, you'll find yourself going along adding bunches of bookmarks to your preferred Web pages without ever bothering to create them in particular subfolders. Then to your dismay, you'll find yourself confronted with a seemingly endless list of unrelated bookmarks every time you open the Favorites Center pane or Explorer bar.

Fortunately, Windows makes it easy to reorganize even the most chaotic of bookmark lists in just a few easy steps:

1. In the Internet Explorer 7 window, click the Add to Favorites button (with the plus sign) or press Alt+Z and then click Organize Favorites on the pop-up menu to open the Organize Favorites dialog box.

   The list box of the Organize Favorites dialog box shows all the subfolders, followed by all the bookmarks in the Favorites folder (similar to the one shown in Figure 4-3).

2. To move a bookmark into one of the subfolders of Favorites, drag its icon and then drop it on the icon of the subfolder. Alternatively, click the favorite to select it and then click the Move button to open the Browse for Folder dialog box. Then click the destination folder in the Browse for Folder dialog box and then click OK.

Figure 4-3

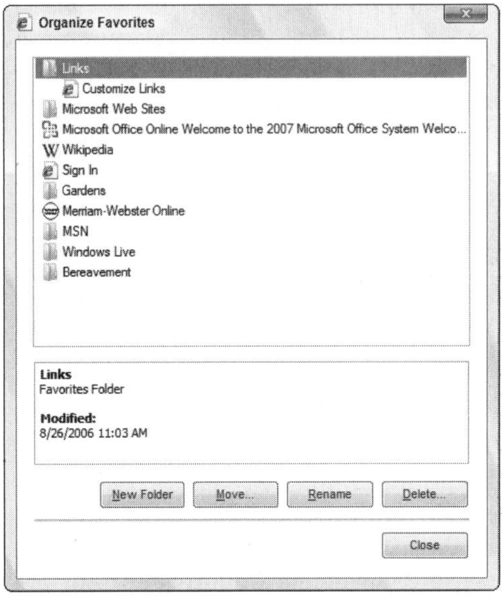

Organize Favorites

Links
  Customize Links
Microsoft Web Sites
Microsoft Office Online Welcome to the 2007 Microsoft Office System Welco...
W Wikipedia
Sign In
Gardens
Merriam-Webster Online
MSN
Windows Live
Bereavement

Links
Favorites Folder

Modified:
8/26/2006 11:03 AM

[New Folder] [Move...] [Rename] [Delete...]

[Close]

Use the following options in the Organize Favorites dialog box to create new folders to hold your bookmarks, to rename bookmarks, or even to get rid of unwanted bookmarks:

✔ To create a new folder, click the New Folder button to add a new folder icon; then type a new name for the folder, and press Enter.

✔ To rename a link to a favorite Web page, click the icon to select it, click the Rename button, edit the item name, and then press Enter.

✔ To delete a link to a favorite Web page, click the icon and then click the Delete button. Click Yes in the Delete File dialog box when it asks whether you're sure that you want to send that particular favorite to the Recycle Bin.

Don't delete or rename the Links folder in the Organize Favorites dialog box. Internet Explorer 7 needs the Links folder so that it knows what items to list on the Links button's continuation menu (when the Links button option is selected in Internet Explorer 7).

You can also use the drag-and-drop method to reorder the bookmarks in the Favorites Center Explorer bar (Ctrl+Shift+I):

✔ To open one of the folders on the Favorites Center Explorer bar to display the folder contents, click the folder icon. Internet Explorer then displays a series of icons for each of the subfolders and bookmarks its contents. To close a folder to hide the contents, click the folder icon again.

✔ To move a bookmark to a new position in the folder, drag that icon up or down until you reach the desired position. As you drag, you see where the item will be inserted by the appearance of a heavy, horizontal I-beam between the bookmarks. You also see where you *cannot* move the icon because of the display of the international no-no symbol.

✔ To move a bookmark icon to a different (existing) folder, drag the book-mark icon to the folder icon. When the folder icon is highlighted, you can drop the favorite icon into it.

Using Internet Explorer 7 tabs

Internet Explorer 7 displays each Web page that you browse in a tab showing the page name. This current tab is not the only one you have in the Internet Explorer window. To add a tab to Internet Explorer, click the New Tab button (the blank button to the immediate right of the current tab in which a page icon appears as soon as you position the mouse pointer on it) or press Ctrl+T.

When you click the New Tab button or press the Ctrl+T key combination, Internet Explorer adds a Welcome to Tabbed Browsing Web page in a new tab that appears to the right of the tab for the page you were viewing. The pro-gram also inserts a Quick Tabs button (shown in the left margin) on the tab row to the immediate right of the Add to Favorites button.

When you navigate to another Web page after adding a new tab with a blank page, Internet Explorer replaces the standard Welcome to Tabbed Browsing page with that page and enters its title in the new tab. You can then go back and forth between the Web page open in the first tab and the one you just navigated to in the new tab by clicking their tabs.

You can also switch between open pages by clicking the Quick Tabs button or pressing Ctrl+Q to display thumbnails of all the pages open on different tabs (see Figure 4-4). Finally, click the thumbnail of the page you want to display in the current tab.

Click the Quick Tabs button or press Ctrl+Q a second time to close the Quick Tabs view and return to the normal page display in Internet Explorer 7. You can also click the drop-down button to the immediate right of the Quick Tabs button to display a list of all the tabs you have open in Internet Explorer (helpful when you have so many tabs open that you can no longer read the names of their pages on the tab bar). To select a new tab and display a new Web page, you simply click its name on this drop-down list.

Note that you can close the tab for an open page's tab in the Quick Tabs view by clicking the close button (with the black X) that appears in the upper-right corner of the title bar of its thumbnail image (opposite the page title). You can also close a tab by clicking the close button that appears to the immediate right of the current page's tab when Internet Explorer is not in Quick Tabs view.

Figure 4-4

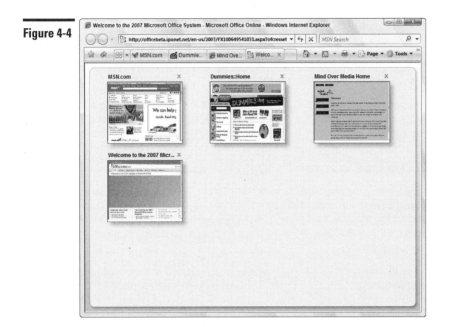

When you exit Internet Explorer 7 after creating a bunch of tabs for the different Web pages you've been visiting, the program displays an alert dialog box asking you if you want to close all the tabs (which you must do by clicking its Close Tabs button in order to shut down th Internet Explorer).

TIP

Click the Show Options drop-down button to display the Open These the Next Time I Use Internet Explorer and the Do Not Show Me This Dialog Again check boxes. Click the Open These the Next Time I Use Internet Explorer check box if you want Internet Explorer to automatically display the same tab arrangement the next time you launch the program. Click the Do Not Show Me This Dialog Again check box before you click the Close Tabs button when you no longer need to be reminded about how to restore multiple tabs from a previous session in Internet Explorer — that way, you'll be able to exit Internet Explorer without having to deal with this alert dialog box again even when you have multiple tabs open in its window.

Saving Web graphics

As you're browsing Web pages with Internet Explorer, you may come upon some sites that offer graphics or other images for downloading. You can save Web graphics on your computer hard drive

✔ As a graphic file for viewing and printing in the Pictures folder by right-clicking the graphic and then clicking Save Picture As on the image shortcut menu.

✔ As the wallpaper for your desktop by right-clicking the graphic and then clicking Set as Background on the image shortcut menu. Click the Yes button in the alert dialog box that appears asking you if you're sure you want to replace the current background.

Keep in mind that when you save a Web graphic as the wallpaper for your desktop, Vista uses its Fit to Screen option to stretch the picture so that it fills the entire desktop (which most often results in a severely distorted image). To center it in the middle of the desktop or to tile the image (by duplicating it across the entire desktop), right-click the desktop, click Personalize on the shortcut menu, and then click the Desktop Background link. Click the Center or Tile option button under How Should the Picture Be Positioned before you click OK.

You can also save a graphic on a Web page as an attachment in a new e-mail message that you can then send to a friend or colleague by right-clicking the image and then clicking the E-mail Picture option on the shortcut menu. An Internet Explorer Security alert dialog may then appear asking your permission to open the Web content on your computer where you click the Allow button to continue. Vista then opens an Attach Pictures and Files dialog box that shows the current size of the image and enables you to select a more or less compressed version to send by clicking its new size on the Picture Size drop-down list. After selecting the size, click the Attach button to open a new message in your e-mail program that you can then address and send. *See* "Windows Mail" later in this part for more information on sending new e-mail messages.

Saving Web pages

Occasionally, you may want to save an entire Web page on your computer (text, hyperlinks, graphics, and all). To save the Web page that currently appears in Internet Explorer 7, click the Page button on the tab row and then click Save As on its drop-down menu to open the Save Webpage dialog box. In this dialog box, you can select the folder in which to save the page, assign a filename to it, and even change its file type.

If the Classic menus are displayed in Internet Explorer, you can also open the Save Webpage dialog box by choosing File⇨Save As on the pull-down menus. If the menus are not displayed, you can press Alt+F+A to open the Save Webpage dialog box.

By default, Internet Explorer saves the Web pages as a Web Archive file with a .mht file extension that this browser can read. If you want to save all the text and graphics on the page as a full-fledged HTML file that any Web browser and many other programs can open, click the Webpage, complete (*.htm, *html) item on the Save as Type drop-down list box of the Save Webpage dialog box before you click the Save button. If you're only concerned about having the text on the page saved in HTML, click the Webpage, HTML only (*.htm, *html) item instead. If you want to be able to use the text on the Web page in any Word processor or with any text editor, click the Text File (*.txt) item on the Save as Type drop-down list box.

After saving a Web page as an HTML file on your hard drive, you can open it in Internet Explorer and view the contents even when you're not connected to the Internet. If your motive for saving the Web page, however, is to be able to view the content when you're not connected to the Internet, you're better off saving the page as a Favorite marked for offline viewing. That way, you can decide whether you want to view other pages linked to the one you're saving, and you can have Internet Explorer check the site for updated content.

You can also e-mail a Web page in the body of a new e-mail message by clicking the Page button and then clicking the Send Page by E-mail item on the drop-down menu. Vista then opens up an Internet Explorer Security dialog box where you click the Allow button. After that, a new e-mail message opens in your computer's e-mail program that you can address and send (*see* "Windows Mail" later in this part for more information on sending new e-mail messages).

When visiting a complex Web site with loads of graphics, you may not want to take the time to send an entire page from the site in an e-mail message. Instead, send a link to the page by clicking Page ▶ Send Link by E-mail to open a new message with your E-mail program containing a link to the page in the body of the message and the name of the page in the Subject field.

Printing Web pages

Many times, when browsing Web pages in Internet Explorer 7, you want to print the pages you visit. Internet Explorer 7 not only makes it easy to print the Web pages you go to see, but also gives you the ability to preview the printout before you commit your printer.

To preview the current Web page, click the drop-down button attached to the Printer button on the tab row (don't click the Print button itself as doing this opens the Print dialog box rather than the Print Preview window) and then click Print Preview on its drop-down menu. Vista then opens the first printed page for the Web page you're printing in a Print Preview window similar to the one shown in Figure 4-5.

If the Classic menus are displayed in Internet Explorer, you can also open the Print Preview window by choosing File⇨Print Preview on the pull-down menus.

Print Document

Portrait   Turn header and footers on and off

Landscape | View full width

Page   View
Setup   full page

Show multiple pages

Change print size

Help

Figure 4-5

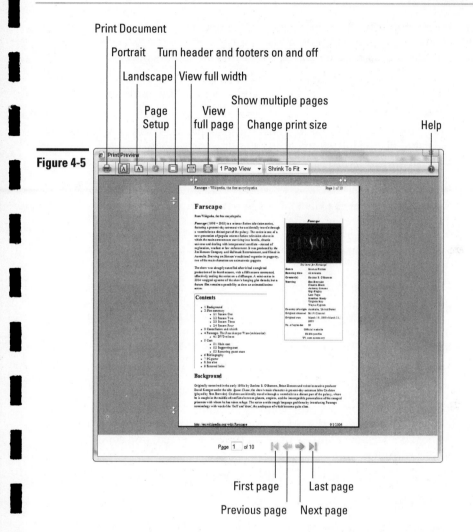

First page | Last page

Previous page   Next page

The Print Preview toolbar at the top of this window contains some important buttons for modifying the view of the pages in the preview window:

> ✔ **Portrait (Alt+O),** to display the printed page in portrait mode, which prints text across the shorter edge of the paper in lines running down the longer edge.

> ✔ **Landscape (Alt+L),** to display the page in landscape mode, which prints text across the longer edge of the paper in lines running down the shorter edge.

✔ **Page Setup (Alt+U),** to open the Page Setup dialog box, where you can change paper size and source as well as add a header and footer for the printout and specify the top, bottom, left, and right margins.

✔ **Turn Headers and Footers On and Off (Alt+E),** to turn off and on the display of any headers and/or footers you specify for the printout in the Page Setup dialog box.

✔ **View Full Width (Alt+W),** to adjust the magnification of the current page so that it fills the full width of the Print Preview window.

✔ **View Full Page (Alt+1),** to adjust the magnification of the page preview so that the full length of the current page fits within the Print Preview window.

✔ **Show Multiple Pages (Alt+N),** to switch between 1-Page View (the default), 2-Page View, 3-Page View, 6-Page View, and 12-Page View settings that determine the number of pages (displayed in the Print Preview window) over which Internet Explorer spreads the printed contents of the current Web page.

✔ **Change Print Size (Alt+S),** to stretch or shrink the printout of the pages a particular percentage of its actual size (between 30% and 200% or a Custom setting). Alternatively, use the Shrink To Fit default setting to have Internet Explorer automatically make all the content fit on the number of pages selected in the Show Multiple Pages drop-down list box.

✔ **Help (F1),** to open a Microsoft Internet Explorer Help window with information on using Print Preview.

The status bar at the bottom of the window contains the following controls for displaying different pages of the printout in the Print Preview window (when the default 1-Page View Show Multiple Pages setting is selected) and sending the printout to the printer:

✔ **Current Page (Alt+A),** to select the text box that displays the number of the current page. Type another page number in this text box and press Enter to display that page of the preview.

✔ **First Page (Alt+Home),** to display the first page of the preview.

✔ **Previous Page (Alt+Left Arrow),** to display the previous page of the preview.

✔ **Next Page (Alt+Right Arrow),** to display the next page of the preview.

✔ **Last Page (Alt+End),** to display the last page of the preview.

✔ **Print Document (Alt+P),** to print the page(s) as it appears in the Print Preview window. Click the Print button (or press Alt+P) to open the Print dialog box.

✔ **Close Print Preview (Alt+C),** to close the Print Preview window without printing the page.

If you choose not to print from the Print Preview window, or you're sure that you don't need to use Print Preview to get the information you want, you can print the Web page currently displayed in Internet Explorer by clicking the Print option on the Page drop-down list or pressing Ctrl+P to open the Print dialog box. In this dialog box, you can specify such options as the printer name, pages to print, and number of copies before you click the Print button to send the pages to the printer.

Working offline

To facilitate the use of RSS feeds (see "Subscribing to RSS Feeds" later in this part) and Web page subscriptions, Internet Explorer 7 supports offline browsing (as opposed to online browsing, which indicates being connected to the Internet). Offline browsing is especially beneficial when you're using a laptop computer and can't get connected to the Internet (as when in transit on a bus, train, or plane). It can also come in handy when you rely on a relatively slow dialup connection (as with 28.8 or 33.3 Kbps modems) to the Internet, enabling you to download Web content during nonpeak hours and browse it with maximum efficiency during the peak surfing hours (thereby totally avoiding the "World Wide Wait").

To turn offline browsing on and off, click Work Offline on the Tools drop-down menu (or you can choose File➪Work Offline if Internet Explorer pull-down menus are displayed or press Alt+F+W when they are hidden). Note that after you put the browsing window in offline mode, it remains in this work mode until you restart your computer. In other words, if you shut down the browsing window and then launch it again during the same work session, it opens in offline mode. If you decide that you want to do some serious online surfing, you need to start by choosing Tools ▶ Work Offline to turn off the offline mode.

When offline mode is on (indicated by a check mark in front of the Work Offline command on the Tools drop-down menu), Windows will not automatically attempt to connect to the Internet, and you can browse only pages stored locally on your computer, such as those that have been downloaded into the *cache* on your computer hard drive. Also known as the Temporary Internet Files, the cache contains all Web pages and their components that are downloaded when you subscribe to Web sites or channels.

TIP

When you browse a Web site offline from a local drive, you have none of the wait often associated with browsing online when connected to the Internet. You may also find, however, that some of the links aren't available for offline viewing. Internet Explorer lets you know when a link isn't available by adding the international "No" or "Don't" symbol (you know, the circle with a backslash in it) to the normal hand mouse pointer.

If you persist and click a hyperlink to a page that has not been downloaded with the hand-plus-Don't-symbol mouse pointer, the browsing window displays a Web Page Unavailable While Offline alert dialog box, indicating that the Web page you requested is not available for browsing. To have Internet Explorer connect you to the Internet and go to the requested page, click the Connect button or press Enter. To remain offline and close the alert dialog box, click the Stay Offline button instead.

Most of the time when browsing offline, you do your local Web surfing in one of two ways:

✔ Visit updated Web pages stored in the cache as Favorites marked for offline viewing. You open these pages by selecting them from the Favorite Explorer bar (opened by clicking the Favorites button) or by choosing them from the Favorites pull-down menu.

✔ Revisit Web pages stored in the cache as part of the History. You open these pages by selecting them from the History Explorer bar, which you open by pressing Ctrl+Shift+H, by clicking the History button on the Explorer toolbar (the one with the arrow curving around backwards), or by clicking View⇨Explorer Bar⇨History on Internet Explorer menu bar.

In addition to using these two browsing methods, you can open Web pages that are stored in folders on local disks, such as the hard drive or a CD-ROM in your CD-ROM drive. The easiest way to open these pages is by selecting the drive letter in the address bar of Internet Explorer. You can also open a local Web page with the Open dialog box (choose File⇨Open when the classic menus are displayed or press Ctrl+O).

Searching from the Live Search text box

The World Wide Web holds an enormous wealth of information on almost every subject known to humanity — and it's of absolutely no use if you don't know how to get to it. To help Web surfers such as yourself locate the sites containing the information you need, a number of so-called *search engines* have been designed. Each search engine maintains a slightly different directory of the sites on the World Wide Web (which are mostly maintained and updated by auto-mated programs called by such wonderfully suggestive names as Web crawlers, spiders, and robots!). Internet Explorer 7 uses the Live Search engine to find your next new favorite Web sites.

Internet Explorer 7 makes it easy to search the World Wide Web from the Live Search text box located to the immediate right of the Address bar. After you click the text box and then enter the keyword or words (known affectionately as a *search string* in programmer's parlance) to search for in this text box, you begin the search by clicking the Search button (the one with the magnifying glass) or by pressing Enter.

Internet Explorer conducts a search for Web sites containing the keywords and then displays the first page of matching results. To visit one of the sites in this list, click its hyperlink. To view the next page of Web search results (assuming that there are more than one page of matches, which they're usually are), click the number of the next page or the Next hyperlink at the bottom of the Windows

Live Search page. To redisplay the search results from a Web page that you visit, click the Back button or press Alt+←.

After you're convinced that you've seen the best matches to your search, but you still haven't found the Web site(s) you're looking for, you can conduct another search in the Live Search text box by using slightly different terms.

 TIP To search for particular information on the Web site you're visiting (as opposed to finding a page on the World Wide Web), click the drop-down button to the immediate right of the Search button and then click Find on This Page on its drop-down menu. Internet Explorer opens a Find dialog box, where you can enter your search text (in the Find text box), and specify whether to match whole words only and case as well as the direction by clicking its Next or Previous button.

Autosearching from the address bar

In addition to searching from the Live Search text box, Internet Explorer 7 enables you to perform searches from its Address bar by using a feature referred to as Autosearching. To conduct an Autosearch from the Address Bar, you need to click the Address bar to select the current entry and then preface the search string with one of the following three terms:

✔ Go

✔ Find

✔ ?

To search for Web sites whose descriptions contain the terms *Thai cuisine,* for example, you could type

```
go Thai cuisine
```

or

```
find Thai cuisine
```

or even

```
? Thai cuisine
```

in the Address bar. After you enter **go**, **find**, or **?** followed by the search string, press the Enter key to have Windows conduct the search.

When you press Enter, Internet Explorer opens the Windows Live Search page with the first 10 to 20 matches to your search string (depending upon your screen resolution).

Adding a search provider to Internet Explorer 7

Live Search is not the only search provider supported by Internet Explorer 7. If you're more confident using another provider such as Google or Yahoo!, you can add it to the Internet Explorer browser and even make it, rather than Live Search, the default search engine. Here's how:

1. Click the drop-down button to the immediate right of the Search button in the Live Search text box and then click Find More Providers on the drop-down menu.

   The program opens the Add Search Providers to Internet Explorer 7 window, similar to the one shown in Figure 4-6.

2. Click the link for the Web Search provider you want to add (AOL, Ask.com, Google, and so on).

   Vista displays an Add Search Provider dialog box asking you if you want to add the selected search provider to Internet Explorer.

3. (Optional) To make the selected search provider the default search engine that Internet Explorer first uses whenever you search the Web, click the Make This My Default Search Provider check box.

4. Click the Add Provider button to close the dialog box and add the provider.

After adding a new search provider to Internet Explorer 7, to use the provider, click its name on the Live Search button's drop-down menu. As soon as you do, its name appears in the erstwhile Live Search text box as in Google, AOL, and so on.

Figure 4-6

TIP

You can also use this four-step procedure to add topical search engines to Internet Explorer 7 such as Amazon, eBay, cnet.com, ESPN, Shopzilla.com, and Wikipedia.org.

REMEMBER

Keep in mind that after you follow this procedure to add Web and topical search providers to Internet Explorer, their names then appear (in alphabetical order) near the top of the Search drop-down menu. This enables you to select a new search provider on the fly simply by clicking the provider's name on this drop-down menu before you conduct a search that would utilize its particular expertise. For example, to quickly find the best price on a new Tablet PC laptop computer, enter **tablet pc** in Internet Explorer's Live Search text box and then select Shopzilla (assuming that you've already added it to Internet Explorer 7) on the Search drop-down menu.

No phishing allowed

Phishing (and, no that's not a misspelling) refers to a very special kind of illegal fishing on the Internet, whereby someone fraudulently poses as a legitimate business entity in order to get you to pony up some very private and sensitive information such as your Social Security number, passwords, and/or credit card numbers, which, if they obtain, they put to no good use (at least as far as you are concerned).

The damage caused by phishing can run the gamut from a simple inability to access your e-mail all the way to some pretty heavy financial losses. To help you guard against this kind of identity theft, Internet Explorer 7 includes a Phishing Filter feature that automatically checks each site you visit to determine whether it might possibly just be somebody's big old phishing hole rather than a legitimate business with whom you can share sensitive information with a modicum of confidence.

If you visit a Web page that is on Microsoft's list of phishing Web sites, Internet Explorer displays a warning Web page and notification on the address bar. You can then continue to browse the site or close it from the warning Web page. If you visit a Web page that is not on this list but which exhibits suspicious characteristics, Internet Explorer only warns you that the site might be a phishing site on the address bar.

If you become suspicious of a particular Web site that you've never visited before, you can have Internet Explorer 7 check the site by clicking Tools ▶ Phishing Filter ▶ Check This Website. A Phishing Filter alert dialog box then appears, telling you that the current Web site address will be sent to Microsoft to check against a list of known Phishing sites. Click OK.

If you're more than a little suspicious of a particular site, you can submit a report to Microsoft indicating that you think this is a Phishing site (so that they can check out the site and, if it proves to be fishy, redline it for other Internet Explorer 7 users) by clicking Tools ▶ Phishing Filter ▶ Report This Website. Click the Submit button in Feedback – Windows Internet Explorer window after clicking the I Think This Is a Phishing Website check box.

Pop-ups anyone?

Perhaps one of the most annoying aspects of browsing the World Wide Web is coming across those pages littered with awful automated pop-up ads. (You know, the ones that appear the moment you load the page, with ads offering you all sorts of unusable stuff and unreal opportunities.) Fortunately, Internet Explorer 7 comes equipped with a Pop-up Blocker feature — turned on by default — that prevents the display of any automated pop-ups on a page that want to magically materialize the moment you load the page.

Internet Explorer lets you know that it has blocked a pop-up on a page by displaying a message to that effect at the top of the page. To go ahead and display an automated pop-up, you then click Show Blocked Pop-up.

If you have a favorite Web site whose automated pop-ups you want to see, you can add that site's Web address to a list of exceptions in the Pop-up Blocker Settings dialog box (opened by clicking Tools ▶ Pop-up Blocker ▶ Pop-up Blocker Settings).

By default, Vista sets the Pop-up Blocker to Medium: Block Most Automatic Pop-ups, meaning that all automated pop-ups on a page that are not on the Trusted sites list (*See* Part 6: Security) are blocked. If you really, really hate pop-ups, you can block them even on a trusted Web site by clicking the High: Block All Pop-ups (Ctrl+Alt to Override) option on the Filter Level drop-down list in the Pop-up Blocker Settings dialog box.

Subscribing to RSS feeds

Internet Explorer 7 now supports *RSS feeds* (RSS either stands for Really Simple Syndication or Rich Site Summary, depending upon whom you ask). RSS feeds are Web feeds that typically provide summaries of particulars types of Web content that you're interested in keeping up-to-date on, although they may occasionally include full text and even some multimedia attachments.

RSS feeds are mostly used by news Web sites such as Reuters, CNN, NPR, and the BBC, to feed their syndicated headlines to the users who subscribe to them (subscribers can then click particular headlines of interest to go to the page containing the full news story). The feeds are also used by Weblog sites to keep their subscribers up-to-date on the latest podcasts and vodcasts posted to the blog. *See* the Tech Talk Glossary at the end of this book if *podcast*, *vodcast*, and *blog* are not yet in your vocabulary.

RSS feeds are normally indicated on a Web page you're browsing by the words *Subscribe* or *Subscribe to This Feed*, with an orange rectangle with radio waves emanating from a single point (same as the Feeds button on the Tab row shown below) or with the letters *RSS* or *XML* in an orange rectangle. Of course, if you're interested in finding RSS news feeds to subscribe to, the easiest way to do this is by doing a Web search for RSS feeds or for a particular news organization (see "Web search" earlier in this part for details).

Internet Explorer 7 indicates that the Web page you're visiting contains RSS feeds by turning the Feeds button on the tab row (shown in the left margin) to orange (so that it matches the color of the RSS rectangles on the page). Then to subscribe to a particular RSS feed on that page, either click its RSS rectangle on the page or click the drop-down list button attached to the Feeds button on the Tab row of the browser and then select the name of the feed in the drop-down list.

After selecting the RSS feed in this manner, you can then subscribe to the feed by clicking the Subscribe or Subscribe to This Feed link on the Web page that lists the current headlines or Webcasts. Figure 4-7 shows you the NPR Topics: Business Web page, to which you can subscribe by clicking its Subscribe to This Feed link.

Figure 4-7

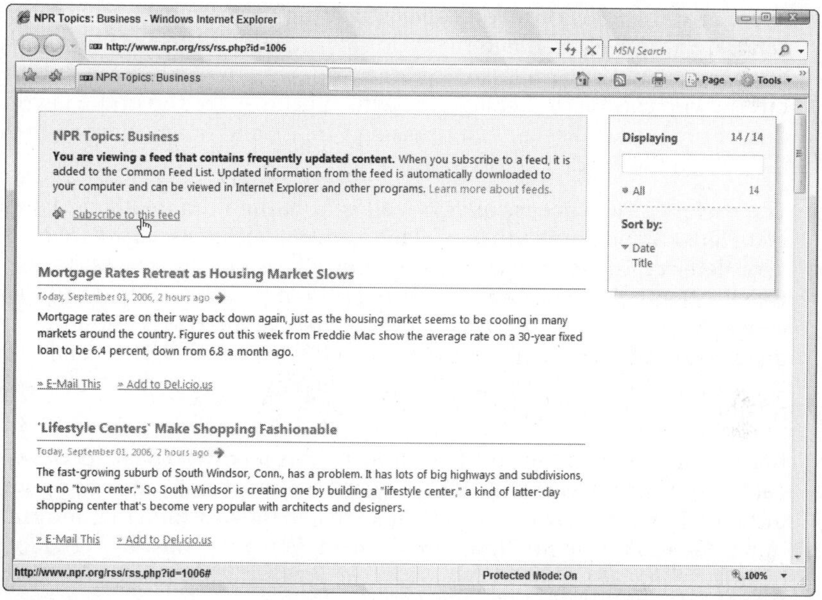

After you click a Subscribe or Subscribe to This Feed link, Internet Explorer opens a Subscribe to this Feed dialog box similar to the one shown in Figure 4-8. You can then change any of the following options in the alert dialog box before you click its Subscribe button to add this RSS feed to your Favorites Center:

- ✔ **Name** text box to modify the name automatically given to the feed by its Web site

- ✔ **Create In** drop-down list box to select a folder other than Feeds in which to add the RSS feed

- ✔ **New Folder** button to create a new folder in which to save the RSS feed

Figure 4-8

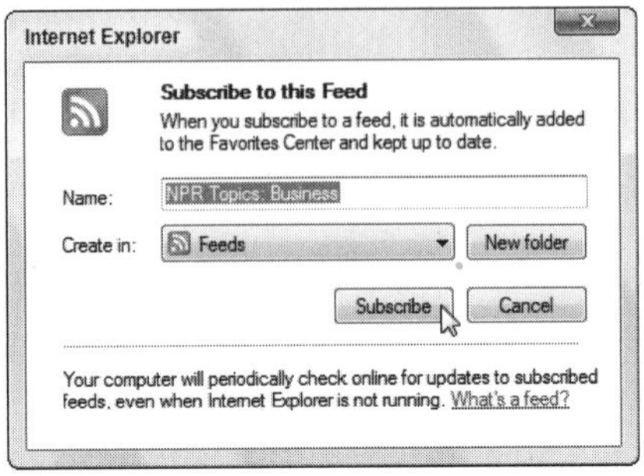

Internet Explorer

Subscribe to this Feed
When you subscribe to a feed, it is automatically added to the Favorites Center and kept up to date.

Name: NPR Topics: Business

Create in: Feeds   New folder

Subscribe   Cancel

Your computer will periodically check online for updates to subscribed feeds, even when Internet Explorer is not running. What's a feed?

After you click the Subscribe button to close this alert dialog box, a message appears at the RSS Feed Web page, indicating that you have successfully sub-scribed to the Web feed and that you can access the RSS feed by clicking the View Feeds link. You can also do this by opening the Favorites Center (the button with the star), clicking the Feeds button at the top of the Favorites Center drop-down list (or just pressing Ctrl+J), and finally clicking the name of the feed in the Feeds Explorer bar.

The easiest way to access an RSS feed is from the Feed Headlines gadget on the Vista Sidebar, one of the three default gadgets automatically displayed (*see* Part 1 for details). To select the RSS feed whose headlines you want displayed in this gadget, position the mouse pointer over the right edge of the Feed Headlines gadget and then click its wrench icon to display the Feed Headlines pop-up dialog box. Click the name of the RSS feed in the Display This Feed drop-down list box and the number of headlines to display in the Number of Recent Headlines to Show drop-down list before you click OK.

Keep in mind that when you're visiting an RSS feed Web page to view its syndi-cated headlines or podcast listings, you access the news story or podcast in Internet Explorer 7 by clicking its link. To see the last time that Internet Explorer downloaded information from an RSS feed Web page, position the mouse pointer over the name of the Web page when the Feeds button is selected in the Favorites Center drop-down list.

Speech Recognition

The Speech Recognition feature in Windows Vista enables you to set up your com-puter to receive voice commands as well as to dictate text in application programs such as Microsoft Word and Excel. In addition, you can configure the Text to Speech feature that reads aloud text in Vista windows and dialog boxes when you turn on the Narrator feature (*see* "Ease of Access Center" in Part 5 for details).

You can set up and fine-tune Speech Recognition by using the links in the Speech Recognition Control Panel window shown in Figure 4-9. To open this window, click the Start ▶ Control Panel ▶ Ease of Access ▶ Speech Recognition Options.

Figure 4-9

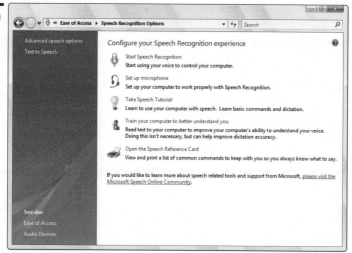

Setting up Speech Recognition

Before you can start barking commands at your Vista computer, you have to get a microphone connected to your Vista PC (preferably one with headphones like the telemarketers you like so well all wear), and then you have to set up the Speech Recognition feature by following these steps:

1. Open the Speech Recognition Control Panel window by clicking Start ▶ Control Panel ▶ Ease of Access ▶ Start Speech Recognition.

   Vista displays a Welcome to Speech Recognition dialog box.

2. Click Next and then select the Headset Microphone, Desktop Microphone, or Other option button in the Select the Type of Microphone You Would Like to Use dialog box.

3. Click Next and then position the microphone connected to your Vista computer next to your mouth. Click Next in the Set Up Your Microphone dialog box.

4. Read the "Peter dictates to his computer . . . " passage in a normal voice and then when you finish dictating this passage, click Next.

   If the computer heard you distinctly, the message, "The microphone is ready to use with this computer" appears in the Your Microphone Is Now Set Up dialog box. If you see a message indicating that the computer did not hear you very well, click the Back button and repeat Step 4, perhaps after adjusting the microphone's position and making sure that it's properly connected to the computer's microphone jack (and not the speaker jack).

5. Click Next in the Your Microphone Is Now Set Up dialog box.

6. Click the Enable Document Review option button in the Improve Speech Recognition Accuracy dialog box and then click Next.

7. Click the View Reference Sheet button in the Print the Speech Reference Sheet dialog box to open a Windows Help and Support window.

8. Click the topics such as Basics, Top 10 Commands, and Commanding Windows to display their tables of commands. Click the Print button on the window's toolbar if you want to print the commands.

9. Click the Close button in the Windows Help and Support window to close it.

10. Click the Next button in the Print the Speech Reference Sheet dialog box to open the Run Speech Recognition Every Time I Start the Computer dialog box.

    By default, Vista selects the Run Speech Recognition at Startup check box. If you don't want Windows to automatically start the Speech Recognition each time you boot Vista, click this check box to clear its check mark before you proceed to Step 12.

11. Click the Next button in the Run Speech Recognition Every Time I Start the Computer dialog box to open the You Can Now Control This Computer By Voice dialog box.

12. Click the Start Tutorial button to run the Speech Recognition Tutorial, which is necessary to train the computer to understand your voice and very good for practice.

After you finish the Speech Recognition Tutorial, Vista automatically returns you to the Speech Recognition Control Panel window. The Sleeping Speech toolbar now appears docked in the center at the top of the Windows desktop.

To undock the Speech Recognition toolbar and move it to a new position on the Vista desktop, drag the toolbar by any area outside the microphone icon, the level meter, Close, and Minimize buttons. To hide the toolbar (while still running the Speech Recognition feature) as an icon in the Notification area of the Windows taskbar, click the Speech toolbar's Minimize button.

Remember that you say "Start Listening" in your microphone whenever you want the sleeping Speech Recognition feature to wake up and start listening to what you have to say!

Changing Speech Recognition settings

After initially setting up Speech Recognition on your Vista computer, you can modify its settings by using the options on the Speech Recognition tab of the

Speech Properties dialog box shown in Figure 4-10. To open this dialog box with this tab selected, click the Advanced Speech Options link in the Speech Recognition Control Panel window.

Figure 4-10

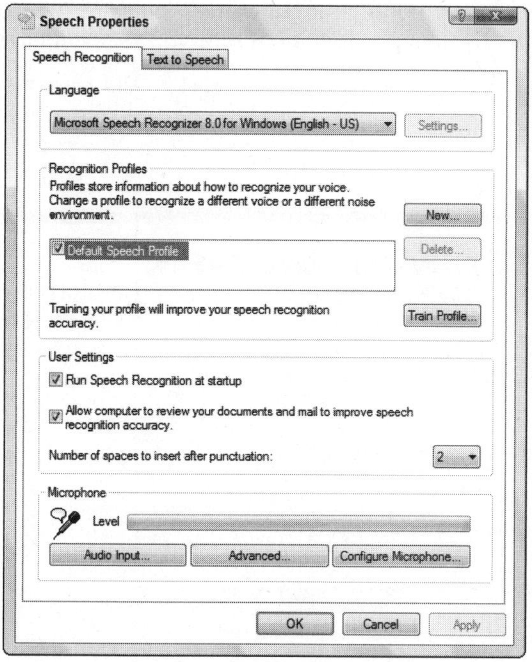

The options on the Speech Recognition tab of the Speech Properties dialog box are divided into four areas:

- **Language,** where you can select a new language other than the default English in which to dictate commands and text (assuming that you installed other Language Packs for use with Windows Vista)

- **Recognition Profiles,** where you can create new speech profiles for different users on the same computer and then select them for use with the Speech Recognition feature

- **User Settings,** where you enable or disable the Run Speech Recognition At Startup and the Allow Computer to Review Your Documents and Mail to Improve Speech Recognition Accuracy check boxes

- **Microphone,** where you can select a new microphone to use in Speech Recognition (by clicking the Audio Input button) and then get it ready for use with Speech Recognition (by clicking the Configure Microphone button)

Windows Fax and Scan

The Windows Fax and Scan utility enables you to send or receive and organize faxes via your Vista computer as well as scan documents and pictures, provided that you have a scanner connected to your computer. You can even use the utility's two features together by faxing a document that you've scanned with it.

To launch the Windows Fax and Scan utility, click Start ▶ All Programs ▶ Windows Fax and Scan. Vista then opens a Windows Fax and Scan window, as shown in Figure 4-11.

Figure 4-11

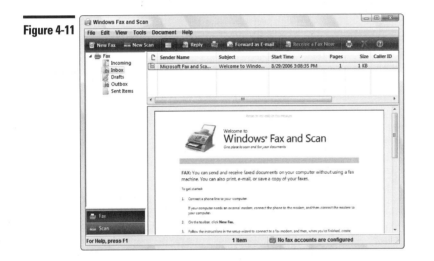

As you can see in this figure, at the bottom of the Navigation pane of the Windows Fax and Scan window you find two buttons: Faxes and Scans. You click these buttons to switch between the fax and scanning features.

To be able to send and receive faxes with Windows Fax and Scan, your computer must either be connected to a fax server that's part of your computer network, or you must have a phone line connected to a fax modem installed on your computer (you can't use separate fax machines). To be able to scan documents and pictures, you must have a scanner installed on your computer.

Sending and receiving faxes

Before you can send and receive a fax with the Windows Fax and Scan utility, you must set up a fax account for yourself. To do this, click Tools⇨Fax Accounts in the Windows Fax and Scan window when the Faxes button is selected. Then click the Add button to open a Create Fax Account dialog box, where you click either the Fax Modem Connection or Windows Fax Server, depending upon whether you use a fax modem or a server to send and receive faxes.

After you set up your fax account, you can then use it to create a new fax to send. Simply click the New Fax button on the toolbar in the Windows Fax and Scan window to open the New Fax dialog box, where you can select a cover page, select the contact to whom to delivery the fax, and input the text of the fax message.

 Don't forget that you can insert text that you've already typed in another document in the body of the fax via the Windows Clipboard (Ctrl+C to copy the selected text and Ctrl+V to insert it into the New Fax dialog box). You can also attach a text document to the fax message with the Attach button on the New Fax toolbar, insert a picture in the body of the fax with the Insert Picture button, and insert a scanned document or picture in the body of the fax with the Insert From Scanner button.

When you finish composing the new fax, you have Vista send it by clicking the Send button in the New Fax dialog box.

To receive a fax when the Windows Fax and Scan window is open, click the Receive a Fax Now button on the window's toolbar.

Scanning documents

Before you can scan a document with the Windows Fax and Scan utility, your scanner must be listed in the Scanners and Cameras Control Panel (Start ▶ Control Panel ▶ Hardware and Sound ▶ Scanners and Cameras). To scan a document, open the Windows Fax and Scan window and then click the Scans button in the Navigation pane before you click the New Scan button on the far left of the window's toolbar.

Vista then opens a New Scan dialog box for your scanner, where you can preview the document and then scan the final version. To save the scanned document, click the Save As button and then enter the filename and select the type of graphics file you want the scanned document to be saved as before you click the Save button.

To automatically forward the document you just scanned as an attachment to a new fax message, click the Forward as Fax button.

 The scan feature in the Windows Fax and Scan utility is set primarily to scan text documents. If you want to scan a photograph or other graphic, keep in mind that you can do this as well directly from within the Windows Photo Gallery (*see* Part 7 for details).

Windows Mail

Windows Mail is the name of the e-mail software installed with Windows Vista. You can use this program to compose, send, and read e-mail messages and to subscribe to the newsgroups supported by your Internet service provider, which enables you to read the newsgroup messages as well as respond to them.

Creating a new e-mail account

The first time you launch Windows Mail by clicking Start ▶ E-Mail, the program leads you through the steps of setting up a new e-mail account. You can also set up a new account from within Windows Mail by following these steps:

1. Choose Tools⇨Accounts to open the Internet Accounts dialog box.

2. Click the Add button to open the Select Account Type dialog box and then, after making sure that E-mail Account is selected, click Next.

3. Enter your name in the Display Name text box and then click Next.

4. Enter your e-mail address in the E-mail Address text box and then click Next to open the E-mail Server Names dialog box.

5. If your incoming e-mail server does not use the POP3 protocol, click IMAP on the My Incoming Mail Server Is a POP3 Server drop-down list box.

   Your ISP's mail server that sends your e-mail messages to the Windows Mail program uses one of two protocols: POP3 (Post Office Protocol version 3) or IMAP (Internet Message Access Protocol, also known as IMAP version 4), just as its mail server that receives the messages you send out through Windows Mail uses the SMTP (Simple Mail Transfer Protocol) protocol.

   Check with your ISP about the type of incoming server when you find out the names of their incoming and outgoing mail servers, which you need in order to set up an e-mail account.

6. Enter the name of your ISP's mail server in the Incoming Mail (POP3 or IMAP) Server text box.

7. Enter the name of the outgoing mail server in the Outgoing Mail (SMTP) Server text box.

8. If your outgoing mail server requires you to enter a user ID and password, click the My Server Requires Authentication check box.

9. Click Next to open the Internet Mail Logon dialog box.

10. Edit the e-mail account name automatically entered in the E-mail Username text box if it is not correct.

11. Enter your logon password in the Password text box and then click OK.

12. Click the Finish button in the Congratulations dialog box to return to the Windows Mail window.

Composing and sending messages

To compose and send a new e-mail message in Windows Mail, follow these steps:

1. Click the Start button and then click the E-Mail button (which lists Windows Mail) at the top of the Start menu to launch Windows Mail in its own window, similar to the one shown in Figure 4-12.

The Windows Mail window contains three panes: on the left, Folders showing the various Local mail folders on your computer; on the right, the larger Windows Mail pane with a list of all the messages currently in your Inbox; and below, the Current Message pane showing the first part of the currently selected message.

2. Click the Create Mail button on the Windows Mail toolbar to open a New Message dialog box, or choose Message⇨New Message (or simply press Ctrl+N) to open a New Message window.

The first thing to do in a new message is to specify the recipient's e-mail address in the To: field (which automatically contains the cursor). You can either type this address in the To: text box or click the To button to display the Select Recipients dialog box, in which you can select the recipients from a list of contacts in your Contacts List or from one of the online directories.

TIP

To send a new message to someone who's already listed in your Contacts List, click the Contacts button on the Windows Mail toolbar and then click the person's name in the Contacts window followed by the E-mail button. Windows Mail then opens a New Message window, with the recipient's e-mail address already entered in the To: field.

Alternatively, you can type the recipient's e-mail address in the text box of the To: field or, if the recipient is listed in your Contact List, click the To button to open the Select Recipients dialog box. Click the name of the recipient in the Name list box, click the To button, and finally click OK.

When composing a new message, you can send copies of it to as many other recipients (within reason) as you want. To send copies of the message to other recipients, type their e-mail addresses in the Cc: field.

3. (Optional) Click somewhere in the Cc: field and then type the e-mail addresses, separated by semicolons (;) in the Cc: field. Alternatively, if the addresses appear in the Contacts List click the Cc button to open the Select Recipients dialog box and then choose the e-mail addresses there (after clicking the names in the Name list box, click the Cc: button to add them to the copy list).

After filling in the e-mail addresses of the recipients, you're ready to enter the subject of the message. The descriptive text that you type in the Subject: field of the message appears in the upper pane of the recipients' Inbox when they read the message.

4. Click somewhere in the Subject: field and then enter a brief description of the contents or purpose of the e-mail message.

In Windows Mail, you can change the priority of the e-mail message from normal to high or low. When you make a message either high or low priority, Windows Mail attaches a priority icon to the message (assuming that the recipients of the message are using Windows Mail, Outlook Express, or Outlook to read their mail) that indicates its relative importance. The high-priority icon has a red flag in front of the envelope, whereas the low-priority icon has an arrow pointing downward.

5. (Optional) To boost the priority of the message, choose Message⇨Set Priority and then choose High in the submenu that appears. To decrease the priority of the message, click the Priority button, and choose Low Priority on the submenu.

6. Click the cursor in the body of the message and then type in the text of the message as you would in any text editor or word processor, ending paragraphs and short lines by pressing the Enter key.

When composing the text of the message, keep in mind that you can insert text directly into the body of the message from other documents via the Clipboard (the old Cut, Copy, and Paste commands).

7. (Optional) If you're not sure of some (or all) of the spelling in the text of the body of the message, you can have Windows Mail check the spelling by inserting the cursor at the beginning of the message text and then clicking the Spelling button on the New Message toolbar or by choosing Tools⇨Spelling on the menu bar (or by pressing F7).

When spell-checking the message, Windows Mail flags each word that it cannot find in the dictionary and tries its best to suggest an alternative.

To replace the unknown word in the text with the word suggested in the Change To text box of the Spelling window, click the Change button or, if it's a word that occurs frequently in the rest of the text, click Change All.

To ignore the unknown word and have the spell checker continue to scan the rest of the text for possible misspellings, click Ignore or, if it's a word that occurs frequently in the rest of the text, click Ignore All.

8. (Optional) To send a file along with your e-mail message, click the Attach button on the New Message toolbar (the one with the paper-clip icon) or choose Insert⇨File Attachment on the menu bar; then select the file in the Open dialog box and click the Open button.

When you include a file with a message, an icon for the file appears in a new Attach field immediately below the Subject field above the body of the e-mail message.

9. To send the e-mail message to its recipients, click the Send button on the New Message toolbar or choose File⇨Send Message on the menu bar (or press Ctrl+Enter or Alt+S).

Windows/Calendar Find

Contacts | Folder List

Figure 4-12

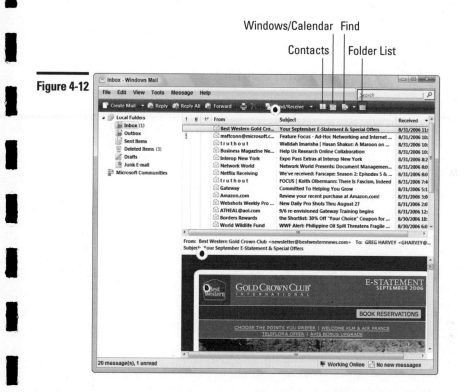

TIP

Note that when composing a new message, you can send blind copies of the message to several recipients by filling in the Bcc: field. To display the Bcc: field between the Cc: and Subject: fields, select View⇨All Headers on the Windows Mail new message menu bar. You can fill in this field with the names of the recipients as you do in the Cc: field (*see* Step 3 in the preceding list). When you add names to the Bcc: field rather than to the Cc: field, none of the Bcc: recipients sees any other names that you've entered. When you add names to the Cc: field, each recipient sees the names of everyone else to whom you've sent this same message.

If you have more than one e-mail account that you've set up in Windows Mail, the New Message dialog box contains a From field at the top of the message header. You can use the drop-down button attached to this field to select from which of your e-mail accounts the new message is to be sent.

TIP If you compose e-mail messages when you cannot get online to send them, choose File⇨Send Later from the New Message window menu bar after you finish composing each message. Windows Mail then displays an alert box indicating that the message will be stored in the Outbox and will be sent the next time you click the Send and Receive button. To send the messages stored in the Outbox when you can connect or are connected to the Internet, just click the Send and Receive button on the Windows Mail toolbar.

Adding recipients to the Contact List

Windows Mail makes it easy to maintain an address book (referred to as Contacts), where you can store the e-mail addresses for all the people you regularly correspond with. If you're switching from some other e-mail program (such as the one that comes with Netscape Navigator), and you've created an address book with that program, you can even import all the addresses into the Contacts List, making it unnecessary to reenter them.

To add a new recipient to the Contacts List, follow these steps:

1. Launch Windows Mail (Start ▶ E-Mail).

2. Click the Contacts button (the one with the address book icon) on the Windows Mail toolbar to open the Contacts window.

3. Click the New Contact button on the toolbar in the Contacts window to open a Properties dialog box for a new contact with the Name and E-mail tab selected.

   ALTERNATIVE You can also choose File⇨New⇨Contact on the menu bar to open this dialog box.

4. Fill in the Name information for the new contact in the various name fields and then select the E-Mail text box, where you type the recipient's e-mail address before clicking the Add button.

   When you click the Add button, Windows Mail adds the e-mail address you entered into the list box, automatically designating it as Default E-Mail.

   If the person you are adding to the Contacts List has more than one e-mail address (as would be the case if, for example, he maintains an e-mail account at home with one address and an e-mail account at work with another address), you can add the additional e-mail address.

5. (Optional) Enter the recipient's alternate e-mail address in the E-Mail text box and then click Add again to add other e-mail addresses for the same recipient.

   If you want to make the second e-mail address the default address that Windows Mail automatically uses when you compose a new message, you need to select the second address in the list box and then click the Set Preferred button.

TIP

To use a contact's alternate e-mail address in a new message, you need to select the person's name in the Select Recipients dialog box and then click the Properties button, where you make the alternate e-mail address the new default with the Set Preferred button.

6. (Optional) If you want to add other information about the contact such as home and work contact information or personal notes, fill in the necessary fields on the appropriate tabs (Home, Work, Personal, or Notes).

7. Click the OK button to close the Properties dialog box.

   Windows Mail returns you to the Contacts window, where an icon for the new contact appears. If you want to see particulars such as the name, e-mail address, business phone, and home phone displayed in this window, you need to select the Details setting on the Views pop-up slider.

8. When you finish adding and modifying contacts in the Contact window, close it by clicking its Close button or choosing File⇨Exit to return to the Windows Mail window.

To import the addresses from an existing address book created with Eudora, Microsoft Exchange, Microsoft Internet Mail for Windows, Outlook Express, Outlook, or Netscape Navigator, or addresses stored in a comma-separated text file, into the Contact List, follow these steps:

1. Launch Windows Mail (Start ▶ E-Mail).

2. Choose File⇨Import⇨Windows Contacts from the Windows Mail menu bar to open the Import to Windows Contacts dialog box.

3. Click the type of address book file you want to import in the list box of the Import to Windows Contacts dialog box and then click the Import button.

4. After Windows Mail finishes importing the names and e-mail addresses of all the contacts in the existing address book (indicated by a slider), close the Import to Windows Contacts dialog box by clicking its Close button to return to the Windows Mail window.

5. Open the Contacts window by clicking the Contacts button.

   Icons for all the contacts in the imported address book now appear in the Contacts window (assuming that this window uses one of the Icons Views). To display a list of the full names along with e-mail addresses and business and home phone numbers in the window, select Details on the Views pop-up slider.

6. (Optional) To filter out all contacts except for those in different groups of the alphabet (A-H, I-P, or Q-Z), click the Name field's drop-down button and then click the check boxes for the group(s) of contacts you want displayed. To sort the contacts in the list on a particular field, click its drop-down button and then click the Sort button (the first time to sort Z-A and

a second to return to the default A-Z sort order). To display the contacts in alphabetical groups (A-H, I-P, and Q-Z), click the Name field's drop-down list box and then click the Group button at the top of the drop-down list.

7. When you finish viewing and arranging the expanded contacts list with the imported contacts, click the Close button in the upper-right corner of the Contacts window to close it.

Reading e-mail

When you use Windows Mail as your e-mail program, you read the messages that you receive in an area known as the Inbox. To open the Inbox in Windows Mail and read your e-mail messages, take these steps:

1. Launch Windows Mail (Start ▶ E-Mail).

2. Click the Send/Receive button on the Windows Mail toolbar, or press Ctrl+M, to have Windows Mail check your Mail server and download any new messages and switch to the Inbox view.

   As soon as you click the Send/Receive button, Windows Mail opens a connection to your Mail server, where it checks for any new messages to download. New messages are then downloaded to your computer. The program also selects the Inbox view so that the Windows Mail pane is replaced with two vertical Inbox panes: the one above, which lists the messages in the Inbox, and the one immediately below, which displays the first part of the text of the currently selected message.

   You can also open this Inbox view either by clicking the Inbox icon in the Folders pane — the status bar at the bottom tells you the total number of messages as well as the number of unread messages in your Inbox.

   Descriptions of any new messages appear in bold at the bottom of the list in the upper pane of the Inbox, which is divided into the following columns: Priority (indicated by an exclamation mark), Attachments (indicated by the paper clip), Flagged Messages (indicated by the flag), From, Subject, and Received (showing both the date and time that the e-mail message was downloaded on your computer).

   TIP Note that mail messages that you haven't yet read are indicated not only by bold type, but also by a sealed-envelope icon in the From column. Mail messages that you have read are indicated by an opened envelope icon.

3. To read one of your new messages, click any column of the description in the upper pane of the Inbox.

   The text of the message that you select then appears in the lower pane of the Windows Mail window, and the From and Subject information appears on the bar right above it. If the message has one or more files attached to it, a paper clip appears on the right side of this bar.

4. (Optional) To open the file or files attached to the e-mail message with its native program (or at least one that can open the file), click the paper-clip icon and then click the name of the file to open in the pop-up menu. To save the attachments as separate files on your hard drive, click Save Attachments on this pop-up menu (or click File⇨Save Attachments on the Windows Mail menu bar) and then select the folder in which to save the files in the Save Attachments dialog box and click Save.

Sometimes, you may need to get a hard copy of the message to share with other, less fortunate workers in the office who don't have e-mail. (If they do have e-mail, forward the message to them instead, as I cover in optional Step 8.)

5. (Optional) To print the contents of an e-mail message, click the Print button on the Windows Mail toolbar or choose File⇨Print (Ctrl+P) and then click Print in the Print dialog box.

Occasionally, an e-mail message contains some information that you want to be able to open and print separately from the other messages in the Windows Mail program.

6. (Optional) To save the contents of an e-mail message as a separate e-mail message file, choose File⇨Save As to open the Save Message As dialog box. If you want to edit the filename, make your changes to the name in the File Name combo box. To save the file in a folder different from the one shown in the Save In field, position the mouse over this field and then click the drop-down button and select a new destination on its list. Alternatively, click the Browse Folders button to expand the Save Message As dialog box and then select a new folder by using its Navigation pane. Then click the Save button.

If the e-mail message uses the High Priority exclamation-mark icon, chances are good that you may have to reply to it right away. You can respond to the message by clicking either the Reply or the Reply All button.

After you click one or the other of these buttons, Windows Mail opens a message window in which

- The sender of the original message is listed as the recipient in the To: field.

- The subject of the original message appears in the Subject: field, preceded by the term Re: (regarding).

- The contents of the original message appear in the body of the reply beneath the heading Original Message, followed by the From:, To:, Date:, and Subject: information from the original message.

7. (Optional) To reply to the author of the e-mail message, click the Reply button on the Windows Mail toolbar. To send copies of the reply to all the

others copied on the original message as well, click the Reply All button instead. Then add the text of your reply above the text of the original message and send the reply (by pressing Ctrl+Enter or Alt+S).

Sometimes, in addition to or instead of replying to the original message, you need to send a copy of it to someone who wasn't listed in the Cc: fields. To send a copy to this person, you forward a copy of the original message to the new recipients of your choosing. When you forward a message, Windows Mail copies the Subject: and contents of the original message to a new message, which you then address and send.

8. (Optional) To forward the e-mail message to another e-mail address, click the Forward button on the Windows Mail toolbar. Then fill in the recipient information in the To: field and, if applicable, the Bcc: or Cc: fields; add any additional text of your own above that of the original message; and send the forwarded message on its way (by pressing Ctrl+Enter or Alt+S).

 If you ever open an e-mail message and then don't have time to really read through it and digest the meaning, you can, if you like, have Windows Mail mark the message as unread to remind you to reread it when you have more time. To mark a read e-mail message as unread, click Edit➪Mark as Unread on the Windows Mail menu bar. Windows Mail then replaces the open-envelope icon in front of the current message with the closed-envelope icon. To temporarily hide all messages in the Inbox except those you haven't yet read, click View➪Current View➪Hide Read Messages on the menu bar. To later redisplay both the read and unread messages in the Inbox, you then click View➪Current View➪Show All Messages.

Keep in mind that as part of the security features in Windows Vista, Windows Mail now automatically blocks the display of all pictures in incoming messages (to prevent the sender from identifying your computer). If you trust the source of the message, you can display the images by clicking the note at the top of body of the e-mail message indicating that the pictures are blocked.

Organizing e-mail

Getting e-mail is great, but it doesn't take long for you to end up with a disorganized mess. If you're anything like me, your Windows Mail Inbox will end up with hundreds of messages, some of which are still unread — and all of which are lumped together in one extensive list.

Windows Mail makes it easy for you to arrange your e-mail messages in folders. To send a bunch of related e-mail messages into a new or existing folder, follow these steps:

1. Launch Windows Mail (Start ▶ E-Mail) *and* then click the Inbox icon in the Folders pane on the left side of the Windows Mail window.

2. Select all the messages that you want to put in the same folder. To select a single message, click the description. To select a continuous series of

messages, click the first one and hold down the Shift key as you click the last one. To click multiple messages that aren't in a series, hold down Ctrl as you click the description of each one.

3. After you select the messages that you want to move, choose Edit⇨Move To Folder on the Windows Mail menu bar (Ctrl+Shift+V) to open the Move dialog box, or you can just drag the message to the folder.

4. Click expand button to the immediate left of the Local Folders icon to display its subfolders (Inbox, Outbox, Sent Items, and so on) and then click the name of the subfolder into which the selected messages are to be moved. If you need to create a new folder for the selected items, click the New Folder button, type the name in the Folder Name text box, and click OK. Then click the Inbox folder icon before clicking the name of the newly created subfolder.

5. Click OK in the Move dialog box to move the messages into the selected folder.

To verify that the items are now in the correct folder, click the folder icon in the outline (beneath the Inbox icon) that appears in the left pane of the Windows Mail window.

TIP Don't forget that the most basic way to organize your e-mail is by sorting all the messages in the Inbox (or any of the other Windows Mail folders, for that matter) by clicking the column button. For example, if you want to sort the e-mail in your Inbox by subject, click the Subject button at the top of the list. So, too, if you want to sort the messages by the date and time received (from earliest to most recent), click the Received button at the top of that column.

Deleting e-mail

When you have messages (especially those unsolicited ones) that you no longer need to store on your computer hard drive, you can move those messages to the Deleted Items folder by selecting them and then choosing Edit⇨Delete (Ctrl+D). You can then get rid of them for good by right-clicking the Deleted Items icon in the Folders bar, clicking Empty Deleted Items Folder, and then clicking Yes in the alert box telling you that you're about to permanently delete the selected messages.

If you receive unsolicited messages from advertisers or people whose e-mail you don't want to receive again in the future, click one of the sender's e-mail messages in the Inbox and then select Message⇨Junk E-mail⇨Add Sender to Blocked Senders List on the menu bar. You then receive an alert dialog box informing you that the person has been added to your blocked senders list and telling you that the sender's message has been moved to the Junk E-mail folder. Click the OK button to close this message dialog box.

TIP

To remove someone you've blocked from your Blocked Senders list so that you can once again get e-mail from that person, open the Junk E-mail folder and then select the sender's message before you choose Message➪Junk E-mail ➪Add Sender to Safe Senders List on the menu bar.

To remove messages from the Inbox without permanently getting rid of them, select them and then press the Delete key. They instantly disappear from the Inbox window. If you ever need them again, however, you can display them by clicking the Deleted Items icon in the Windows Mail window Folder pane. If you find a message in the Deleted Items folder that you intended to keep, drag its message icon and drop it on the Inbox folder (or whatever other special folder you've created for your mail messages) in the Folders pane.

Windows Meeting Space

Vista's Windows Meeting Space feature enables you to share documents, programs, and even your Windows desktop with up to ten other networked computers that are also running Windows Vista (sorry, Windows XP people). The great thing about Windows Meeting Space is that, although it can take advantage of a formal network that uses a dedicated network server, it can also make use of an informal peer-to-peer or ad hoc wireless network by creating the network right at the time new computers join the collaborative session (the very essence of ad hoc). All you need are Vista computers that can connect to one another through Ethernet cabling or a wireless connection. *See* Part 3 for more information on networking in Vista and the various types of networks it supports.

Setting up Windows Meeting Space

Before you and your fellow Vista computer users can get together and collaborate your socks off, you need to set up Windows Meeting Space. To do this, follow these steps:

1. Click Start ▶ All Programs ▶ Windows Meeting Space to open the Windows Meeting Space Setup dialog box.

PERMISSION

2. Click the Yes, Continue Setting Up Windows Meeting Space and then click the Continue button in the User Account Control permission dialog box.

   The People Near Me dialog box appears.

3. Click OK in the People Near Me dialog box to sign you into this utility each time Windows starts.

   The Windows Meeting Space window then appears.

4. Click the Start a New Meeting link to display the Meeting Name and Password text boxes.

5. Edit the default session name containing your name and the current time in the Meeting Name text with a descriptive name and then enter a password of at least eight characters in the Password text box (see Figure 4-14).

   Click the View Characters check box if you want to be able to see the characters as you enter them.

6. (Optional) If you need Vista to create a new ad hoc, peer-to-peer wireless network for the collaborative session, click the Options link. Next click the Create a Private Ad Hoc Wireless Network check box and, if you're not in the U.S.A., click it in the Select Your Country or Region drop-down list before you click OK.

7. Click the Create a Session button (the one with the arrow pointing to the right).

Vista then creates the session and displays a Windows Collaboration window with the name of the session similar to the one shown in Figure 4-13. From this window, you can then invite the participants with whom you will then share resources such as documents, programs, and your computer's desktop.

Figure 4-13

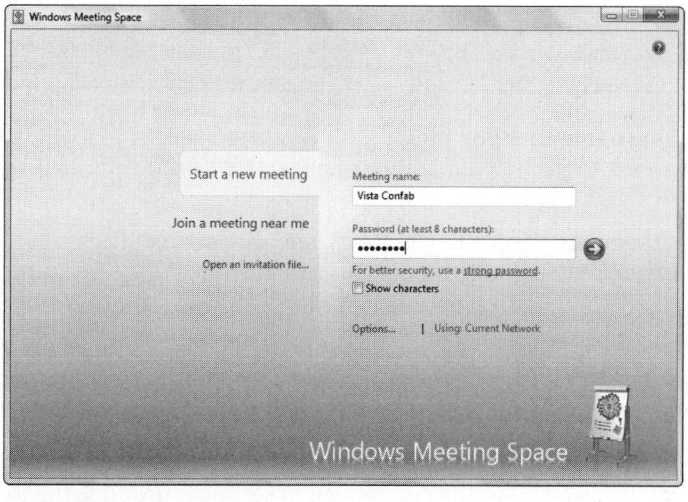

People Near Me

You can use Vista's People Near Me feature to identify yourself for potential collaborative sessions by using the Windows Collaboration feature. To sign into People Near Me, you follow these steps:

1. Click Start ▶ Control Panel ▶ Network and Internet ▶ People Near Me to open the People Near Me dialog box with the Sign In tab selected.

2. (Optional) Edit the name automatically entered in Type the Name You Want Other People to See text box if you want another name to appear in the Windows Meeting window.

3. (Optional) If you don't want Vista to automatically sign you into People Near Me each time you start the computer, clear the check mark from the Sign Me In Automatically When Windows Starts check box.

4. (Optional) If you want Vista to include a picture of you when sending invitations to a collaborative session, click the Include My Picture When Sending Invitations check box.

5. (Optional) If you want to restrict the invitations to participants to only those on your Trusted contacts list (*see* Part 6: Security), click Trusted Contacts on the Allow Invitations From drop-down list.

6. (Optional) To sign yourself into People Near Me each time you start your computer, click the Sign Me in Automatically When Windows Starts check box.

7. Click the Sign In tab in the People Near Me and then click the People Near Me option button.

8. Click OK to close the People Near Me dialog box.

Inviting participants to the session

The next thing to do after you create your Meeting Space is to invite all the people you want to participate in the collaborative session. To do this, you follow these simple steps:

1. Click the Invite People link in the Windows Meeting Space window to open the Invite People dialog box.

2. Click the check boxes in front of the names of all the people you want to participate in the collaborative session in the Invite People list box.

   Note that the names of the folks that appear in the Invite People list are just those who are currently signed into People Near Me.

3. (Optional) If you don't want your participants to have to enter the password you assigned to the session when setting it up, click the Require People Near Me to Enter a Session Passphrase check box to remove its check mark.

4. Click the Send Invitations button.

As soon as you click Send Invitations, Vista closes the Invite People dialog box and sends messages to all those you selected as participants. Vista then displays an invitation on the Vista desktop of each participant. After a participant clicks the Accept button, the Windows Collaboration window opens on her desktop, where she then enters the session password — assuming that you left the Require People Near Me to Enter a Session Passphrase check box selected in the Invite People dialog box — to join the session.

 To invite people who are not currently signed into People Near Me, click the Invite Others button in the Invite People dialog box and then click Send an Invitation in E-mail in the Choose an Option for Inviting Other People dialog box to open a new e-mail message. The message not only invites the potential participant to your collaborative session but also gives him instructions on joining the session by using a file that's automatically attached to the new message.

Sharing computer resources

After you've set up the session, invited your participants and had them join, you're ready to start sharing various computer resources with them (see Figure 4-14). You can share documents as handouts that are copied to each participant's computer, application programs you're currently running, or even your Windows Vista desktop, using one of the two following options:

- **Share** to enable session participants to view application programs that are running on Vista or the Vista desktop — click the Share button or the Share a Program or Your Desktop link in the Meeting Space window and then click the program, file, or Desktop icon in the Start a Shared Session dialog box before you click the Share button.

- **Add** to send documents that you designate as handouts with all the session participants, enabling them to make changes to the document one at a time during the collaborative session.

When you're ready to terminate a collaborative session that you've created, click Meeting ▶ Exit. Vista then asks whether you want to save any handouts distributed during the collaborative session.

Sharing programs, files, or your Vista desktop

After selecting a running program, file, or your Vista desktop to share with all the session participants, all changes that you make in the program, to the file, or on the Windows desktop show up in all the participants' Windows Meeting Space windows on their computers. To stop sharing an application, file, or the desktop, click the Stop Sharing button on the bar above the program's or file's window. Alternatively, when presenting your desktop, click the Stop Sharing link that appears in the You Are Presenting Your Desktop area in your Windows Collaboration window.

 To see how a shared application or your Vista desktop appears on the participants' computers, click the Show Me How My Shared Session Looks on Other Computers link that appears in the You Are Presenting Your Desktop area in your Windows Meeting Space window.

Figure 4-14

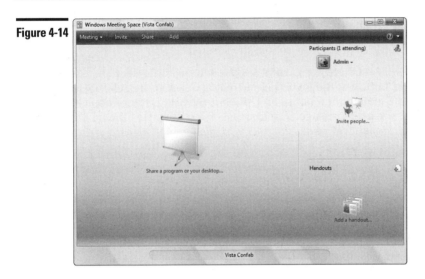

Presenting a document as a handout

To open a document that you're sharing as a handout in the Windows Meeting
Space window on the participants' computers, right-click the handout's icon in
the Handouts section of your Meeting Space window and then click Open With
on its shortcut menu and then click the name of the program in the Open With
dialog box before you click OK. All during the time you present this document,
all the changes you make to the file immediately appear in all the documents
displayed in the participants' Meeting Space windows.

To hand control of the document to another participant so that he can make
changes to it, click Control ▶ Give Control To followed by the participant's name
on the continuation menu. To take back control later in the session, click
Control ▶ Take Control. To display the presented document on a network projector to which you have access, click Options ▶ Connect to a Projector and
then click the name of the networked projector.

When you're finished presenting a document, click Options ▶ Show Windows
Meeting Space window in the upper-right corner of the application in which the
file is open and then click the Stop Sharing link in the middle of your Meeting
Space window. You can then close the document (and decide whether to save
the changes made to it during the session and, if so, under what filename).

Part 5

System Maintenance

The foremost utility for system maintenance in Windows Vista is the Control Panel, as shown in the following figure. The Control Panel enables you to control computer settings relating to both hardware components and Windows software. In addition, this part gives you the specifics on synchronizing files on your computer with other devices, backing up the data on your computer, moving your system settings from your current computer to another, and keeping your copy of the Windows Vista operating system up-to-date.

In this part . . .

- ✔ Backing up your computer system
- ✔ Changing your computer's settings with the Control Panel
- ✔ Restoring your computer system to a prior state
- ✔ Getting automatic Windows updates

Backup and Restore Center

The Backup and Restore Center encompasses a File and Folder Backup utility that enables you to make, compare, or restore backup copies of selected files and folders on your computer, as well as the CompletePC Backup utility that enables you to back up your entire hard drive (unless you're running the Home Basic or Vista Home Premium versions, in which case you don't have this program). Use these utilities to maintain copies of all the files you can't live without, in case (knock on wood) anything ever happens to your computer or the hard drive.

To open the Backup and Restore Center, click Start ▶ Control Panel ▶ Back Up Your Computer. Vista then opens the Backup and Restore Center window in Figure 5-1.

Figure 5-1

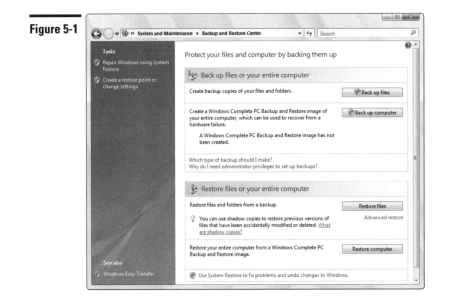

File and Folder Backup

To use the File and Folder Backup utility to make backups of just certain folders and files on your computer, follow these steps:

1. Click the Backup Files button in the Back Up Files or Your Entire Computer section of the Backup and Restore Center window (Start ▶ Control Panel ▶ System and Maintenance ▶ Back Up Your Computer).

2. Click the Continue button in the User Account Control dialog box to open the Back Up Your Files window.

3. Select the drive or network folder where you want the backup of your computer's folder and files to be stored.

   To back up the files on another local hard drive, select it in the On a Hard Disk , CD, or DVD drop-down list box. To back up the files on a CD or DVD disc, select your computer's CD/DVD drive letter in the drop-down list box and then be sure to insert a blank CD or DVD disc into this drive.

   To back up the files on a network drive, click the On a Network option button and then enter the folder's pathname or use the Browse button to select the folder in the Browse for Folder dialog box.

4. Click Next to open the Which File Types Do You Want to Backup? window. In this window, clear the check boxes for any types of files that you don't want included in the backup.

   By default, the File and Folder Backup utility includes all types of files, pictures, documents, music, video, e-mails, and recorded TV. The only files that are not included in the backup are system files and temporary files.

5. Click Next to open the How Often Do You Want to Create a Backup? dialog box.

6. Select how often (Daily, Weekly, or Monthly), on what day of the week or month, and at what time Vista is to perform the file and folder backup.

7. Click the Save Settings and Start Backup command button.

Vista then displays the Backup Up Files dialog box, which keeps you informed of the backup progress. The operating system backs up all the selected files, first by creating a shadow copy of the files and then by actually copying them to the designated drive, disc, or network folder. While Windows performs the backup, you can continue to work.

To call a halt to a backup before Vista finishes copying all the files, click the Stop Backup button in the Backup Files dialog box.

CompletePC Backup

To use the CompletePC Backup utility to make a complete backup of all the files on your computer's hard drive, follow these steps:

1. Click the Back Up Computer button in the Back Up Files or Your Entire Computer section of the Backup and Restore Center window.

2. Click the Continue button in the User Account Control dialog box to open the Windows Complete PC Backup window.

3. Select an alternate hard drive or the letter of your computer's CD/DVD drive where you want Vista to make the backup of your computer's hard drive.

   To back up the files on another local hard drive, select it in the On a Hard Disk drop-down list box. To back up the files on one or more DVD discs, click the On One or More DVDs option button and then select your computer's CD/DVD drive letter in the drop-down list box. Be sure to insert a blank DVD disc into this drive.

4. Click Next to open the Confirm Your Backup Settings dialog box, where the letter of your computer's hard drive appears in the Backup Location list box.

5. Click the Start Backup button.

Vista then displays the Windows Complete PC Backup dialog box, which keeps you informed of its progress in making the backup. If you're backing up the computer to DVD discs, Vista displays dialog boxes prompting you to insert and label all the DVD discs needed to do the backup. If a DVD disc that you insert needs formatting, a dialog box prompting you to format that disc then also appears.

Restoring files to your computer

After using the File and Folder Backup or the CompletePC Backup utility to back up certain files or your entire computer, you can then use the Backup and Restore Center to restore the backed-up files if you ever need to due to a hard drive malfunction or reformatting.

To restore files and folders backed up with the File and Folder Backup utility, follow these steps:

1. Click the Restore Files button in the Restore Files or Your Entire Computer section of the Backup and Restore Center window.

   Vista opens a window entitled, What Do You Want to Restore?

2. Make sure that the Files From the Latest Backup option button is selected, and then click Next.

   Vista opens a window entitled, Which Files and Folders Do You Want to Restore?

3. Select the Restore Everything in This Backup check box or browse for the individual files or folders to restore.

4. Click Next and then click the Start Restore button in the Where Do You Want to Save the Recovered Files? window with the In the Original Location option button selected.

To restore files backed up with the CompletePC Backup utility, click the Restore Computer button in this same Restore Files or Your Entire Computer section of the Backup and Restore Center window.

Be *very* cautious about using the Restore Computer feature of the Backup and Restore Center: When you click the Restore Computer button, Vista displays an alert dialog box informing you that as part of restoring your computer, Vista will reformat your hard disk, thereby destroying all of its data (this includes all Windows files, program files, and document files you've created).

Therefore, you only want to proceed with restoring an entire computer backup when you know that your backup disk or discs contains the latest backups of all your files and you don't care about losing all the data on your hard drive. If this is the case, follow these steps:

1. Click the Close button in the Backup and Restore Center alert dialog box, insert the system image backup DVD in your computer's DVD drive or, if the image backup is on an external drive, connect it to your computer and then click the Start button and click Restart on the Shut Down Options button's pop-up menu to reboot your computer.

    Proceed to Step 2 while the computer is rebooting.

2. Hold down the F8 key during reboot to start Vista in the Windows Recovery Environment.

3. Click Windows System Image Backup in the Windows Recovery Environment and then let it guide you through the process of backing up your entire computer.

Control Panel

The Control Panel in Windows Vista is the place to go when you need to make changes to various settings of your computer system. To open the Control Panel window, click the Start button on the taskbar and then click Control Panel on the Start menu.

In Vista, you can view the Control Panel in two different views:

- ✔ Category view (the default), which contains links representing groups of related Control Panel programs displayed in columns (see Figure 5-2)

- ✔ Classic view, where the individual Control panel program icons are displayed in rows running down and across the window (see Figure 5-3)

To switch from Category view into Classic view, click the Classic View link in the Control Panel window's navigation bar. This link appears immediately underneath the bold Control Panel Home heading. To switch back into Category view, click the Control Panel Home link that appears in smaller type above the now bold Classic view heading.

As you see in Figure 5-2, in Category View, Vista organizes the Control Panel window into ten categories, ranging from System and Maintenance to Additional Options. To open a window with the Control Panel options for any one of these categories, simply click the category's hyperlink.

Figure 5-2

In Figure 5-3, you notice that when the Control Panel window is in Classic view, Vista displays an alphabetical listing of all the Control Panel options on your system with a program icon and name from Add Hardware to Windows Update. To view and possibly change the settings for a particular Control Panel option in Classic view, you need to double-click the Control Panel program icon.

If you're running Vista on a laptop computer, the Control Panel has an extra Mobile PC category that appears between the Programs and User Accounts and Family Safety categories.

The following table gives you a descriptive list of all the Control Panel categories except for Additional Options (which varies according to your computer's configuration) and including Mobile PC for laptops that appear in the Control Panel window when you have it in Category view. Use this table to figure out what type of computer settings you can change by clicking each category's hyperlink.

The Groups of Category Links in the Control Panel Home

Click this Category Link	To Display These Groups of Links
System and Maintenance	Welcome Center, Backup and Restore Center, System, Windows Update, Power Options, Indexing Options, Problem Reports and Solutions, Performance Information and Tools, Device Manager, and Administrative Tools

Click this Category Link	*To Display These Groups of Links*
Security	Security Center, Windows Firewall, Windows Update, Windows Defender, Internet Options, Parental Controls, and BitLocker Drive Encryption (if your version of Vista supports this utility)
Network and Internet	Network and Sharing Center, Internet Options, Offline Files, Windows Firewall, People Near Me, Sync Center
Hardware and Sound	Printers, AutoPlay, Sound, Mouse, Power Options, Personalization, Scanners and Camera, Keyboard, Device Manager, Phone and Modem Options, Game Controllers, Windows SideShow, Pen and Input Devices, Color Management, and Tablet PC Settings
Programs	Programs and Features, Windows Defender, Default Programs, Windows Sideshow, Windows Sidebar Properties, and Get Programs Online
Mobile PC (laptops only)	Windows Mobility Center, Power Options, Personalization, Tablet PC Settings, Pen and Input Devices, and Sync Center
User Accounts and Family Safety	User Accounts, Parental Controls, Windows CardSpace, and Mail
Appearance and Personalization	Personalization, Taskbar and Start Menu, Ease of Access Center, Folder Options, Fonts, and Windows Sidebar Properties
Clock, Language, and Region	Date and Time, and Regional and Language Options
Ease of Access	Ease of Access Center and Speech Recognition Options

As you can see from this table, Vista's Control Panel programs are numerous, and different categories have duplicate links for opening the same Control Panel windows or dialog boxes. The following sections give you detailed information on the most commonly used Control Panel groups: System and Maintenance, Hardware and Sound, Clock, Language, and Region, and Ease of Access.

See Part 1 for information on customizing your computer with the Personalization and Windows Sidebar Properties Control Panel programs.

See Part 2 for information on using the Programs and Default Programs Control Panel programs.

See Part 3 for information on configuring and changing network settings with the Network and Internet Control Panel options.

See Part 4 for information on configuring and using speech recognition and text to speech with the Speech Recognition Control Panel options.

See Part 6 for information on configuring and changing your computer's security settings by using the Security Control Panel option.

Figure 5-3

System and Maintenance

When you click the System and Maintenance link in the Control Panel home window when the Category view is selected, Vista opens a new window (see Figure 5-4) containing the following groups of options:

- ✔ **Welcome Center** to open the welcome screen to your computer window that automatically appears each time you boot your computer until you deselect the Run at Startup check box. This window displays basic information about your computer, including Windows edition, processor, memory, video adapter, and the computer name, manufacturer, and model, along with links such as Add New Users and What's New in Windows.

- ✔ **Backup and Restore Center** to launch the Windows Backup utility, which allows you to back up all or just certain files on your computer's harddrive as well as restore them (*see* "Backup and Restore Center" for details earlier in this part).

✔ **System** to open a window displaying information about your computer system such as rating (based on its processor, memory, hard drive, and graphics capability), memory, and type of operating system (32-bit or 64-bit) and the edition of the Windows operating system including the product key.

✔ **Windows Update** to open the Windows Update window, where you can check for updates to the Windows Vista operating system (**see** "Windows Update" for details later in this part).

✔ **Power Options** to open the Power Options Control Panel window, where you can select or edit a power scheme that determines when and if Windows should turn off your monitor or power down your hard drive after so many minutes of inactivity. You can also use the Require a Password on Wakeup link in the Navigation pane to designate whether to shut down the computer or put it to sleep when you click the Power button on your computer, and whether to require you to enter your password when you wake your computer from sleep (see "Restart, Sleep/Hibernate, Lock, Log Off, and Shut Down" in Part 2).

✔ **Indexing Options** to open the Indexing Options dialog box, where you can designate which user's files on your computer to include and which to exclude from indexing for the purpose of doing Searches (**see** "Search" in Part 1).

✔ **Problem Reports and Solutions** to open a Problem Reports and Solutions window displaying links to solutions for Vista problems your computer is experiencing.

✔ **Performance Rating and Tools** to open a window displaying ratings for and ratings of your PC in five performance areas, (processor, memory, hard drive storage, graphics, and gaming graphics), and detailing any issues that are adversely affecting your computer's performance.

✔ **Device Manager** to open the Device Manager dialog box, which displays all the devices installed on your computer and tells you whether they are all working properly.

✔ **Administrative Tools** to open the Administrative Tools Control Panel window, which contains shortcuts to a number of utilities used by the Systems Administrator to review and control your computer. (Don't fool with these options unless you know what you're doing.)

Hardware and Sound

When you click the Hardware and Sound link in the Control Panel home window when the Category view is selected, Vista opens a new Hardware and Sound window (see Figure 5-5) displaying a long list of links to hardware devices from printers to Tablet PC settings (even when you don't have a Tablet PC and have no use for the settings).

Figure 5-4

Among the most commonly used of Hardware and Sounds options are the following:

- ✔ **Printers** enables you to change the settings for the printers you've installed on your computer as well as add a new local or network printer (*see* "Printers" later in this part for details).

- ✔ **AutoPlay** enables you to designate which Windows program to use in playing various types of media files (*see* "AutoPlay" later in this part for details).

- ✔ **Sound** enables you to manage your sound devices and assign new sounds to common Windows events (*see* "Manage Audio Devices and Sound Themes" later in this part for details).

- ✔ **Mouse** enables you change the settings for your mouse (*see* "Mouse" later in this part for details).

- ✔ **Scanners and Cameras** enables you to transfer images from digital scanners or cameras to your computer (*see* "Scanners and Cameras" later in this part for details).

Printers

When you click the Printers link under Hardware and Sound in the Control Panel home window or on the Hardware and Sound Control Panel window, Vista opens a Printers Control Panel window that displays all the printers (physical, virtual, local, and network) installed on your computer.

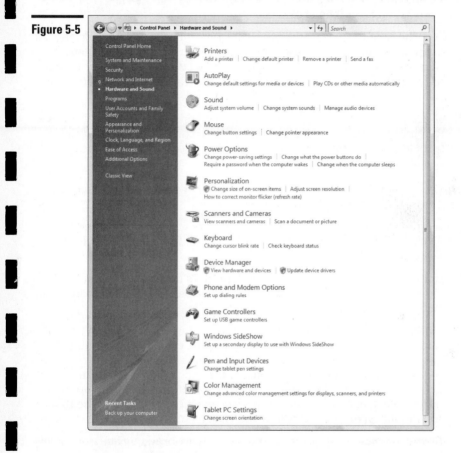

Figure 5-5

To add a new local printer to your computer system in the Printers window, follow these steps:

1. Click the Add a Printer button on the Printers window toolbar to start the Add Printer Wizard, choose the option that applies to you and click Next.

2. Select the port for the printer to use in the Use the Existing Port drop-down list box in the Choose a Printer Port dialog box and then click the Next button.

3. Click the manufacturer and the model of the printer in the Manufacturers and Printers list boxes, respectively, of the Install the Printer Driver dialog

box. If you have a disk with the software for the printer, put it into your floppy or CD-ROM drive and then click the Have Disk button: Select the drive that contains this disk in the Copy Manufacturer's Files From drop-down list box and then click OK.

4. Click the Next button to advance to the Type a Printer Name dialog box. If you want, edit the name for the printer in the Printer Name text box. If you want to make the printer that you're installing the default printer that is automatically used whenever you print from Windows or a Windows pro-gram, leave the Set as the Default Printer check box selected.

5. Click the Next button to advance to the final Add Printer Wizard dialog box. To print a test page from your newly installed printer, select the Print a Test Page check box. Click the Finish button or press Enter to finish installing the new printer.

To use the Add Printer Wizard to install a printer that's available through your Local Area Network, follow slightly different steps:

1. Click the Add a Printer button on the Printers window toolbar and then click the Add a Network, Wireless or Bluetooth Printer option before you click Next.

2. After Vista is finished searching for all printers on your network and all wireless printers in your vicinity, click the name of the printer to install in the Searching for Available Printers list box, and then click Next.

3. (Optional) If the printer you want to install is not on this list or Vista fails to find and list the network or wireless printer, click the The Printer That I Want Isn't Listed link. To browse for the printer on the network, click the Browse for a Printer option button and then click Next. To enter the path-name for the printer, leave the Select a Shared Printer by Name option button selected, and then type the pathname in its text box or use the Browse button to locate it before you click Next.

   If you can't locate the printer on the network by browsing and don't know its pathname but do happen to know its IP (Internet Protocol) address, click the Add a Printer Using a TCP/IP Address or Hostname option button before you click Next. Then enter the IP address in the Hostname or IP Address text box, its port in the Port Name text box, and click Next. Vista will then detect the printer, using the address you provide. After Windows locates the printer, click Next.

4. In the Type a Printer Name dialog box, edit the name for the printer in the Printer Name text box if you want. To make the printer that you're installing the default printer that is automatically used whenever you print from Windows or a Windows program, leave the Set as the Default Printer check box selected.

5. Click the Next button to advance to the final Add Printer Wizard dialog box. To print a test page from your newly installed printer, select the Print a Test Page check box. Click the Finish button or press Enter to finish installing the new printer.

In addition to installing new printers in the Printers Control Panel window, you can use it to change settings and to control the jobs you send to a printer:

✔ To share a printer, assuming that the administrator of the computer has configured the Windows firewall to permit printer sharing (*see* Part 6), right-click its printer icon and then click Sharing on its shortcut menu. Click the Share This Printer option button and give the printer a share name in the text box provided.

✔ To change the default printer for your computer programs, right-click the printer's icon and then click Set as Default Printer on its shortcut menu.

✔ To change the layout, paper, and print quality settings for a particular printer, right-click its printer icon and then click the Printing Preferences on its shortcut menu.

✔ To pause a print job that is in progress by the printer currently selected in the Printers Control Panel window, double-click the printer icon to open its window and then click Printer⇨Pause Printing.

✔ To open the currently selected printer when it's processing or printing a print job to view the status of the jobs in the print queue or to cancel print jobs, click the See What's Printing button on the toolbar of the Printers Control Panel window. To cancel a job, click it in the queue and then click Document⇨Cancel.

TIP To be able to print documents directly from Windows Vista, create a desktop short-cut to your printer by right-clicking its icon in the Printers Control Panel window, selecting Create Shortcut, and then drag the icon of the file you want printed and drop it on the printer's desktop shortcut. Vista responds by opening that file in the program associated with its file type. That program then immediately sends the file to that printer for printing.

AutoPlay

When you click the AutoPlay link in the Hardware and Sound Control Panel window, Vista opens an AutoPlay Control Panel window. This window displays all the various types of audio, video, and still digital image files that you can have on your computer in the Media column on the left. You can then have a particular program such as the Windows Media Player or Media Center open certain kinds of media files, or have Vista take a particular action with certain types of media. For example, you can have Vista open them from Windows Explorer or burn them to disc by selecting Windows Media Player in the drop-down list box to the immediate right of that kind of media file.

See "Media Center" and "Windows Media Player 11" in Part 7 for details on using these Vista programs to play your media files.

Manage Audio Devices and Sound Themes

When you click the Manage Audio Devices link in the Hardware and Sound Control Panel window, Vista opens the Sound dialog box, which contains the following three tabs:

- ✔ **Playback,** which lists all the audio output and output audio devices connected to your computer. To review the properties for a particular device or modify its parameters, click the device to select it and then click the Properties button to open a Properties dialog box for that device showing all the options you can change.

- ✔ **Recording,** which enables you to select a new recording device such as external microphone or line in.

- ✔ **Sounds,** where you can modify or create a new sound scheme that determines what sounds, if any, to play when particular events take place, such as closing programs, displaying an alert box, receiving new e-mail, emptying the Recycle Bin, and so on.

To manage the overall volume setting for your computer and for the applications on your system that play sound, either click the Adjust System Volume link under Sound in the Hardware and Sound window or click the speaker icon in the Notifications area of the taskbar and choose Mixer. Vista then opens a Volume Mixer dialog box containing both a Device and Applications slider that you can drag up to increase the volume or down to decrease it. Note that you can move the Applications volume slider independently of the Device slider.

Mouse

When you click the Mouse link under Hardware and Sound in the Control Panel home window or on the Hardware and Sound Control Panel window, Vista opens a Mouse Properties dialog box. you can modify the settings for your mouse, including switching the primary and secondary buttons, changing the double-click speed, and selecting new pointer icons and pointer movement options for the mouse. If your mouse has a wheel, you can also modify the behavior of rolling the wheel one notch.

Scanners and Cameras

When you click the Scanners and Cameras option in the Hardware and Sound Control Panel window, Vista opens a Scanners and Cameras dialog box showing all digital scanners and cameras currently connected to your computer.

If you don't see your scanner or camera listed in this dialog box and you've previously installed it, click the Refresh command button. Click the Add Device button and then follow the steps by using the Scanner and Camera Installation Wizard if you need to install the device.

To get information about a particular scanner or camera that's connected to your computer and possibly adjust its settings, click its icon in the Scanners and Cameras dialog box and then click the Properties command button.

To scan a text document with a scanner shown in the Scanners and Cameras dialog box, you need to use the Windows Fax and Scan utility — *see* "Windows Fax and Scan" in Part 4. To scan a graphic image or photo, you can also scan right from within the Windows Photo Gallery — *see* "Windows Photo Gallery" in Part 7.

Clock, Language, and Region

When you click the Clock, Language, and Region link in the Control Panel home window, Vista opens a new Clock, Language, and Region Control Panel window containing the two following links:

🖙 **Date and Time** to open the Date and Time Properties dialog box, where you can reset the date and time, add up to two additional clocks, and synchronize the time on your computer to Internet time. (*See* the "Date and Time" section that follows.)

🖙 **Regional and Language Options** to open the Regional and Language Options dialog box, where you can change the way numbers, currency, dates and times are normally displayed in Windows, change the locality of your computer, and add new languages and keyboards to use. (*See* "Regional and Language Options" later in this part.)

Date and Time

When you click the Date and Time link in the Clock, Language, and Region Control Panel window, Vista opens the Date and Time Properties dialog box with the Date and Time tab selected, as shown in Figure 5-6. You can use the options on this tab to correct the date or time used by your computer as well as to update your time zone and observance of daylight savings time. Note that Vista uses the date and time information displayed on the tab of this dialog box not only to date-stamp files that you create and modify, but also for its time display at the far right of the Notification area of the Windows taskbar. (To display the current date including the day of the week, position the mouse pointer over this time display.)

You can use the options on the Additional Clocks tab to keep tabs on the local time in two other time zones besides your own. Just click either of the Show This Clock check boxes and then select the time zone in the associated dropdown list box for the new clock. Give it a name in its Enter Display Name text box before you click OK.

After adding additional clocks, you can check their local time anytime you want simply by clicking the local time that appears at the far right of the Notifications area of the Windows taskbar. Doing this displays a Date and Time Settings pop-up bar that contains a monthly calendar with the current date highlighted along with analog representations of all your clocks on your computer with their current time. (Simply click anywhere on the desktop outside this Date and Time Settings bar to hide its display.)

Figure 5-6

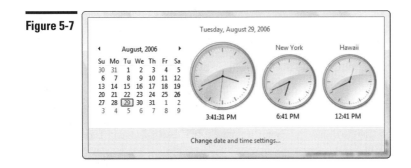

Figure 5-7 shows the Date and Time Settings bar that appears when I click the local time displayed on my taskbar. This display contains a calendar with the current month, lists the current time, and shows all the clocks I've created. In this figure, you can see that I've created two additional clocks: a New York clock, so I always know my publisher's local time, and a Hawaii clock, so that I know the local time of the place where I'll be when this book is done! To get rid of this date and time display, simply click anywhere on the desktop outside of its graphic.

Figure 5-7

TIP

To have Vista display a temporary pop-up display that lists the current date and the time for the system clock and each of the clocks you've created, simply position the mouse pointer on the time in the Notification area. This pop-up display then disappears the moment you move the mouse pointer off the time in the Notification area.

You can synchronize the time shown in the Time text box on the Date and Time tab with one of the various online time servers (such as `time.windows.com` or `time.nist.gov`). To do so, click the Change Settings button on the Internet Time tab. Next, simply select the time server to use in the Server drop-down list box in the Internet Time Settings dialog box that appears. Click the Update Now button.

Regional and Language Options

When you click the Regional and Language Options link in the Clock, Language, and Region Control Panel window, Windows opens the Regional and Language Options dialog box with the Formats tab selected, as shown in Figure 5-8. Here, you can customize the default number, currency, and date formats on your computer by clicking the Customize This Format button, and then clicking the appropriate tab (Numbers, Currency, Time, or Date) in the Customize Regional Options dialog box. Use the individual drop-down lists boxes to modify all the settings of the selected format that you need to change.

To select a new country location for your computer, click the Location tab in the Regional and Language Options dialog box and then select the new country in the Current Location drop-down list box.

To switch to a new keyboard or language or to make changes to the language bar settings, click the Keyboard and Languages tab in the Regional and Language Options dialog box, and then click the Change Keyboards command button to open the Text Services and Input Languages dialog box. There, you can use the options on the General tab to add and select new input languages for Windows as well as a new keyboard layout for those languages.

To control how the Language bar (which enables you to switch from using one language to another while working in Windows programs) appears on the desktop, click the Language Bar tab in the Text Services and Input Languages dialog box. Use its option buttons and check boxes to modify its desktop behavior.

To change the hot keys you can use to switch from one language to another in Windows (instead of having to do this from the Language bar), click the Advanced Key Settings tab in the Text Services and Input Languages dialog box and then click the language for which you want to select a set of predefined hot keys. Click the Change Key Sequence command button to open the Change Key Sequence dialog box. There, click the option button for the predefined sequence under Switch Input Language before you click OK.

To add or remove languages on your computer, click the Install/Uninstall Languages button on the Keyboard and Languages tab of the Regional and Language Options dialog box. After you click the Continue button in the permissions dialog box that appears, Vista opens the Install or Uninstall Display Languages window where you either click Install Languages to add new languages (provided that you have already copied their language files on your

computer and know their location) to the computer, or Remove Languages to
delete them.

Figure 5-8

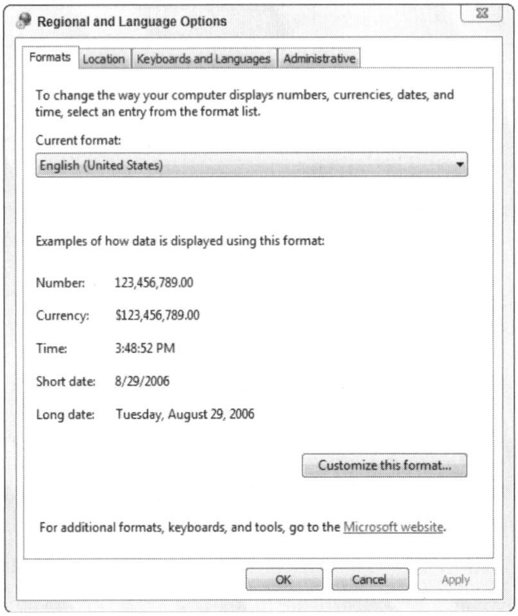

Ease of Access Center

When you click the Ease of Access link in the Control Panel Home window, Vista
opens an Ease of Access Control Panel window that contains the following two
links:

- ✔ **Ease of Access Center** to open an Ease of Access Center Control Panel
  window, which contains a whole range of options for aiding users with various degrees of vision and hearing impairments.

- ✔ **Speech Recognition Options** to open a Configure Your Speech Recognition
  Experience Control Panel window, where you can set up speech recognition on your computer enabling you to issue voice commands as well as
  dictate text in Windows application programs. (**See** "Speech Recognition"
  in Part 4 for details).

When you click the Ease of Access Center link, the Ease of Access Center
Control Panel window, shown in Figure 5-9, appears. The controls in this window
enable you to change a number of keyboard, sound, display, and mouse settings
that can make using the computer easier if you have less-than-perfect physical
dexterity. The Quick Access to Common Tools section of this window contains
the following options in two columns:

✔ **Start Magnifier** to turn on and off the Magnifier dialog box that shows each element of the screen magnified many times. Use the settings in the Microsoft Screen Magnify dialog box that appears when you first turn this feature on to control various settings, including whether the Screen Magnify window appears full-screen at start-up and assigning a new magnification factor (2x is the default).

✔ **Start On-Screen Keyboard** to turn on and off the display of the On-Screen Keyboard. The On-Screen Keyboard enables you to make text entries by clicking its keys to input letters, numbers, and punctuation, plus the accelerator keys (Shift, Ctrl, and Alt), function keys (F1 through F12), and cursor keys (Tab, Home, End, ←, ↑, →, ↓, and so on). Don't confuse this On-Screen Keyboard window with the Input PC Panel. The Input PC Panel enables you to make keyboard entries via written inputs with the mouse or a special pen tablet connected to your PC or directly on the screen of a Tablet PC running Windows Vista for Tablet PCs.

✔ **Start Narrator** to turn on and off the Narrator feature that reads aloud the names of each key you press, all system messages and on-screen messages that you receive, as well as all menu and toolbar options you select with the mouse.

✔ **Set Up High Contrast** to turn on and off High Contrast, which displays all Windows elements in very high contrasting colors. Click the Choose a High Contrast Color Scheme link to open the Appearance Settings dialog box, where you can select the high contrast color scheme to use.

TIP

Vista automatically uses the Text to Speech feature to narrate the name of each check box option while highlighting it whenever the Ease of Access Center Control Panel is open, provided that you don't clear the Always Read This Section Aloud and the Always Scan This Section check boxes at the bottom of this section.

In addition to these options in the Quick Access to Common Tools section, this window contains the following links in the Explore All Settings section that you can use to make your PC easier to use:

✔ **Use Computer without a Display** to open a window of audio accessibility options, including Narrator and Audio Description, that make it possible for a user with a hearing impairment to interact with the computer through audio cues

✔ **Make the Computer Easier to See** to open a window of visual accessibility options, such as turning on the Magnifier and changing the size of text and icons that make it easier for a user with a visual impairment to see and decipher screen elements

✔ **Use the Computer without a Mouse or Keyboard** to open a window containing options for activating the On-Screen Keyboard and enabling you to configure and activate Speech Recognition (*see* Part 4) on your computer

✔ **Make the Mouse Easier to Use** to open a window with mouse settings you can adjust, including activating Mouse Keys, which enables you to use the numeric keypad to move the mouse

✔ **Make the Keyboard Easier to Use** to open a window with keyboard options that you can adjust, including Mouse Keys (see above), Sticky Keys, Toggle Keys (to sound a tone when you press the Caps Lock, Num Lock, or Scroll Lock keys), and Filter Keys

✔ **Use Text or Visual Alternatives for Sounds** to open a window of visual accessibility options, including turning on Sound Sentry to display visual on-screen warnings (rather than audible ones), and text captions for spoken dialog when that's available

✔ **Make It Easier to Focus on Tasks** to open a window containing options for configuring and turning on the Narrator as well as Sticky Keys, Toggle Keys, and Filter Keys, and to control Windows on-screen animations

Figure 5-9

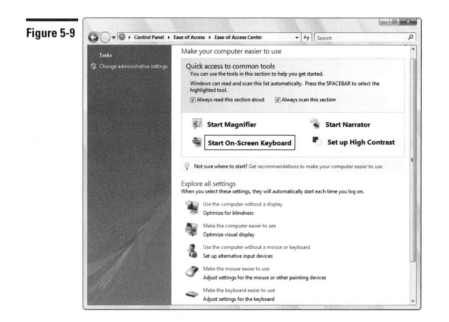

System Restore

System Restore enables you to turn back the clock on your computer system. For example, say that you're about to install a antivirus software program that you suspect will change a number of system settings. Before installing and using this software, you can use the System Restore accessory to create a restore point. That way, in the unlikely event that you find that the new software destabilizes your computer when it changes your system settings, you can remove the offending software (with the Add or Remove feature — *see* "Program Management" in Part 2) and then use the System Restore accessory to go back to the systems settings that were in effect at the restore point (that is, before the new software had a chance to mess with them).

Before you use the System Restore program, you need to create a protection point to which the system can later be restored:

1. Open the Backup and Restore Center window (Start ▶ Control Panel ▶ System and Maintenance ▶ Backup and Restore Center) and then click the Create a Restore Point or Change Settings link in the Navigation pane.

2. Click the Continue button in the User Account Control dialog box.

    Vista opens the System Properties dialog box with the System Protection tab selected.

3. Click the Create command button.

    Vista opens the System Protection dialog box with the heading Create a Restore Point.

4. Enter a descriptive name for the new protection point in the text box in the System Protection dialog box (note that Vista automatically adds the date and time to this description); then click the Create button.

    When creating this name, make sure that you enter a name that clearly indicates to you the current state of your computer, as in "Prior to ACME Anti-Virus Install."

    When Vista completes the creation of the restore point, an alert box appears.

5. Click OK to close the alert dialog box indicating that the protection point was successfully created.

After you create a protection point for your Windows settings, you can restore your system to that point by taking these steps:

1. Click the Start button and then type **sy** in the Start Search text box. Click System Restore in the Programs List, and then click the Continue button in the User Account Control dialog box to open the first System Restore dialog box entitled Restore System Files and Settings.

    If the System Properties dialog box is still open, you can also open this dialog box by clicking the System Restore command button on the System Protection tab.

2. By default, the Recommended Restore option button is selected to undo the most recent updates to your computer. To select one of the restore points you created (as outlined in the preceding steps), click the Choose a Different Restore Point option button before you click Next.

   Vista opens the second System Restore dialog box, entitled Choose a Restore Point.

3. Click Next to open the System Restore dialog box entitled Confirm Your Restore Point dialog box where you click the Finish button and then click Yes in the alert dialog box that tells you that you can't interrupt the restoration process nor can you undo the procedure until it's finished.

   As soon as you click Yes, the screen displays a bar showing the Windows progress in preparing your system for restoration and restoring your system settings. As soon as Windows finishes restoring your settings, it will automatically restart your computer so that the newly restored settings are put into effect. Windows will then display a System Restore screen indicating that your system settings were successfully restored.

4. Click the Close button in the System Restore window to close the System Restore accessory.

 TIP If you use System Restore only to discover that the restore point you selected made Windows Vista run even worse than it did before you did the restoration (heaven forbid!), you can undo the restoration by launching System Restore and then clicking Undo System Restore: Restore Operation for the date and time of this restoration. Click Next and then follow Steps 3 and 4 in the preceding list.

Windows Update

The Windows Update feature notifies you of the latest updates and bug fixes for the Windows Vista operating system directly from the Microsoft Web site. You can set Windows Update to automatically download Vista updates on a regular schedule and have it either ask you to install them on your computer or install them automatically.

To launch Windows Update, click Start ▶ All Programs ▶ Windows Update. Vista then opens a Windows Update window similar to the one shown in Figure 5-10. This window informs you of any updates that have been downloaded but not yet installed and enables you to install them by clicking the Install Updates button. It also enables you to review all the updates that have been made to your system by using the Windows Update feature (by clicking the View Update History link in the Navigation pane).

Figure 5-10

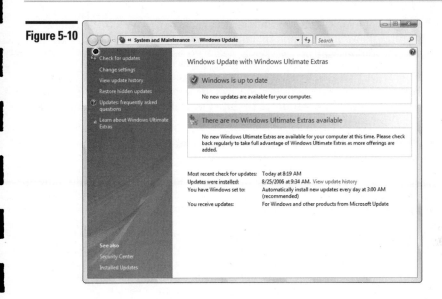

You can also open the Windows Update window from the Control Panel Home window by clicking the Check for Updates link under Security, or from the Windows Security Center window (Start ▶ Control Panel ▶ Check This Computer's Security Status) by clicking the Windows Update link in its Navigation pane.

To turn automatic updates off and on, as well as to modify how often Windows checks for and downloads and/or installs updates, follow these steps:

1. Open the Windows Update window (Start ▶ All Programs ▶ Windows Update) and then click the Change Settings link in its Navigation pane.

Windows opens a Change Settings Control Panel window similar to the one shown in Figure 5-11, where Vista automatically selects the Install Updates Automatically (Recommended) option button.

2. (Optional) To change how often and at what time Vista installs new updates to your computer, click the Install New Updates drop-down list button and select the day of the week (Every Sunday through Every Saturday). Next click the Time drop-down list button and select the time of day (12:00 AM midnight to 11:00 PM).

3. To prevent Vista from automatically downloading and installing updates on your computer, click the appropriate option button for the type of updating you want to put into effect:

- **Download Updates but Let Me Choose Whether to Install Them** to have Windows automatically check for and download critical and security updates. You can then review them in the Windows Update Control Panel window and install them if you choose by clicking the Install Updates button.

- **Check for Updates but Let Me Choose Whether to Download and Install Them** to have Windows only check for updates and install them when you open the Windows Update Control Panel window and click the Download and Install button.

- **Never Check for Updates (Not Recommended)** to turn off the Windows Updates feature entirely.

4. (Optional) Click the Include Recommended Updates When Downloading, Installing, or Notifying Me About Updates check box to have Vista check for optional recommended updates.

Keep in mind that when you select this check box, Windows Update not only checks for critical updates to Windows System files but also for optional updates to your system (such as the latest drivers for hardware on your system) that can greatly improve the performance of your system.

5. Click OK or press Enter to close the Change Settings window.

Click the View Update History link in the Windows Update window to open the View Update History window, which displays a complete log of all updates made to your computer with Windows Update. This update log includes the name of the update, its current status, type (Recommended or Important), as well as the date of installation.

Figure 5-11

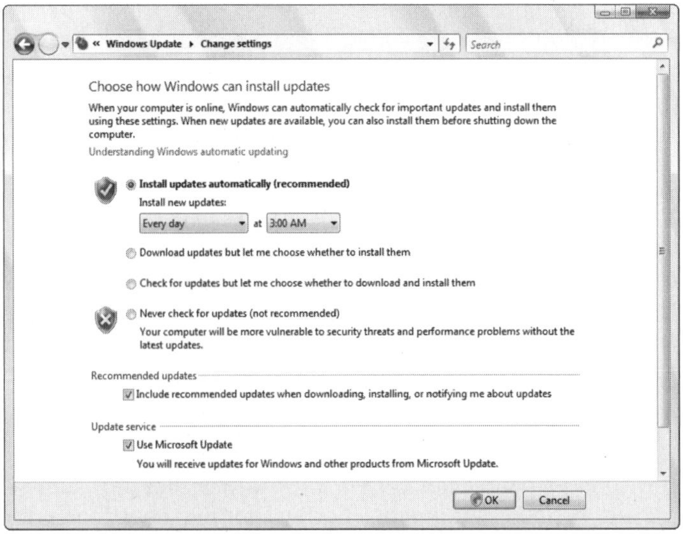

Choose how Windows can install updates

When your computer is online, Windows can automatically check for important updates and install them using these settings. When new updates are available, you can also install them before shutting down the computer.

Understanding Windows automatic updating

- ● **Install updates automatically (recommended)**
  Install new updates:
  Every day ▼ at 3:00 AM ▼
- ○ Download updates but let me choose whether to install them
- ○ Check for updates but let me choose whether to download and install them
- ○ Never check for updates (not recommended)
  Your computer will be more vulnerable to security threats and performance problems without the latest updates.

Recommended updates
  ☑ Include recommended updates when downloading, installing, or notifying me about updates

Update service
  ☑ Use Microsoft Update
  You will receive updates for Windows and other products from Microsoft Update.

OK   Cancel

Part 6

Security

In Windows Vista, your computer's security and integrity are paramount concerns. In addition to the Security Center, shown in this figure, which has been carried over from earlier versions of Windows, the Enterprise and Ultimate versions of Vista introduce BitLocker drive encryption, which protects all the files in your computer's System folder. And, all versions of Vista include Windows Defender (previously known as Microsoft AntiSpyware) — a utility that works with Internet Explorer and Windows Mail to protect your computer from spyware.

In this part . . .

- ✔ Turning on BitLocker drive encryption
- ✔ Setting up parental controls
- ✔ Monitoring the security of your PC with the Security Center
- ✔ Setting up and maintaining user accounts on your PC
- ✔ Monitoring the computer for harmful software with the Windows Defender

BitLocker Drive Encryption

The BitLocker Drive Encryption feature offered in the Enterprise and Ultimate versions of Windows Vista enables you to protect your hard drive by encrypting all its files and thus protecting them from unauthorized access and use. When you encrypt a drive, all files that you store on that drive are automatically encrypted, including any shared files (*see* "Sharing files" in Part 2).

To access this security feature, click Start ▶ Control Panel ▶ Security ▶ BitLocker Drive Encryption to display the BitLocker Drive Encryption Control Panel window.

Before you can turn on BitLocker Drive Encryption for your computer, your machine must meet the following criteria:

✔ Your computer's hard drive must be formatted by using the NTFS system rather than the FAT or FAT32 file system.

✔ Your NTFS-formatted hard drive must be partitioned into two volumes: one that holds the drive with the operating system files (typically the C: drive) that BitLocker encrypts, and another partition that remains unencrypted in order to start the computer.

✔ Your computer must support and be equipped with a separate TPM (Trusted Platform Module) module or a USB flash drive on which BitLocker stores a recovery key. You'll need the recovery key to once again access the files on a BitLocker encrypted drive that Vista has locked up in response to a perceived security threat.

Don't attempt to engage BitLocker Drive Encryption on your computer if it does not meet these three criteria or your user account is not an administrator type. Also, be aware that if you turn on BitLocker encryption and Vista then detects any condition that it looks upon as a security risk (such as disk errors and changes to the computer's BIOS or Windows start-up files), it will then lock the drive. Should this happen, you *must* be able to produce the BitLocker recovery key and password in order to be able to access your hard drive's data files!

Parental Controls

Vista offers a set of parental controls to help control how children sharing the computer can use it. Vista's Parental Controls enable you to set limits on children's access to Web pages on the Internet, the hours they can use the computer, as well as the games they can play.

To open the Parental Controls window where you can set these limits for particular users, click Start ▶ Control Panel ▶ Security ▶ Parental Controls. Then click the name of the user for whom you want to set certain limits in the Choose a User and Set Up Parental Controls area of this window. Vista then opens a User Controls window for the user you select, similar to the one shown in Figure 6-1.

Figure 6-1

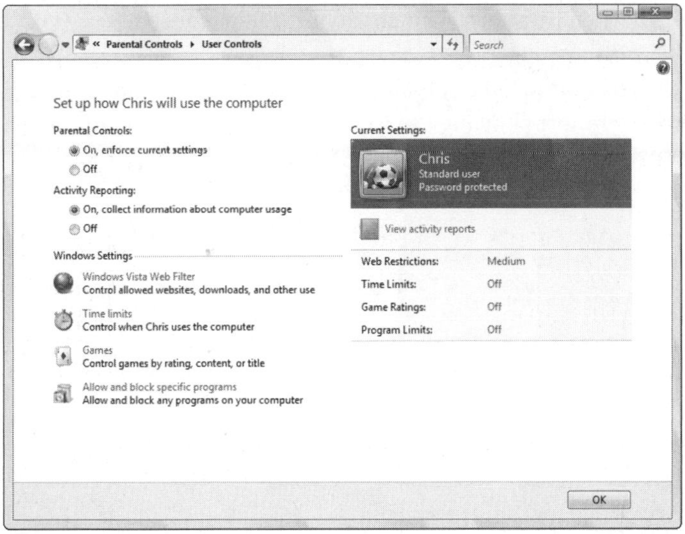

Set up how Chris will use the computer

Parental Controls:
- On, enforce current settings
- Off

Activity Reporting:
- On, collect information about computer usage
- Off

Windows Settings

Windows Vista Web Filter
Control allowed websites, downloads, and other use

Time limits
Control when Chris uses the computer

Games
Control games by rating, content, or title

Allow and block specific programs
Allow and block any programs on your computer

Current Settings:

Chris
Standard user
Password protected

View activity reports

Web Restrictions:	Medium
Time Limits:	Off
Game Ratings:	Off
Program Limits:	Off

OK

This User Controls window enables you to make the following changes to the selected user's settings:

- ✔ **Parental Controls** to turn on and off the enforcement of the parental control settings you put in place.

- ✔ **Activity Reporting** to turn on and off activity reporting that collects information about the selected user's computer usage.

- ✔ **Windows Vista Web Filter** to open a Web Restrictions window for the user (see Figure 6-2) where you can block particular Web sites, choose a restriction level of Web filtering (from Custom to High), select the type of Web content you want to block (from Alcohol to Weapons), and block downloading Internet files.

- ✔ **Time Limits** to open the Time Restrictions window for the user, where you can drag through the hours squares in the hours/days of the week matrix for each of the days you want to block computer usage — all red squares in the matrix represent hours that the user cannot log on the computer.

✔ **Games** to open the Game Controls window for the user where you can block the playing of particular computer games by the game's rating or content, or block its usage by name.

✔ **Allow and Block Specific Programs** to open the Application Restrictions window for the user, where you can click the check box for each program on the computer to which you want to allow access. Note that the selected user will then be able to launch any program whose check box you select in this window.

✔ **View Activity Reports** to open an Activity Viewer window containing a summary report showing the weekly computer activity of the user for whom you're setting these controls.

Figure 6-2

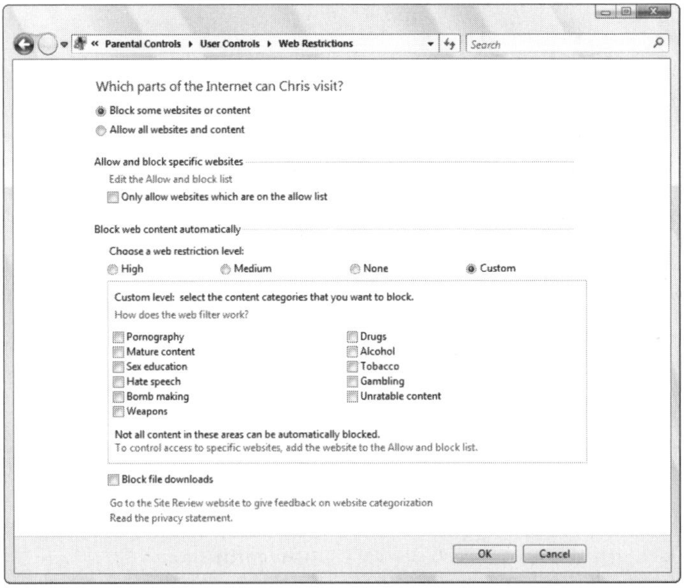

Security Center

The Windows Security Center window enables you to keep a watchful eye on all your computer's security settings. To open the Windows Security Center window, similar to the one shown in Figure 6-3, click Start ▶ Control Panel ▶ Security ▶ Security Center and then click expand buttons to the right of Firewall, Automatic Updating, Malware Protection, and Other Security Settings.

Figure 6-3

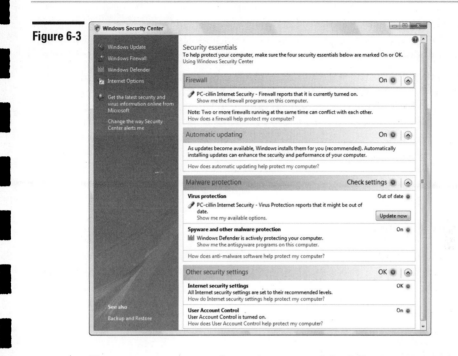

Here, you can see at a glance the status of the following security settings:

- ✔ **Firewall** displays whether the Windows firewall protection that helps block harmful information from entering your network from the Internet is active — to change the firewall settings, click the Windows Firewall link in the Security Center's Navigation pane.

- ✔ **Automatic Updating** displays whether the Windows Update program that checks online for important Windows updates that it can then download is operative — to change the Windows Update settings, click the Windows Update link in the Security Center's Navigation pane (*see* "Windows Update" in Part 5 for more information).

- ✔ **Malware Protection** displays whether your computer is running a third-party Virus Protection program and lets you know whether the Windows Defender anti-spyware program is running — to obtain information on various Virus Protection programs, click the Find a Program button. To change the Windows Defender settings, click the Windows Defender link in the Security Center's Navigation pane (*see* "Windows Defender" later in this part).

- ✔ **Other Security Settings** indicates the overall status of your computer's Internet security settings and your user account — to change your Internet security settings, click the Internet Options link in the Security Center's Navigation pane.

Click the Get the Latest Security and Virus Information from Microsoft link to go online to the Microsoft Security Web page, read the latest security and virus bulletins, and download important security updates for Windows Vista.

Clicking the Change the Way Security Center Alerts Me link in the Security Center's Navigation pane and then clicking the Don't Notify Me and Don't Display the Icon (Not Recommended) button in the Windows Security Center dialog box halts all security alerts. Don't do this unless you're certain that you no longer want Vista to display alerts in the Notification area of the taskbar when a threat to computer's security arises or one of your security utilities is inadvertently disabled.

User Account Control

The User Accounts Control Panel window (see Figure 6-4) contains the controls for adding users and changing the properties of existing user accounts on your computer.

Figure 6-4

To open the User Accounts Control Panel window, click Start ▶ Control Panel ▶ User Accounts and Family Safety ▶ User Accounts.

Managing your own account

The User Accounts Control Panel window contains the following links that enable you to make changes to your own account:

✔ **Create a Password for Your Account** to create a password for your account that you must reproduce each time you log on to, start, or unlock your computer. (*See* "Restart, Sleep/Hibernate, Lock, Log Off, and Shut Down" in Part 2.) If you already have a password assigned, you see a Change Your Password link you can click to modify your password and a Remove Your Password link you can click to delete your password without assigning a new one (assuming that you can correctly reproduce your current password).

✔ **Change Your Picture** to select a new picture to represent you on top of the Start menu and on various Vista start-up and welcome screens.

✔ **Change Your Account Name** to assign a new name to your account.

✔ **Change Your Account Type** to change your account type from Administrator to Standard User to restrict your ability to make changes to computer settings that affect its security — note that you can only change your account status from Administrator to Standard User provided that at least one other user account is currently designated as an administrator.

Managing other user accounts

If your user account is designated Administrator, you can not only make changes to your account name and your account type, but you can also manage other user accounts on the computer.

To add or make changes to other accounts on the computer, click the Manage Another Account link in the User Accounts Control Panel window. Doing this opens a Manage Accounts window.

To create a new account in the Manage Accounts window, click the Create a New Account link and then enter the account name. Designate the account as either Standard User or Administrator before you click the Create Account button.

Too many administrators on a single computer make it impossible to keep centralized control over the number and type of user accounts created on it. Therefore, keep the number of administrator accounts to a bare minimum. (I recommend just one, or perhaps two, if several people share the same computer and only one of them might be available when you need to make security setting changes on the machine.)

To modify the settings for an existing user account, click the name of the account you want to change to open the Change an Account window, which contains the following links:

✔ **Change the Account Name** to assign a new name to the user's account.

✔ **Create a Password** to create a password for the user's account that he must reproduce each time he logs on to, starts, or unlocks his computer (*see* "Restart, Sleep/Hibernate, Lock, Log Off, and Shut Down" in Part 2).

- ✓ **Change the Picture** to select a new picture to represent the user at the top of his Start menu and on various Vista start-up and welcome screens.

- ✓ **Set Up Parental Controls** to open the Parental Controls window where you can restrict the user's access to Web pages on the Internet, the hours he can use the computer, as well as the games he can play (*see* "Parental Controls" earlier in this part).

- ✓ **Delete the Account** to get rid of the account when it's no longer needed.

Changing the User Account Control status

If your user account is designated as Administrator, you can use the Turn User Account Control On or Off link at the bottom of the links in the User Accounts window to turn off the User Account Control for your computer by clearing the Use User Account Control (UAC) to Help Protect Your Computer check box in the Turn User Account Control On or Off window.

Although turning off UAC is not normally recommended, especially when you share the computer with several different people whose accounts are not designated as Administrator, you may want to do this if you are the sole user of the computer (as in a home situation) and you're not in an environment where other people (like roommates or friends who stop by) can mess up your settings. That way, you're no longer bothered by all those pesky permission alert dialog boxes each and every time you need to tweak the slightest of the computer's security settings.

Windows Defender

The Windows Defender enables you to scan your computer for any type of spyware that might have infected your computer (especially if you use Internet Explorer to subscribe to online services or make online purchases). To open the Windows Defender window similar to the one shown in Figure 6-5, click Start ▶ Control Panel ▶ Security ▶ Windows Defender.

After the Windows Defender window is open, you can click the Scan button to have Vista perform a quick scan of your computer and report on any spyware anomalies.

Figure 6-5

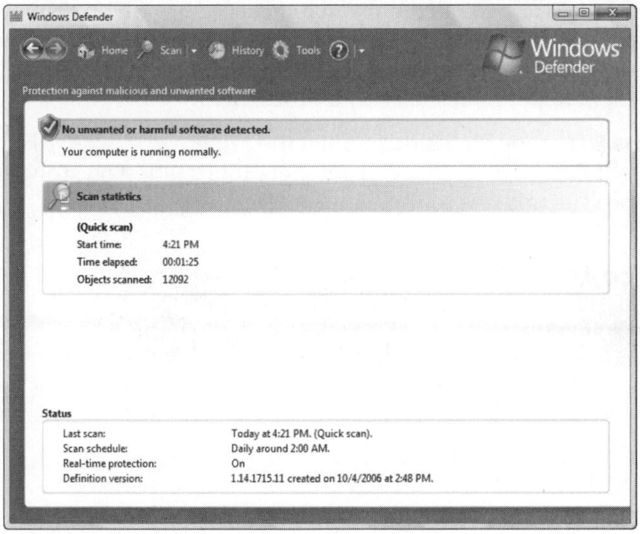

In addition, you can click the Tools button to display the Tools and Options screen of the Windows Defender shown in Figure 6-6. This screen includes the following options:

- ✔ **Options** to open the Options screen, where you can determine when or if automatic scanning takes place, what actions Vista is to take when it locates a potential spyware program, and turn on and off real-time protection (that alerts you right at the time a spyware program tries to install itself), as well as select the software and settings that you want Windows Defender to monitor.

- ✔ **Microsoft SpyNet,** to join the Microsoft SpyNet online community to share information about how Windows Defender responds to suspected spyware programs.

- ✔ **Quarantined Items,** to display all the programs that Windows Defender has quarantined by preventing them from running until you give the approval.

- ✔ **Software Explorer,** to open the Software Explorer window, which displays the classification of all the programs on your computer that Windows Defender monitors. The Software Explorer lets you to remove or just disable start-up programs or programs that are currently running on your computer. In addition, it lets you block incoming connections made to Web sites when Internet Explorer is running. You can also use the Software Explorer to reenable any programs that you previously disabled.

✔ **Allowed Items,** to open the Allowed Items window, which displays all the programs you've allowed despite warnings of their potential spyware status by Windows Defender and enables you to clear particular programs so that the Defender once again monitors them.

✔ **Windows Defender Web site,** to open the Windows Defender Home page in Internet Explorer, where you can get more information on stopping spyware as well as updates to the Windows Defender.

Figure 6-6

Part 7

Entertainment

Windows Vista is full of fun stuff to keep you entertained. In Vista, the diversions run the gamut from games to making your computer a part of your larger home entertainment center, thanks to Windows Media Center, shown in the following figure. Also part of the fun is Movie Maker, a video-editing program that you can use to turn your video clips into digital movies; Windows Media Player 11, which you can use to rip tracks from audio CDs as well as to play CDs and DVDs; and Windows Photo Gallery, which helps you organize your digital photos.

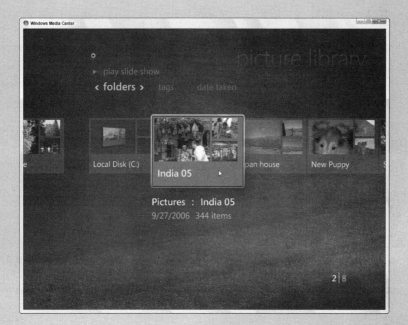

In this part . . .

- ✔ **Playing games on your PC**
- ✔ **Listening to music, viewing photos, and watching TV with the Media Center**
- ✔ **Playing music and DVDs with Windows Media Player**
- ✔ **Creating your own movies with Windows Movie Maker**
- ✔ **Maintaining your digital photos in the Windows Photo Gallery**

Games

Let the games begin! To open the Game window similar to the one shown in Figure 7-1 in Windows Vista, all you have to do is click Start ▶ Games. To play any of the games included with Vista, click the game to select it and then click the Play button on the Games window toolbar. Vista then opens the game in its own window.

Figure 7-1

Keep in mind that when you click a game in the Games window, the Details pane not only displays general information about the game's publisher and developer but also the date you last played the game. In addition, the Preview pane displays the game's rating: And, by the way, you don't have to worry about the content: All games supplied with Vista are rated E for Everyone.

You can get help on the rules for playing the game you've selected by clicking Help⇨View Help on the game window's pull-down menu or by pressing F1. If you have to close a game before you've had a chance to win, Vista gives you the option of saving the game in its present state when you close the game's window.

If you always want Vista to save your game when you exit it, click the Always Save Game on Exit check box before you click the Save button.

The next time you open the game that you've saved, Vista opens a Saved Game Found alert dialog box that asks you if you want to continue your saved game. To open the saved game rather than start a new one, click the Yes button in this alert dialog box.

Media Center

Windows Vista now integrates the Media Center as a part of its entertainment programs. Originally developed as an interface for the so-called Media Center PC (a computer running Windows XP that's specially configured for playing multimedia and often is equipped with a TV tuner card and a special wireless remote), you can use the Vista version of this nifty application to play music, view your digital pictures, play movies, and even watch and record TV (assuming that your computer is equipped with a TV tuner card).

Keep in mind that you can connect your computer that runs the Media Center for Vista to your home entertainment center by purchasing the Media Center Extender. You can connect your computer to your Xbox 360 by purchasing Media Center Extender for Xbox.

The first time you launch the Media Center, you see the Welcome to the Media Center Wizard that walks you through the steps of setting up the center for your screen display and configuring it to receive a TV signal and download the online TV guide, if your computer's equipped with a TV tuner card.

Thereafter, when you launch the Media Center (Start ▶ All Programs ▶ Media Center), the program opens full screen in a predominantly dark-blue window similar to the one shown in Figure 7-2. Because the Media Center options are designed to be accessed by using a special Media Center remote control (included with many Media Center PCs and with some brands of Media Center TV tuner cards) as well as with a standard computer mouse, its interface is much more fluid than what you find in other conventional Vista application windows (including the Windows Media Player) and dialog boxes.

The first thing you notice about the Media Center interface is the amount of audio and visual feedback it provides. At the time you launch the program and each time you select a menu option thereafter, Vista provides you with distinctive (and fairly harmonious) tones and clicks as well as visual clues to let you know which menu option you're about to select and when you've actually selected it.

The next thing to note is how easily you can cycle up and down through the main menu options either by positioning the mouse pointer on the up and down arrowheads (which look like white greater-than and less-than symbols rotated 90 degrees) or, if your mouse has a center wheel, by rolling it forward and backward to speed (and I do mean speed) through them. After you've highlighted the option you want, you can select it and display its submenu options by clicking the mouse button.

If you're using the Media Center remote control, you move up and down through the main menu options by pressing the device's up and down arrowheads (the black triangles pointing up and down). Click the OK button the center of the remote (separating these arrowheads) to select the main option you want.

Figure 7-2

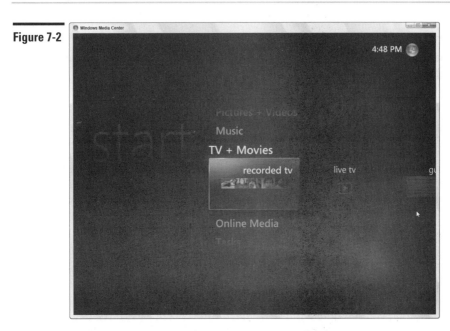

The Media Center's main menu options include

- ✔ **TV + Movies** to access live TV, recorded TV, and the online TV guide (if your computer has a TV tuner card and is connected to a cable or satellite dish), to play movies on DVD that you've inserted into your computer's DVD drive, and to get a listing of all the movies currently playing (assuming that you have a TV tuner card in your computer), or to search for movies on your computer by title, actor, or director

- ✔ **Online Media** to play your favorite games on the computer or access the Showcase, where you can sign up for special online services such as Comedy Central, MSN Remote Record (to schedule your TV recordings on the Web), ABC Enhanced TV and ABC Family, AOL Music, Napster, and MTV Overdrive to download music, and Movielink and CinemaNow to download movies

- ✔ **Tasks** to burn media files stored on your computer's hard drive to a CD or DVD (assuming that your computer has DVD recording capabilities), synchronize media between your computer and another device connected to it, shut down the Media Center, or add the Media Center Extender or Media Center Extender for Xbox and to change your Media Center settings

- ✔ **Pictures + Videos** to access the digital photos that are stored in your picture library, which you can then view as a slideshow, or to access the video files in your video library, which you can then play in the Media Center window

- ✔ **Music** to access your music library and play tunes saved in it or to listen to your favorite Internet radio stations

When you select the main menu option you want in the vertical listing, Media Center lists its submenu options horizontally. To view more submenu options, move the mouse pointer to the right, highlighting each one as you go, and then click the mouse button to select the one you want to use.

If you're using the Media Center remote control, press the right arrowhead key (with the black triangle pointing to the right) to highlight each option in succession and then click the OK button to select the one you want to use.

Some submenu options lead to yet further levels of suboptions. Keep in mind, however that you can always return to the previous level, all the way back to the main menu, by clicking the Back button (the black arrow pointing left that appears in a bar at the top of the Media Center window whenever you position the mouse pointer in this vicinity) or by pressing the Back button (which is labeled and uses the same black left-pointing arrow) when using the Media Center remote control.

When it's TV time

Who needs a separate TV when the Media Center is completely capable of playing your favorite TV shows right on your computer's fancy new 20-inch flat panel display? All you need to make this happen in Vista's Media Center is for your computer to be equipped with a TV tuner card and hooked up to your local cable system or a satellite TV dish.

To watch TV on your PC, you follow these steps:

1. Launch the Media Center by choosing Start ▶ All Programs ▶ Media Center.

   Press the green button (sporting the Windows four-color flag logo) on the Media Center remote control.

2. Highlight TV + Movies on the Media Center main menu and then click the Live TV option.

   Press the Live TV button on the Media Center remote.

3. Select the channel you want to watch either by entering the channel number from the keyboard and then pressing Enter, pressing the ↑ or ↓ key and then pressing Enter, or by clicking the CH plus (+) or minus (–) buttons on the playback controls displayed in the lower-right corner of the Media Center window when you position the mouse pointer in this area.

   Use the numeric keypad to type in the channel number.

4. To adjust the volume, click the plus (+) or minus (–) buttons that appear after the speaker icon on the playback controls displayed in the lower-right corner of the Media Center window when you position the mouse pointer in this area.

Click the plus (+) or minus (–) pad of the button marked Vol on the Media Center remote.

5. (Optional) To record the show you're watching, click the Record button on the playback controls displayed in the lower-right corner of the Media Center window.

Click the Record button on the Media Center remote.

Selecting TV programs to record

Instead of recording TV programs as you're watching them, you can use your TV guide to schedule recording ahead of time. That way, not only can you watch them whenever you want to, you can also use the Skip button (the one with the triangle pointing right against a vertical bar) either on the Media Center's playback controls or on the Media Center remote control to skip over all those annoying commercials.

To have the Media Center record a program, follow these steps:

1. Launch the Media Center by choosing Start ▶ All Programs ▶ Media Center.

Press the green button (sporting the Windows four-color flag logo) on the Media Center remote control.

2. Highlight TV + Movies on the Media Center main menu and then click the Guide option to display the online TV guide where you can select the program to record.

Press the Guide button on the Media Center remote.

3. Use the arrow keys on the keyboard to select the time and channel of a program playing sometime later in the day that you want the Media Center to record in the on-screen TV guide.

4. Press the Enter key to display a Program Info screen and then click its Record button — note that the program now displays a red dot in the TV guide indicating that it will be recorded.

Press the Record button on the Media Center remote.

If you want the Media Center to record all episodes of the show you've selected, click the Record Series button on the Program Info Media Center screen rather than the Record button.

TIP ◢ If you decide that you don't want to record one of the programs that you've selected for recording, click the program in the on-screen TV Guide and then click the Do Not Record button in the Program Info screen.

Watching recorded programs

After recording TV programs on your computer's hard drive, you can use the Media Center to play them back at any time you want. To do this, launch the Media Center and then highlight TV + Movies and then click Recorded TV (or press the Recorded TV button if your Media Center remote control has this button) to open the Recorded TV screen in the Media Center, similar to the one shown in Figure 7-3.

Figure 7-3

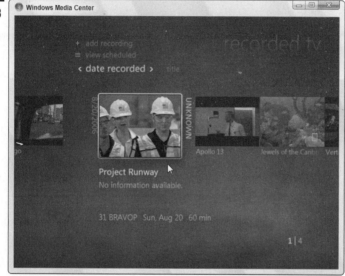

To play one of the recorded TV programs, click its thumbnail, press the Enter key to open its Program Info screen, and click its Play button.

The Media Center automatically deletes recorded programs according to the Keep Until settings (often a particular date or until the disk space is needed). To prevent Media Center from deleting a recorded program that you haven't yet seen, click the Keep Until button in the Program Info screen and then click the Keep Until I Watch or Keep Until I Delete items.

Playing your favorite tunes

You can use the Media Center rather than the Windows Media Player to play the music you've stored on your computer's hard drive. To do this, launch the Media Center and then click Music ▶ Music Library (or press the My Music button on the Media Center remote control) to open the Music Library screen in the Media Center.

To play a song, click its album thumbnail in the Music Library screen. To play all the tracks on the album, click the Play Album button in the Album Details screen. To play a single track from the album, click its name and then click the Add to Queue button or the Play button in the on-screen playback controls.

Playing your much-loved movies

The Media Center (as well as the Windows Media Player) can play movies stored on DVD disc — either those that you create with the Windows DVD Maker or professionally produced DVDs that you purchase or rent. To play a DVD with Media Center, insert the DVD disc you want to play in your DVD drive. Launch the Media Center and then click TV + Movies ▶ Play DVD (or press the DVD Menu button on the Media Center remote control) to open the DVD's main menu, where you can then select the option you want such as Chapter List, Language Selection, Bonus Materials, Play or Play Movie, and the like.

Click the Pause button if you need to temporarily pause the movie. If you click the Stop button on Media Center playback controls or press it on the remote control, the Media Center displays a screen of options, including Resume to resume the movie from the frame where you selected Stop, Restart to restart the movie from the beginning, and Eject to open the DVD drive so you can remove the disc.

Viewing your preferred photos and videos

Instead of using the Windows Photo Gallery to view the digital photos you store on your computer and the Windows Media Player to play back your videos (both of which are discussed later in this part), you can use the Media Center. To view your photos, launch Media Center and then click Pictures + Videos ▶ Picture Library (or press the My Pictures button on the Media Center remote control).

The Media Center then displays all the digital photos it has catalogued in your Picture Library by date. To display the photos by folder, click the Folders option. To open a folder and display its photos, click its name. Figure 7-4 shows you the photos stored in a folder called Tibet in the Pictures folder on my hard drive as they appear in my Picture Library in the Media Center.

To scroll quickly (and I do mean, quickly) through the photos, position the mouse pointer on the left or right edge of the screen with the displayed thumbnails. A < or > symbol appears on the screen as you fly through the thumbnails. When you locate a photo that you want to view full size in the Picture Library screen or an image that want to be the first in a slide show, click its thumbnail. To manually scroll through the photos, press the → or ← key. To start a slide show that automatically scrolls through each of the images one after the other, click the Play button in the on-screen playback controls. (You can also start a slide show from the very first photo by clicking the Play Slideshow link in the Picture Library.)

Figure 7-4

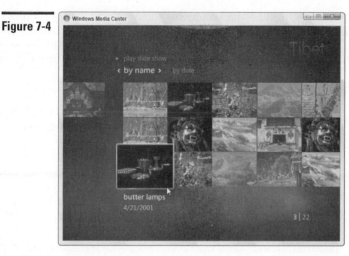

If you want to play a video you've stored on your computer rather than view photos, all you need to do is open the Video Library by clicking Pictures + Videos ▶ Video Library from the Media Center Start screen (or by pressing the My Videos button on the Media Center remote control). To play a video in the library, you simply click its thumbnail.

Windows DVD Maker

Vista's new Windows DVD Maker program enables you to burn video DVDs by using digital photos or videos you've saved on your computer that you can then play back in stand-alone DVD players connected to a TV. Best of all, this handy little program lets you create menus for your video DVD just like those created for professional movies released on DVD disc for purchase or rent. All you need is a DVD drive on your computer that is capable of writing DVDs and a blank DVD disc.

To create a new video DVD disc with Windows DVD Maker, follow these steps:

1. Insert a blank DVD disc into your computer's DVD drive.

2. Click Start ▶ All Programs ▶ Windows DVD Maker to launch Windows DVD Maker.

3. (Optional) If the Share Your Memories on a DVD start screen appears (because you didn't remove the check mark from the Don't Show This Page Again check box), you must click the Choose Photos and Videos command button in the initial Windows DVD Maker window to open the Add Pictures and Video to the DVD screen.

4. Click the Add Items button on the Windows DVD Maker window's toolbar to display the Add Items to DVD dialog box.

5. Select all the digital videos you want to add to your DVD by clicking the appropriate media folder in the Favorite Links section of the Navigation pane and then selecting their file icons before you click Add.

   Hold down the Ctrl key and click individual icons to select multiple video files for the DVD.

6. Replace the title with the current date that automatically appears in the Disc Title text box in the lower portion of the Windows DVD Maker window with a title that you want to appear on the DVD menu.

7. (Optional) After selecting all the video files for the DVD, select the video thumbnail and then use the Move Up or Move Down button to modify the order in which they automatically play on the DVD.

8. (Optional) Click the Options link to the immediate right of the Disc Title text box to open the DVD Options dialog box, and then make any necessary changes to how the DVD plays, its aspect ratio (4:3 or 16:9), or its video format (NTSC or PAL) before you click OK.

   If you're making the DVD for a DVD player sold in the United States you won't need to change the Video Format option from NTSC to PAL.

9. Click Next to open the Ready to Burn Disc screen in the Windows DVD Maker window (see Figure 7-5).

10. Click the thumbnail with the type of menu style you want your DVD disc to use in the Menu Styles list box on the right side of Windows DVD Maker window.

    Note that you can click the Menu Text button to customize the text that appears on the buttons used by the menu style you select. You can also click the Customize Menu button if you want to modify certain aspects of the menu style, including adding a foreground or background video as well as a menu audio track that plays until the user selects one of the menu options.

11. (Optional) Click the Preview button on the Windows DVD Maker window's toolbar to preview it and then, after experimenting with the menu and previewing your video content, click OK.

12. Click the Burn button below the Menu Styles list box to start burning your videos to the DVD disc.

After you click Burn, a Burning dialog box appears, which keeps you informed of the progress of the burn. After the entire project is burned to disc, Windows DVD Maker automatically ejects the DVD disc.

Figure 7-5

If you want to make another copy of the DVD, replace the ejected disc with a new blank disc and then click the Make Another Copy of This Disc link in the Your Disc Is Ready dialog box. If you don't want to make another copy, remove the ejected disc, close the DVD drive door, and then click the Close button in the dialog box instead.

> **TIP** When using Windows DVD Maker to create a slide show of a selection of your digital photos, click the Slideshow button on the Windows DVD Maker window's toolbar so that you can customize the number of seconds each photo in the slide show is displayed, the type of transition to use when going from one image to another, and to add any background music you want playing during the show.

Windows Media Player 11

You can use Windows Media Player 11 to play audio, video, and animation files that you either save on your computer or (if you have a fast connection to the Internet, also known as *broadband*) play online as they're being downloaded to your computer (a technique known as *streaming*). This means that you can use Windows Media Player to play Internet radio stations, as well as to view video clips from trailers from upcoming movies. Of course, the most important thing is that Windows Media Player also plays all the MP3 (short for MPEG3, which is a compression scheme developed by the motion picture entertainment industry) audio files that you've downloaded from your favorite music Web sites, including URGE, the most recent addition to Napster, Rhapsody, and all the rest.

To launch the Windows Media Player, click the Media Player button (shown in the left margin) on the taskbar's Quick Launch toolbar or click Start ▶ All Programs ▶ Windows Media Player. You're able to use Windows Media Player in one of three modes:

> ✔ **Full mode** (Ctrl+1) shown in Figure 7-6 (the default)

> ✔ **Skin mode** (Ctrl+2) shown in Figure 7-7

> ✔ **Minimized mode** on the Vista taskbar shown in Figure 7-8

 TIP 🎯 When the Media Player is in Full Mode, you can collapse it into a compact mode wherein only the name of the song playing along with the Stop, Previous, Play/Pause, Next, Mute, and Volume buttons are displayed. To do this, click the Switch to Compact Mode button. (This button then turns into a Return to Full Mode button that you can click to restore Full Mode.)

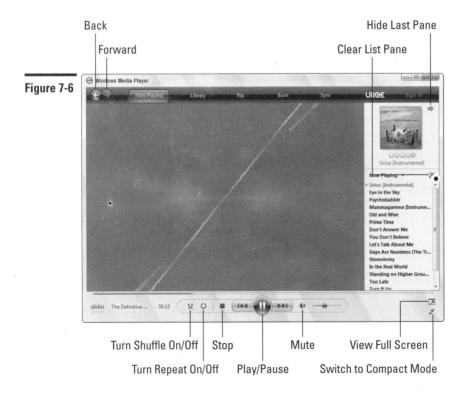

Figure 7-6

Back

Forward

Hide Last Pane

Clear List Pane

Turn Shuffle On/Off   Stop   Mute   View Full Screen

Turn Repeat On/Off   Play/Pause   Switch to Compact Mode

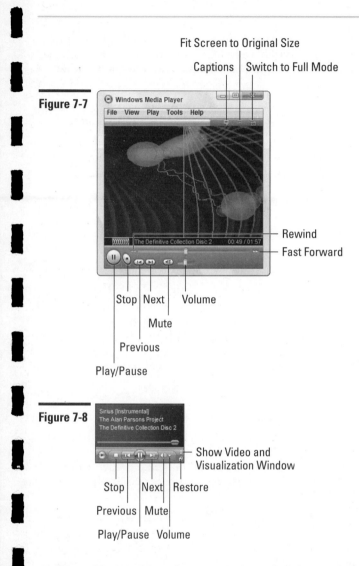

Figure 7-7

Fit Screen to Original Size
Captions
Switch to Full Mode
Windows Media Player
File View Play Tools Help
The Definitive Collection Disc 2
00:49 / 01:57
Rewind
Fast Forward
Stop
Next
Volume
Mute
Previous
Play/Pause

Figure 7-8

Sirius [Instrumental]
The Alan Parsons Project
The Definitive Collection Disc 2
Show Video and Visualization Window
Stop
Next
Restore
Previous
Mute
Play/Pause
Volume

TIP

You can also play music or watch videos in full-screen mode by pressing Alt+Enter or by clicking the View Full Screen button in the lower-right corner when the Windows Media Player is in full mode. In full-screen mode, the music visualization or video takes up the entire screen except for a bar at the bottom that contains the playback controls and an Exit Full-Screen Mode button on the far right.

When you use Windows Media Player in full mode, the program displays a toolbar at the top of the window that contains a number of buttons that you can use to switch between the types of media that you're playing, and to control how you view and play them:

- **Now Playing:** Media Player shows the video you're playing or represents the audio you're playing with some sort of visual pattern representing the sounds.

- **Library:** Media Players shows you all the music on your computer and enables you to select audio files to play and arrange them into playlists.

- **Rip:** Media Player rips the tracks from an audio CD that you insert in your computer's CD/DVD drive.

- **Burn:** Media Player burns tracks saved in your music library to a CD disc in your CD/DVD drive.

- **Sync:** Synchronizes content to and from a compatible portable device you have connected to your computer such as a portable MP3 player.

- **URGE:** Connects you to the URGE music store, where you can purchase tunes for playback on Windows Media Player. If you sign up for an URGE subscription, the Media Player then adds a Sign In button to the right of the URGE button. After you sign in, you can play snippets of your favorite tunes and possibly download them. (**See** "When you get the URGE for music" later in this part for details.)

Now Playing

When you click the Now Playing button on the Media Player's toolbar, the program shows you the video movie or video DVD you're playing. If you're playing music instead of video in the Media Player, the program then represents the sounds visually. You can then use the buttons on its playback controller (see Figure 7-6) to manage the playback.

When the Play List pane is displayed in the Now Playing view (Now Playing ▶ Show List Pane), you can select a new track to play from the currently playing CD or playlist, a new video, or a new chapter in the currently playing DVD by double-clicking their names in the list.

 To change the visualization for audio, click Now Playing ▶ Visualizations and then click the type of visualization (Album Art, Alchemy, Bars and Waves, or Battery), followed by the name of the visualization (when there's more than one). To tweak to the audio and video settings for the Media Player, click Now Playing ▶ Enhancements ▶ Show Enhancements. Click the ▶ button to cycle through the various enhancements: Graphic Equalizer, Media Link for E-Mail, Play Speed Settings, Quiet Mode, SRS WOW Effects, Video Settings, Color Chooser, and Crossfading, and Auto Volume Leveling, or click these items on the Enhancements submenu listed below the Show Enhancements item.

Using the Media Library

The Media Library in the Windows Media Player enables you to view and organize all the various types of media files (music, photos, video, and recorded TV) that Media Player can deal with currently in your Media Library. When you first open the Media Library by clicking the Library button on the Media Player toolbar, the music category is automatically selected (as shown in Figure 7-9 when the List pane is closed). All the music files found on your computer appear in Expanded Tile view in alphabetical order by artist and album.

View Options

Layout Options

Show List Pane

Figure 7-9

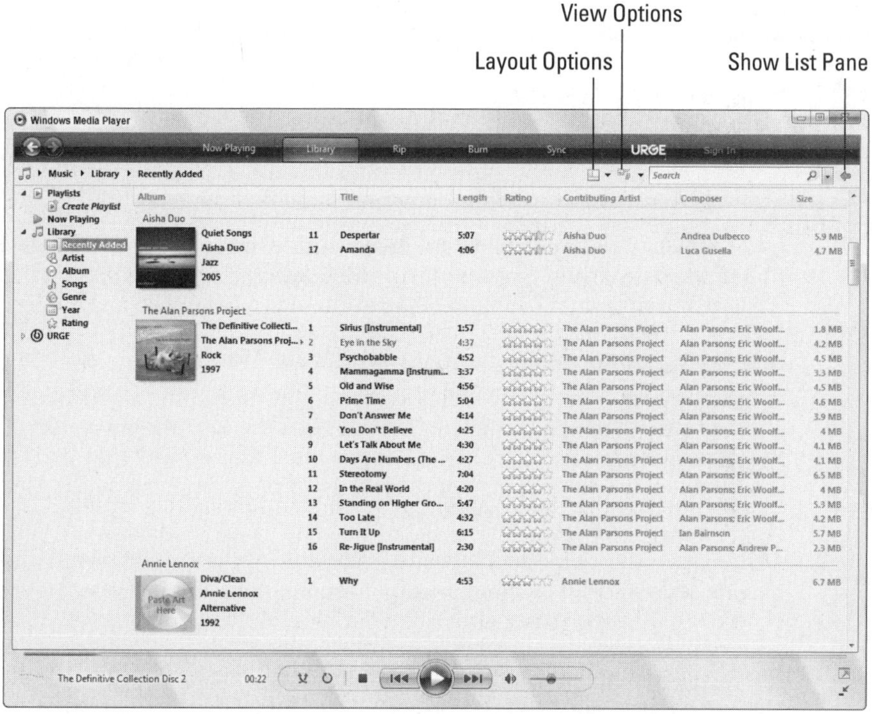

You can then reorder this list of music files by selecting another link — Recently Added, Artist, Album, Songs, Genre, Year, or Rating — in the Navigation pane and then selecting another view on the View Options button's drop-down list.

TIP

Vista automatically adds all media files that it finds in the Documents folder to the Media Library of the Windows Media Player. To manually add other media files to the Media Library, click Library ▶ Add to Library to open the Add to Library dialog box. Click the Advanced Options button and then select all the folders and drives in the list box whose media files you want added to the Library.

Creating playlists

To select the music you want to play in the Media Player, simply drag the icon of album or songs you want to hear to the List Pane (in the area that says "Drag Items Here") and then click the Play button on the playback controller at the bottom of the window.

To save the list of songs you've manually assembled in the List Pane as a playlist that you can then later play by simply selecting the playlist's name in the Media Player's Navigation pane, click the Save Playlist button at the bottom of the List Pane and then enter a name for the new playlist in the text box that appears above the first song selection. Press Enter.

After creating a playlist, you can play its songs simply by opening the Media Library, locating the playlist in the Playlists section of the Navigation pane, and then dragging it to the List Pane.

You can edit the contents of a playlist at any time after creating it. To remove a song from the list, right-click it and then click Remove From List on its shortcut menu. To change the order of a song in the list, right-click it and then click Move Up or Move Down on its shortcut menu as needed to get it into the desired position in the list. To add a new song to the playlist, drag its icon from the Media Library and drop it at the desired position in the list in the List Pane.

Displaying other media types in the Media Library

You can use the Windows Media Player to play more than audio files. To display another type of media file in the Library, click the Library button and then select the type of media: Pictures, Video, or Record TV, assuming that you have a TV tuner connected to your computer and use a program such as the Media Center to record TV programs. (*See* "Media Center" earlier in this part for details.)

Although Windows Media Player 11 is capable of displaying digital photos and playing recorded TV programs, I don't recommend Media Player as your first choice for showing either type of media files. Instead, use the Windows Photo Gallery to manage and view your photos (*see* "Windows Photo Gallery" later in this part): It enables you tag and edit photos and has a terrific slide show. Use Media Center to play your recorded TV programs because it enables you to fast-forward through those awful, incessant commercials (and Windows Media Player does not).

Ripping and burning CDs

You can use the Rip button on the Windows Media Player toolbar to rip tracks from audio CDs you own for playback on your computer or on a compatible portable MP3 player. Likewise, you can use its Burn button to burn tracks to a blank CD disc.

To rip tracks from an audio CD and save them on your computer's hard drive, insert the audio CD into your computer's CD/DVD drive, and then click the Rip button on the toolbar. The Media Player then opens a screen, similar to the one shown in Figure 7-10, displaying all the tracks on the CD along with the status of the burn progress for each track. Be aware that Media Player automatically copies all tracks in the Windows Media Audio file format. To rip the tracks by using the more compressed MP3 file format, you need to click Rip ▶ Format ▶ MP3 before you insert the audio CD in the computer's drive.

Figure 7-10

To burn tracks to a blank CD disc, insert the blank disc in your computer's CD/DVD drive and then click the Burn button on the Media Player toolbar. The Media Player then displays a Burn List in the List Pane where you assemble the tracks you want to copy to a blank CD disc by dragging their album and song icons from the Media Library, or by dragging their playlists and then dropping them on the "Drag Items Here" section.

After you've assembled all the tracks in the order in which you want them copied in the Burn List, click the Start Burn button at the bottom of the List Pane in the Media Player.

When you get the URGE for music

URGE is the name of the new online MTV Networks digital music service integrated into Windows Media Player 11. URGE offers you the opportunity to either purchase music by the song or by the album. You can also sign up for one of two monthly download subscriptions: All Access, which allows unlimited download and playback on just your computer, or the All Access To Go service, which allows unlimited download and playback on your computer as well as four other machines, including portable MP3 players such as the iriver clix and the Creative ZEN Vision:M.

To access the URGE online music store, click the URGE button at the far-right end of the Windows Media Player toolbar. The first time you click this button, a Confirm Software Download dialog box appears that asks for confirmation in downloading the URGE software and accepting the store's end user license agreement. After clicking the I Accept button and downloading the software, the URGE Home screen appears in the Windows Media Player window. Here, you can sign up and start purchasing and downloading the music you want to listen to.

After establishing an account at the URGE Web site, you can click any of the links that appear in the upper part of the Windows Media Player window when you mouse over the Guide button: MTV, VH1, CMT, Informer Blogs, Feature Stories, Playlists, Radio, New Releases, Charts, Genres, or Feeds. Figure 7-11 shows the URGE Home displaying its latest offerings in the Windows Media Player window.

Using the Media Guide

The Windows Media Player gives you access to all the various media files on its WindowsMedia.com Web site. These media files include videos of the latest song releases, video clips for the latest TV shows, movie releases, and top news stories as well as video games and online radio stations whose music you can play with the Windows Media Player.

Figure 7-11

To display the Media Guide in the Media Player window, click URGE ▶ Media Guide. Then click the link at the top of the Media Guide screen to access the part of the guide you're interested in browsing: Music, Movies, Entertainment, Radio, Current Events, or Site Index.

Keep in mind that many of the clips available for download from the WindowsMedia.com Web site are quite large in size and therefore require a broadband Internet connection if you want to download them sometime in the 21st century. Also, remember that after clicking a link to a video file in the Media Guide, you still need to click the Now Playing button in order to actually be able to see the video as it's playing in the Media Player.

Synching up with a portable MP3 player

If you own a compatible portable MP3 player such as the iriver clix or a Creative ZEN Vision:M, you can synchronize the music files (as well as photos and videos, if your device can display and play them) in your Media Library with the portable device.

To do this, first connect your portable device to the computer and then, if a dialog box asking you to sync with Windows Media Player doesn't automatically appear, launch the Media Player and then click the Sync button on its toolbar. Next, drag all the media files (including playlists) you want to copy onto the portable device from the main area of the Media Player to the Sync List in its Reader pane, and then, finally, click the Start Sync button at the bottom of the pane.

To display media files that you want to add to the Sync List, expand the Playlists or Library link in the Navigation pane and then click the particular link of interest to display its files or click the Library button and select the media type on its pop-up menu (Music, Pictures, Video, or Recorded TV). After displaying the media files you want to add, click the Sync button again to display the Sync List where you can add them.

If your portable device is capable of displaying photos and playing videos, you can sync these files as well by dragging them to the Sync List.

The Windows Media Player then displays each of the files you added to the Sync List in the main area of the Windows Media Player, showing you the progress on synchronizing each file. To stop the synchronization before all the files you added to the Sync List are copied, click the Stop Sync button. When Media Player finishes synchronizing all the files added to the Sync List, it then displays the free space left on your portable device at the top of the Reader pane.

Windows Movie Maker

You can use the Windows Movie Maker program to capture video and audio clips, which you can then edit and arrange into your very own movies. You can play these movie files on your computer or distribute them to family, friends, and colleagues by e-mail so that they can play them on their computers.

Launch Windows Movie Maker by selecting Start ▶ All Programs ▶ Windows Movie Maker. Windows Movie Maker opens its program window full screen, similar to the one shown in Figure 7-12 (except that yours doesn't have any content in it).

The Windows Movie Maker window is divided into several different sections:

- ✔ **Task Area,** which contains links to all the common Movie Maker tasks and subdivided into three major tasks: Import for bringing video clips into a collection; Edit for adding video effects, transitions, and titles; and Publish To for rendering the final movie so that you can save it on your computer, send in an e-mail message, upload it to a Web site, or transfer it to a tape on a digital video camera.

- ✔ **Collections Area,** which shows thumbnails of the various still graphic images, video clips, and audio clips in that collection that you can add to your movie by dragging them to the storyboard area or by clicking the thumbnail and pressing Ctrl+D.

Figure 7-12

✔ **Storyboard Area** or **Timeline Area** along the bottom of the window, which either contains the storyboard view (the default), indicating the progression of the movie video clips, or the timeline view (View⇨Timeline or Ctrl+T), indicating the order and duration of both the video and audio (in separate tracks).

✔ **Preview Area,** which displays whatever video image or clip is selected in the Collections Area. You can also use this area to preview the movie that you're putting together by clicking the various control buttons (which use the standard VCR-control symbols) or by dragging the slider bar located under the preview window.

Importing media files and capturing video clips

To add the media clips for your movie, you have a choice between importing existing media files and capturing video clips directly from your video camera:

✔ Import sound files, graphic images, and video clips into the collections area (by clicking the Import Media button or pressing Ctrl+I) and then selecting the audio files, photos, video clips, or even finished movies to add in the Import Media Items window.

✔ If you've attached a movie camera to your computer, you can digitally capture video footage as clips to add to your movie project by clicking the From Digital Video Camera link in the Tasks area or press Ctrl+R and then entering a name for the clip, the location, and the video file format in the Import Video: Microsoft DV Camera and VCR window. Leave the Import the Entire Videotape to My Computer option button selected to record all of its scenes or, after cueing up the tape to the place you want to start importing, click the Only Import Parts of the Videotape to My Computer option button.

TIP

After capturing your video footage into individual date-and-time-stamped video clips, Movie Maker automatically adds them to the Collections Area. From there, you can add the clips to your project in the Storyboard or Timeline by dragging them to it or by selecting them and pressing Ctrl+D.

Assembling media files in your movie

To assemble the graphic images, sound files, and video clips you've added to your movie project, you sequence them in the work area in one of two views:

✔ Choose the Storyboard View (View⇨Storyboard) to add video clips or still graphic images to the movie — you can also use this view to check and alter the order and duration of these video elements.

✔ Choose the Timeline View (View➪Timeline), shown in Figure 7-13. to add audio clips to the track beneath the video or to add a title overlay that appears in all video clips (or both) — you can also use this view to change the sequence of the audio clips in relation to the video elements in the movie.

To preview your edits to get an idea of how they will play in the final version of the movie, choose Play➪Play Storyboard, press Ctrl+W, or click the Play button on the controls under the Preview area (the one with the triangle pointing to the right). To pause the movie, press Ctrl+W again or click the Pause button in the preview controls (the one with the two vertical bars). To save your editing work, choose File➪Save Project (Ctrl+S) and give the project a new filename. Windows Movie Maker automatically appends the filename extension MSWMM (for Microsoft Windows Movie Maker) to whatever filename you give the project.

Adding special effects to clips

Movie Maker includes a variety of special effects that you can apply to the clips you've added to your movie. These effects run the gamut from the 3D Ripple effect all the way to the Zoom, Focus Upper Right effect. They also include the ever-popular Fade In, From Black to fade the image in from a solid black background and Fade Out, To Black to fade out the image to a solid black background.

Figure 7-13

To add a special effect to a clip in the project, click the Effects link in the Edit section of the Tasks Area to display a list of all the special effects supported by Windows Movie Maker. To preview a particular effect, click its thumbnail in the Collections Area and then click the Play button (the one with the triangle pointing right) in the Preview Area.

After you locate the special effect that you want to use, drag the effect's thumbnail from the Collections Area and then drop it on the clip in the Storyboard. Movie Maker then adds a star icon to the lower-left corner of the clip in the Storyboard indicating that you've added an effect to it. To delete an effect from a clip, all you have to do is right-click this star icon and then click Remove Effects Del on its shortcut menu.

TIP You can add comic effects to your video clips with the Slow Down, Half effect that plays the video footage at half normal speed and the Speed Up, Double effect that plays the footage at twice normal speed.

Adding transitions

Transitions are the effects that smooth out the changeover from one clip to the next in the movie project. In Windows Movie Maker, the transitions run the gamut from Bars, Horizontal to Zig Zag, Vertical.

To add a transition between two clips in the project, click the Transitions link in the Edit section of the Tasks Area to display a list of all the transitions supported by Windows Movie Maker. To preview a particular transition, click its thumbnail in the Collections Area and then click the Play button (the one with the triangle pointing right) in the Preview Area.

After you locate the transition you want to use, drag the transition's thumbnail from the Collections Area and then drop it on the blank square between the two clips in the Storyboard. Movie Maker then adds the transition's icon to a square between those clips in the Storyboard, indicating the type of transitions you've added. To delete a transition, click its icon in the Storyboard and then press the Delete key.

Adding movie titles and credits

Windows Media Player enables you to add credits to the beginning or end of your movie as well as to add titles to individual photo and video clips. To add titles and credits to your movie, you need to click the Titles and Credits link in the Edit section of the Task Area and then click one of the following links that then appear in the Where Do You Want to Add a Title? section of the Windows Movie Maker window:

- **Title at the Beginning** to add a title as the very first frame of your movie

- **Title Before the Selected Clip** to add a title to a new frame that is inserted immediately in front of the clip that's currently selected in the Storyboard

✔ **Title Overlay on the Selected Clip** to add a title to the frame that's currently selected in the Storyboard

✔ **Credits at the End** to add movie credits as the final frame of the movie

After you finish adding the text for your title, click the Add title to insert its text into the movie project.

Publishing the final movie

When you finish your edits and are satisfied with the final version, you need to convert your Windows Movie Maker project into a movie that Windows Media Player can use. To do this, click the Publish button on the Windows Movie Maker toolbar or choose File⇨Publish Movie on the menu bar (Ctrl+P) to open the Publish Movie dialog box entitled Where Do You Want to Publish Your Movie?. (Be sure that you don't use File⇨Save Project, because that action saves the project file only for playing in Windows Movie Maker.)

If you know the type of media to which you want to publish your movie project, you can just click its link (This Computer, DVD, Recordable CD, E-Mail, or Digital Video Camera) in the Publish To section of the Tasks area.

In the initial Publish Movie dialog box, choose the movie location (This Computer, DVD, Recordable CD, E-Mail, or Digital Video Camera) and then click the Next button to open the screen entitled, Name the Movie You Are Publishing.

Then edit the movie title (as in *Puppy Play*) if you want it to be different from the movie project name in the File Name text box. Select the folder in which to save the movie in the Publish To drop-down list box before clicking Next to open the Publish Movie dialog box entitled Choose the Settings for Your Movie (see Figure 7-14).

Note that when saving the movie to your hard drive, this screen of the Publish Movie dialog box also prompts you to select the video quality, which directly affects its file size. (Higher quality equals a larger file size.) By default, Vista selects Best Quality for Playback on My Computer. If space is at a premium on your system, click the Compress To option button and then use the spinner buttons to select a smaller compressed size. Alternatively, click the More Settings option button, which enables you to create a smaller-size movie file by selecting the device it's going to be played back on (DVD, DVD Widescreen, HD, Low Bandwidth, or VHS Quality) and the rate at which the video data can be sent (Mbps for megabits per second or Kbps for kilobytes per second).

After you finish specifying the vital information for the type of location you select, Vista publishes the movie by saving your movie to the designated location in the selected format.

Figure 7-14

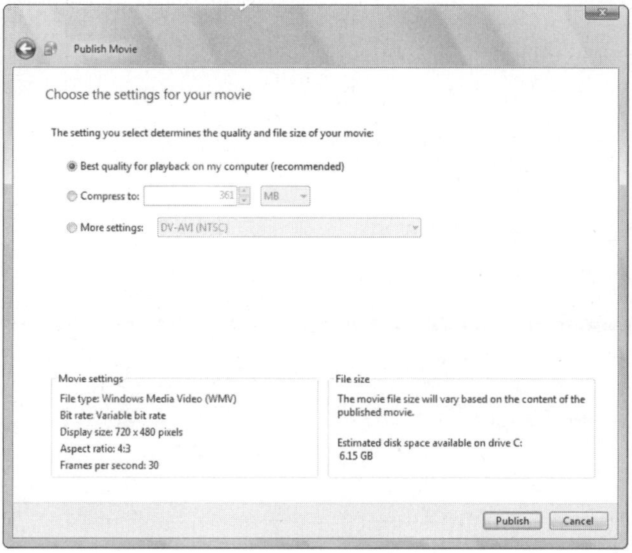

When Windows Movie Maker finishes publishing the movie, Vista automatically plays it in Windows Media Player when you click the Finish button. If you don't want to view the movie right away, click the Play Movie When I Finish check box to remove its check mark before you click the Finish button.

Then after closing the Windows Movie Maker window, you can test out your finished movie in the Windows Media Player: Simply open the folder where the movie was saved and double-click the file icon to open both the movie file and Windows Media Player and then click the Play button.

Windows Photo Gallery

The Windows Photo Gallery is a brand-new Windows Vista utility that enables you to more easily keep track of and manage the digital photos and videos that you save on your computer. To open the Windows Photo Gallery window similar to the one shown in Figure 7-15, click Start ▶ All Programs ▶ Windows Photo Gallery.

When you first open the Windows Photo Gallery window, the All Pictures and Videos favorite link is selected in its Navigation pane so that thumbnails of all the photo and video media files on your computer are displayed, grouped by the date they were taken.

Figure 7-15

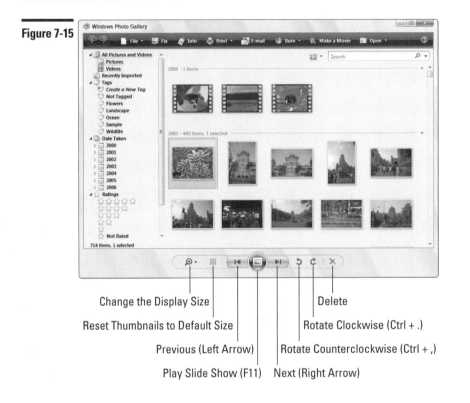

Change the Display Size   Delete

Reset Thumbnails to Default Size   Rotate Clockwise (Ctrl + .)

Previous (Left Arrow)   Rotate Counterclockwise (Ctrl + ,)

Play Slide Show (F11)   Next (Right Arrow)

 Keep in mind that you can change the orientation of any photo displayed in the Gallery that was taken when you rotated the camera 90 degrees to the left or right so as to fit a tall image in the picture. Simply click the Rotate Counterclockwise button in the image controls at the bottom of the window or press the Ctrl+comma (,) key combination to rotate counterclockwise. To rotate clockwise, click the Rotate Clockwise button or press the Ctrl+period (.) key combination.

 When you click the Change the Display Size button in the image controls at the bottom of the Gallery window, a slider appears that you can drag up and down to quickly make all the media files' thumbnails larger or smaller. Then click the Set Default Thumbnail Size button to its immediate right or press Ctrl+0 (zero) to immediately reset all the thumbnails to their original, default size in the Gallery.

To filter which media files are displayed in the Windows Photo Gallery window, expand the desired category link in the Navigation pane by clicking the ▶ symbol in front of the link name and then click the filtering criterion in the list. For example, to display only pictures taken in 2006 in the Windows Photo Gallery, I would first click Pictures in the All Pictures and Videos category followed by 2006 in the Date Taken category.

To change the view used to display the photo and video media files shown in the Windows Photo Gallery, click the Choose a Thumbnail View button to the immediate left of the Search box and then click the desired menu item:

✔ **Thumbnails** (default) to display just the thumbnail pictures for each photo and video media file displayed in the Gallery

✔ **Thumbnails with Text** to add text to each media file thumbnail displayed in the Gallery, reflecting the Arrange By option currently selected (dates, if Date Taken is selected, filenames if File Name is selected, and so on)

✔ **Tiles** to display the media files displayed in the Gallery as tiles, that is, as thumbnails arranged in two columns with pertinent information including filename, file size, duration (for video), image size (for photos), five-star rating, and caption (if assigned) displayed to the immediate right of the thumbnail image

✔ **Group By** to determine whether the media file thumbnails displayed in the Gallery are ordered into groups and, if so, using what attribute (Date Taken, File Size, Image Size, Rating, and so on)

✔ **Sort By** to determine the order in which the media file thumbnails displayed in the Gallery appear (sorted by Date Taken, File Size, Image Size, Caption, File Name, and so on in either Ascending or Descending order)

✔ **Table of Contents** to add a column to the Windows Photo Gallery with links representing the major attributes selected with the Group By option that you can click to jump immediately to that group in the Gallery window

✔ **Refresh** to have Vista do a search for all the newly added photo and video media files in the folders you've added to the Windows Photo Gallery

The toolbar at the top of the Windows Photo Gallery window contains the following buttons that you can use to manage your photo and video media files:

✔ **File** to perform all file-related tasks on selected files including duplicating, renaming, copying, and deleting them as well as adding new folders to the Gallery, importing images from a scanner or camera, and syncing images and videos to a compatible portable device.

✔ **Fix** to open a selected photo in a special Gallery window containing controls for adjusting the image's color and exposure, cropping the image, and fixing red eye (*see* "Fixing a photo" later in this part).

✔ **Info** to display a Reader pane on the right side of the Windows Photo Gallery window containing a thumbnail with all vital information about a photo or video, such as ratings, search tags, and, in the case of photos, a caption. (*See* "Adding ratings, tags, and captions" later in this part.)

✔ **Print** to print all selected photos in the Gallery or to open the Order Prints dialog box, where you can select an online printing company from which you can order professional prints of your photos.

✔ **E-mail** to open a new e-mail message in Windows Mail with the selected media files attached. When you select photos to attach to a new message, Vista first opens an Attach Pictures and Files dialog box, where you can select the size of the images in the Picture Size drop-down menu (Smaller: 640 x 480, Small: 800 x 600, Medium: 1024 x 768, Large: 1280 x 1024, or No Compression), which is very helpful in controlling file size, before clicking the Attach button.

✔ **Burn** to open a drop-down menu from which you can choose either of the following:

 • Video DVD to add the selected media files to an Add Pictures and Video to the DVD screen in the Windows DVD Maker. (*See* "Windows DVD Maker" earlier in this part.)

 • Data Disc to burn them to a CD or DVD data disc in your computer's CD/DVD drive.

✔ **Make a Movie** to import the files into a new movie project in the Windows Movie Maker. (*See* "Windows Movie Maker" earlier in this part.)

✔ **Open** to open up the selected photos in some other graphics editing program on your computer such as Microsoft Office Picture Manager or Vista's Paint program.

Keep in mind that you can select photo and media files in the Windows Photo Gallery by positioning the mouse pointer over each thumbnail and then clicking the check box that appears in the upper-left corner of the thumbnail. Photos and videos selected in this manner then remain selected (indicated by the blue highlighting around their thumbnail images), enabling you to scroll through the other thumbnails adding others, until you click the mouse in a blank area between the thumbnails. The great thing about this method of selecting media files (as opposed to Ctrl+clicking, Shift+clicking, or dragging through the thumbnails) is that you can deselect a media file simply by positioning the mouse over its thumbnail and then clicking its check box again to clear its check mark *without* automatically deselecting all the other selected media files in the Gallery.

Playing a slide show

Windows Photo Gallery has a great slide show feature that enables you to view all the photos and videos in the gallery (or all those whose thumbnails you've selected beforehand) full screen in their current sequence in the Gallery.

To start the slide show, simply click the Play SlideShow button (in the center of the image controls at the bottom of the Windows Photo Gallery window) or press F11. Vista then begins the show by displaying the first media file in the Gallery (or the first one of those you've selected) full screen. In the case of photos, Vista displays them for a several seconds before dissolving into the next image.

To display the slide show's playback controller, simply position the mouse pointer at the bottom of the screen near the center. To select another effect such as pan and zoom that makes it feel like the lens is moving in the photo, click the Themes button at the far left of this controller, and then click the effect you want to use on this button's pop-up menu. (To once again view the videos and photos, using the default dissolve effect, click the Fade item at the top of this menu.)

To change the amount of time that photos are displayed in the slide show, click the button with the picture of the gear on it (to the immediate right of the Themes button) and then click Slow to increase the time or Fast to decrease the time on the pop-up menu. To randomize the order in which the images are shown, click Shuffle on this pop-up menu.

If you want to take manual control of the photo portion of the slide show, click the Play button in the center of the controller first to change it to Pause and then click the Pause button to both pause the show and turn the button back into Play. To advance to the next photo in the sequence, click the Next button on the controller or press the → key. To return to the previous photo in the sequence, click the Previous button on the controller or press the ← key.

When you're finished enjoying the slide show and want to return to the Windows Photo Gallery, click the End Slide Show button on the right of the controller.

Adding ratings, tags, and captions

Clicking the Info button on the Gallery's toolbar displays a special Preview pane to the Windows Photo Gallery window (see Figure 7-16) that enables you to add five-star ratings and search tags to selected photo and video thumbnails that you can then use in filtering the media files displayed in the Gallery. In the case of photos, you can also add captions to the files that appear beneath the photo's thumbnail when you select Tiles as the view and can be used in the Gallery's Search text box to quickly filter the images.

To rate the selected media file shown in the Preview pane, click the star you want to give it (between one and five, from left to right, with one as the lowest and five stars as the highest).

To add tags to the selected media file, click the Add Tags button in the Preview pane, and then enter each search tag in the text box that appears and then press Enter. (You can add as many tags as you want in this manner.)

To rename a photo that the camera automatically named, such as DSC_0034.jpg, click the generic filename near the bottom of the Preview pane and then edit the name before you click outside its outline. Note that the photo's filename does not appear in this pane if you've already assigned a descriptive name to it. In that case, to rename the photo, you have to open its folder in the Documents window and use Vista's rename command (**see** Part 2).

Figure 7-16

To add a caption to a photo, click its <Add Caption> button near the bottom of the Preview pane and then enter the caption in the text box that appears and press Enter.

TIP

To filter out all media files besides those that carry a particular five-star rating, expand the Ratings category in the Navigation pane and then click the number of stars from five down to one that represents the rated images you want displayed. To filter out all media files besides those that have a certain tag, expand the Tags category in the Navigation pane and then click the tag for the images you want displayed.

Fixing a photo

You can use the Fix button on the Window Photo Gallery's toolbar to edit photos in the gallery that need some touching up. When you click Fix after selecting a photo's thumbnail in the Gallery, Vista displays the image in the Gallery along with five buttons on the right, representing the types of fixes you can make to it (see Figure 7-17).

Figure 7-17

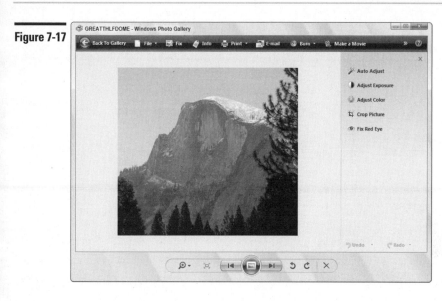

These buttons enable you to make the following modifications:

- **Auto Adjust** to have Vista automatically adjust the image's exposure and color — click the Undo button or press Ctrl+Z to restore the original settings.

- **Adjust Exposure** to display Brightness and Contrast sliders that you can drag to manually adjust the brightness and contrast level in the image.

- **Adjust Color** to display Color Temperature, Tint, and Saturation sliders that you can drag to manually adjust the color in the image.

- **Crop Picture** to display a cropping frame in the image that you can position and size (by dragging its corners) to indicate where Vista should crop the image when you click the Apply button. Click the Rotate Frame button if you need to change the orientation of the cropping frame.

- **Fix Red Eye** to remove red eye from subjects in the photo by drawing a rectangle around the eye. Before you draw the rectangle, you may want to click the Changes the Display Size button in the image controller and drag its slider up to zoom in on the subject whose eye needs fixing.

After you finish making all the modifications to the image that you want to make, click the Back to Gallery button to return to the normal Windows Photo Gallery window display and, at the same time, have Vista save the changes to the graphics file. If, however, you decide that you don't want to keep all the changes, press Ctrl+R. Click the Revert button in the Revert to Original alert dialog box that appears asking you to confirm reverting back to the original version of the photo.

Glossary: Tech Talk

accessories: Tiny (by Microsoft standards) auxiliary programs shipped with Windows Vista, such as Calculator, Notepad, Paint, Sound Recorder, and the like, that aren't really necessary to run your computer but can be really handy. Click Start ▶ All Programs ▶ Accessories to see the complete list.

Aero Glass: Aero is a "backcronym" (that's an acronym consciously created after the fact) that stands for *Authentic*, *Energetic*, *Reflective*, and *Open*, the keywords coined by the Microsoft engineers to describe the design objectives for Windows Vista. In a nutshell, Aero Glass refers to the highly transparent, more reflective, smoothed out, and less jagged look and feel of Vista graphical user interface.

applications: A techie way of saying "programs" — you know, the things that make your computer run around the room and jump through hoops.

blog: *See Weblog.*

browsing offline: *See work offline.*

Clipboard: The place in your system memory where items you want to cut or copy from one place to another are stored. The Clipboard is available in most Windows programs that you run, most notably Microsoft Office.

context menu: *See shortcut menu.*

Control Panel: Refers to the collection of utilities that enables you to customize the many Windows Vista settings available for your computer.

desktop: The basic background for the Windows Vista environment made up of the background graphic, Windows taskbar, Sidebar, and Recycle Bin. The desktop is the place from which you start and end your work session with a Windows computer.

dialog box: A special, limited type of window that contains any number of buttons, boxes, tabs, and sliders, which you use to specify a whole bunch of settings all at once in Windows Vista or in any other particular Windows program you have open.

DOS: An acronym for disk operating system. DOS is almost irrelevant with the advent of Windows Vista. You can, however, open a command window with an old-fashioned DOS prompt within Windows Vista — simply type **cmd** in the Start Search box on the Start menu and then click the C:\ cmd on the Start menu to open its window; if you really miss that kind of stuff!

e-mail: Electronic mail. You send and receive e-mail in Windows Vista with Windows Mail.

filename: The name you give your files, silly. I'm only bringing it up here because Windows Vista allows users to name their files and folders with up to 255 characters, including spaces. Imagine that.

firewall: A system designed to prevent unauthorized access to your computer system through the Internet or a network to which it is connected. A firewall can be implemented through hardware or software or a combination of the two. Vista implements a software form of firewall that blocks all suspect data entering or leaving the system.

folder: A data container that holds files, other folders, or a combination of the two. Folders used to be called *directories,* even though their icons look like folders.

gadgets: Little desktop programs such as the Slide Show, Clock, and Feed Viewer (for RSS feeds) that normally run in the Sidebar on the right side of the Windows Vista screen. You can add more gadgets to the Sidebar and even create gadgets of your own. **See also** *RSS feed* and *Sidebar.*

HTML (HyperText Markup Language): The traditional computer programming language for the Web (traditional since 1989–1990, when the World Wide Web and HTML language first began to make themselves a presence in the world). HTML can run on almost any computer platform and can combine text with pictures, sounds, and other multimedia enhancements.

HTML document: *See Web page.*

hyperlink: Text or graphics images that you click with the mouse to take you to a certain Web destination (or, rather, have that Web destination appear in your browser window). You can spot a hyperlink when the mouse pointer changes to an outline of a hand. Also, words or other text hyperlinks are almost always underlined text and in blue — which, after you follow the link, changes to purple.

hypertext: Text to which a hyperlink is attached.

icon: A small picture used in Windows Vista to make your computer a more GUI (*gooey,* as in *Graphical User Interface*) place to be. Icons identify all manner of objects associated with your computer and positively run rampant in Windows Vista.

Internet: A large number of computers of all types all hooked together all around the World. The popular multimedia part of the Internet is the World Wide Web.

Internet Explorer: The Microsoft Web browser that connects you to the Internet and enables you to browse the Web pages on the World Wide Web (**see** *Web browser*). Internet Explorer also opens files on the same computer on which it's running and displays the local files as Web files.

intranet: A small-scale version of the Internet that works the same way as the Internet, but only the authorized members of the corporation or organization that sponsors the intranet get to use it.

Media Center: The name of the full-screen program in Windows Vista that gives you access to all the photos, music, videos, and, if your computer is equipped with a TV tuner card, TV programs.

multimedia: Yeah! It's what we want: music, color, sound, and video — all the stuff that separates the computer experience from just plain document text on a monochromatic screen. Vista, more than any other version of Windows, supports multimedia throughout, from the desktop Sidebar to the new version of Windows Media Player and the newly integrated Media Center.

phishing: Pronounced just like *fishing,* the activity of trying to catch our finny friends in the deep blue sea, the people who do indulge in *this* kind of illegal "sport" are casting about for a very special kind of flounder. It refers to the crooked practice of attempting to swindle you online (usually through e-mail messages) by obtaining personal and profitable information such as passwords, Social Security numbers, and credit card numbers. Microsoft's new Internet Explorer 7 supports a form of antiphishing software that tries to identify suspicious Web sites.

podcast: A method of downloading or streaming audio or video files on the Internet for playback on personal computers and other portable devices. Commonly, podcasts represent single episodes of a Web "show" that are updated on a regular basis such as daily or weekly. *See also RSS feed* and *vodcast*.

properties: A description of the settings assigned to folders and files in Windows Vista. A listing of all the properties is found in a special dialog box that you access through the folder's or file's shortcut menu.

Recycle Bin: The trash can of Windows Vista, where you can drag the files, directories, and other stuff that you want to get rid of. Somebody at Microsoft was positively gushing with political correctness when he or she named this thing, because nobody is going to drive up, take the stuff you throw away, and make something wonderful and new with it.

RSS feed: Depending upon whom you talk to, RSS stands for Really Simple Syndication, Rich Site Summary, or even RDF (Resource Description Framework) Site Summary. It refers to a type of Web feed syndication used by a lot of news Web sites, weblogs, and podcasts. RSS feeds often provide summaries with links to full Web content and are now fully supported in Windows Internet Explorer 7. *See also podcast.*

ScreenTips: Windows Vista extensively uses ScreenTips to provide a way of adding commentary or footnotes to features. When you run your mouse pointer over a certain part of the screen, a little black-outlined, pale-yellow rectangle pops up with some more or less informative text. In some cases, such as with some Internet search results, this text can amount to a paragraph's worth of context-sensitive material.

search: The ability to search for any program, folder, and file simply by entering part of its name or, in the case of text documents, its contents in any of the Search text boxes that appear on the Start menu (where it's called Start Search) as well as all the Explorer windows in Vista.

shortcut: A remarkable way in Windows Vista to open a favorite document, folder, Web page, or program directly from the desktop of your computer without needing to know its real whereabouts.

shortcut menu: A pull-down menu containing commands that relate directly to the object to which they're attached. Shortcut menus can be found almost everywhere in Windows Vista. They're attached to program, folder, or file icons, toolbar buttons, and even the desktop itself. To open a shortcut menu, simply right-click the object in question. Also known as a *context menu.*

Sidebar: The bar with all gadget thingamajigs including the slide show, clock, and RSS Viewer that appear on the right side of the Windows Vista desktop. *See also Gadgets.*

SideShow: No, this does not refer to all of Microsoft's hype around the introduction and rollout of Windows Vista — it's the new technology that enables you run gadgets on auxiliary laptop computer displays when the machine is in Sleep mode and on certain compatible devices such as PDAs and smart cellphones.

Start menu: The mother of all pull-down menus in Windows Vista. Located by clicking the ever-present Start button on the far left at the very beginning of the taskbar, it contains almost all the commands you'll ever need to use.

taskbar: The bar at the bottom of Windows Vista that contains the Start button, buttons for all open programs and windows currently in use, and the Notification area with the clock and other little icons letting you know what system utilities are running and alerting you to any system problems.

toolbar: A bar containing a row of buttons that perform the routine tasks you used to have to do with pull-down menus or keystroke combinations in the old days of Windows XP.

vodcast: Either stands for video podcast or video on demand (VOD) podcast. It refers to the online delivery via downloading or streaming of video clips using RSS feed technology. *See also* podcast and *RSS feed*.

Weblog: A contraction of Web log that is normally shortened to just *blog*. It refers to a form of online publication that is periodically updated and whose updates appear in reverse order (most to least recent). The most basic form of a blog is a Web diary dedicated to chronicling a person's day-to-day thoughts and activities, although blogs can cover any subject and are often professionally maintained.

Web browser: A program, such as Microsoft Internet Explorer 7, Firefox, or Opera, which enables the user or client to visit various Web sites and experience the content found there.

Web page: The basic display unit of the World Wide Web: When you see something on the Internet, it is most likely a Web page. The Web page itself may be composed of a number of parts, including the HTML source and various multimedia images.

window: The basic on-screen box used in Windows Vista to contain and display each and every program you run on your computer.

wizards: A particular set of dialog boxes used in Windows Vista and other Microsoft products to step the user through complex procedures, such as installing a new printer, sending a fax, or performing coronary angioplasty.

work offline: When you aren't connected to the Internet and you use a browser (like Internet Explorer 7) to browse Web pages or e-mail and newsgroup messages that have been downloaded onto your own computer, you're working offline. With the advent of RSS feeds and Web page subscriptions, you can have new content automatically downloaded during the wee hours of the night, when you're not bothered by Internet traffic and lengthy downloads. You can then view the downloads offline at your leisure.

XML (Extensible MarkUp Language): Like its cousin HTML (HyperText Markup Language, which renders Web pages on the Internet), XML is a markup language that uses codes called *tags* to define the documents structure and appearance. Unlike HTML, whose tags are all predefined and set in stone (at least until a new version comes out), XML is extensible in the sense that you (well, actually not you, but a programmer) can define and create new tags as needed for any particular project. Also, XML actually describes the structure and meaning of its data, whereas HTML only defines how its data looks (and beauty, as they say, is only skin-deep). It is this latter quality that makes XML so valuable in terms of sharing data among different incompatible systems, making it easy to reuse the data wherever it's needed. (Now, aren't you sorry you asked?)

Index

Notes

Notes

BUSINESS, CAREERS & PERSONAL FINANCE

0-7645-5307-0   0-7645-5331-3 *†

Also available:
- Accounting For Dummies †
  0-7645-5314-3
- Business Plans Kit For Dummies †
  0-7645-5365-8
- Cover Letters For Dummies
  0-7645-5224-4
- Frugal Living For Dummies
  0-7645-5403-4
- Leadership For Dummies
  0-7645-5176-0
- Managing For Dummies
  0-7645-1771-6

- Marketing For Dummies
  0-7645-5600-2
- Personal Finance For Dummies *
  0-7645-2590-5
- Project Management
  For Dummies
  0-7645-5283-X
- Resumes For Dummies †
  0-7645-5471-9
- Selling For Dummies
  0-7645-5363-1
- Small Business Kit For Dummies *†
  0-7645-5093-4

HOME & BUSINESS COMPUTER BASICS

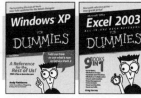

0-7645-4074-2   0-7645-3758-X

Also available:
- ACT! 6 For Dummies
  0-7645-2645-6
- iLife '04 All-in-One Desk Reference
  For Dummies
  0-7645-7347-0
- iPAQ For Dummies
  0-7645-6769-1
- Mac OS X Panther Timesaving
  Techniques For Dummies
  0-7645-5812-9
- Macs For Dummies
  0-7645-5656-8
- Microsoft Money 2004 For Dummies
  0-7645-4195-1

- Office 2003 All-in-One Desk
  Reference For Dummies
  0-7645-3883-7
- Outlook 2003 For Dummies
  0-7645-3759-8
- PCs For Dummies
  0-7645-4074-2
- TiVo For Dummies
  0-7645-6923-6
- Upgrading and Fixing PCs
  For Dummies
  0-7645-1665-5
- Windows XP Timesaving
  Techniques For Dummies
  0-7645-3748-2

FOOD, HOME, GARDEN, HOBBIES, MUSIC & PETS

0-7645-5295-3   0-7645-5232-5

Also available:
- Bass Guitar For Dummies
  0-7645-2487-9
- Diabetes Cookbook For Dummies
  0-7645-5230-9
- Gardening For Dummies *
  0-7645-5130-2
- Guitar For Dummies
  0-7645-5106-X
- Holiday Decorating For Dummies
  0-7645-2570-0
- Home Improvement All-in-One
  For Dummies
  0-7645-5680-0

- Knitting For Dummies
  0-7645-5395-X
- Piano For Dummies
  0-7645-5105-1
- Puppies For Dummies
  0-7645-5255-4
- Scrapbooking For Dummies
  0-7645-7208-3
- Senior Dogs For Dummies
  0-7645-5818-8
- Singing For Dummies
  0-7645-2475-5
- 30-Minute Meals For Dummies
  0-7645-2589-1

INTERNET & DIGITAL MEDIA

0-7645-1664-7   0-7645-6924-4

Also available:
- 2005 Online Shopping Directory
  For Dummies
  0-7645-7495-7
- CD & DVD Recording For Dummies
  0-7645-5956-7
- eBay For Dummies
  0-7645-5654-1
- Fighting Spam For Dummies
  0-7645-5965-6
- Genealogy Online For Dummies
  0-7645-5964-8
- Google For Dummies
  0-7645-4420-9

- Home Recording For Musicians
  For Dummies
  0-7645-1634-5
- The Internet For Dummies
  0-7645-4173-0
- iPod & iTunes For Dummies
  0-7645-7772-7
- Preventing Identity Theft
  For Dummies
  0-7645-7336-5
- Pro Tools All-in-One Desk
  Reference For Dummies
  0-7645-5714-9
- Roxio Easy Media Creator
  For Dummies
  0-7645-7131-1

WILEY

SPORTS, FITNESS, PARENTING, RELIGION & SPIRITUALITY

0-7645-5146-9   0-7645-5418-2

Also available:

Adoption For Dummies
0-7645-5488-3

Basketball For Dummies
0-7645-5248-1

The Bible For Dummies
0-7645-5296-1

Buddhism For Dummies
0-7645-5359-3

Catholicism For Dummies
0-7645-5391-7

Hockey For Dummies
0-7645-5228-7

Judaism For Dummies
0-7645-5299-6

Martial Arts For Dummies
0-7645-5358-5

Pilates For Dummies
0-7645-5397-6

Religion For Dummies
0-7645-5264-3

Teaching Kids to Read
For Dummies
0-7645-4043-2

Weight Training For Dummies
0-7645-5168-X

Yoga For Dummies
0-7645-5117-5

TRAVEL

0-7645-5438-7   0-7645-5453-0

Also available:

Alaska For Dummies
0-7645-1761-9

Arizona For Dummies
0-7645-6938-4

Cancún and the Yucatán
For Dummies
0-7645-2437-2

Cruise Vacations For Dummies
0-7645-6941-4

Europe For Dummies
0-7645-5456-5

Ireland For Dummies
0-7645-5455-7

Las Vegas For Dummies
0-7645-5448-4

London For Dummies
0-7645-4277-X

New York City For Dummies
0-7645-6945-7

Paris For Dummies
0-7645-5494-8

RV Vacations For Dummies
0-7645-5443-3

Walt Disney World & Orlando
For Dummies
0-7645-6943-0

GRAPHICS, DESIGN & WEB DEVELOPMENT

0-7645-4345-8   0-7645-5589-8

Also available:

Adobe Acrobat 6 PDF
For Dummies
0-7645-3760-1

Building a Web Site For Dummies
0-7645-7144-3

Dreamweaver MX 2004
For Dummies
0-7645-4342-3

FrontPage 2003 For Dummies
0-7645-3882-9

HTML 4 For Dummies
0-7645-1995-6

Illustrator CS For Dummies
0-7645-4084-X

Macromedia Flash MX 2004
For Dummies
0-7645-4358-X

Photoshop 7 All-in-One Desk
Reference For Dummies
0-7645-1667-1

Photoshop CS Timesaving
Techniques For Dummies
0-7645-6782-9

PHP 5 For Dummies
0-7645-4166-8

PowerPoint 2003 For Dummies
0-7645-3908-6

QuarkXPress 6 For Dummies
0-7645-2593-X

NETWORKING, SECURITY, PROGRAMMING & DATABASES

0-7645-6852-3   0-7645-5784-X

Also available:

A+ Certification For Dummies
0-7645-4187-0

Access 2003 All-in-One Desk
Reference For Dummies
0-7645-3988-4

Beginning Programming
For Dummies
0-7645-4997-9

C For Dummies
0-7645-7068-4

Firewalls For Dummies
0-7645-4048-3

Home Networking For Dummies
0-7645-42796

Network Security For Dummies
0-7645-1679-5

Networking For Dummies
0-7645-1677-9

TCP/IP For Dummies
0-7645-1760-0

VBA For Dummies
0-7645-3989-2

Wireless All In-One Desk Reference
For Dummies
0-7645-7496-5

Wireless Home Networking
For Dummies
0-7645-3910-8

HEALTH & SELF-HELP

0-7645-6820-5 *†   0-7645-2566-2

Also available:
- Alzheimer's For Dummies
  0-7645-3899-3
- Asthma For Dummies
  0-7645-4233-8
- Controlling Cholesterol For Dummies
  0-7645-5440-9
- Depression For Dummies
  0-7645-3900-0
- Dieting For Dummies
  0-7645-4149-8
- Fertility For Dummies
  0-7645-2549-2

- Fibromyalgia For Dummies
  0-7645-5441-7
- Improving Your Memory For Dummies
  0-7645-5435-2
- Pregnancy For Dummies †
  0-7645-4483-7
- Quitting Smoking For Dummies
  0-7645-2629-4
- Relationships For Dummies
  0-7645-5384-4
- Thyroid For Dummies
  0-7645-5385-2

EDUCATION, HISTORY, REFERENCE & TEST PREPARATION

0-7645-5194-9   0-7645-4186-2

Also available:
- Algebra For Dummies
  0-7645-5325-9
- British History For Dummies
  0-7645-7021-8
- Calculus For Dummies
  0-7645-2498-4
- English Grammar For Dummies
  0-7645-5322-4
- Forensics For Dummies
  0-7645-5580-4
- The GMAT For Dummies
  0-7645-5251-1
- Inglés Para Dummies
  0-7645-5427-1

- Italian For Dummies
  0-7645-5196-5
- Latin For Dummies
  0-7645-5431-X
- Lewis & Clark For Dummies
  0-7645-2545-X
- Research Papers For Dummies
  0-7645-5426-3
- The SAT I For Dummies
  0-7645-7193-1
- Science Fair Projects For Dummies
  0-7645-5460-3
- U.S. History For Dummies
  0-7645-5249-X

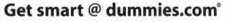

Get smart @ dummies.com®

- **Find a full list of Dummies titles**
- **Look into loads of FREE on-site articles**
- **Sign up for FREE eTips e-mailed to you weekly**
- **See what other products carry the Dummies name**
- **Shop directly from the Dummies bookstore**
- **Enter to win new prizes every month!**

* Separate Canadian edition also available
† Separate U.K. edition also available

Available wherever books are sold. For more information or to order direct: U.S. customers visit www.dummies.com or call 1-877-762-2974.
U.K. customers visit www.wileyeurope.com or call 0800 243407. Canadian customers visit www.wiley.ca or call 1-800-567-4797.